GREEK
FOR THE
REST OF US

Also by William Mounce

Basics of Biblical Greek Grammar and *Workbook*
Basics of Biblical Greek Vocabulary Cards
Basics of Biblical Greek Vocabulary Audio CD
Basics of Biblical Greek Get an A! Study Guide
Biblical Greek: A Compact Guide
The Morphology of Biblical Greek
A Graded Reader of Biblical Greek
The Analytical Lexicon to the Greek New Testament
Greek for the Rest of Us: The Essentials of Biblical Greek
Greek for the Rest of Us: Get an A! Study Guide
*Mounce's Complete Expository Dictionary of
Old and New Testament Words*
*Interlinear for the Rest of Us: The Reverse Interlinear for
New Testament Word Studies*
*The Zondervan Greek and English Interlinear New Testament
(NASB/NIV, NIV/KJV, TNIV/NLT)*
Pastoral Epistles (Word Biblical Commentary)
Why I Trust the Bible
*The Crossway Comprehensive Concordance of the Holy Bible:
English Standard Version*

THIRD EDITION

GREEK
FOR THE
REST OF US

LEARN GREEK TO STUDY
THE NEW TESTAMENT WITH
INTERLINEARS AND BIBLE SOFTWARE

WILLIAM D.
MOUNCE

ZONDERVAN
ACADEMIC

ZONDERVAN ACADEMIC

Greek for the Rest of Us
Copyright © 2003, 2013, 2022 by William D. Mounce

Published in Grand Rapids, Michigan, by Zondervan. Zondervan is a registered trademark of The Zondervan Corporation, L.L.C., a wholly owned subsidiary of HarperCollins Christian Publishing, Inc.

Requests for information should be addressed to customercare@harpercollins.com.

Zondervan titles may be purchased in bulk for educational, business, fundraising, or sales promotional use. For information, please email SpecialMarkets@Zondervan.com.

Library of Congress Cataloging-in-Publication Data

Names: Mounce, William D., author.
Title: Greek for the rest of us : learn Greek to study the New Testament with Interlinears and Bible
    Software / William D. Mounce.
Description: Third edition. | Grand Rapids : Zondervan, 2022. | Includes index.
Identifiers: LCCN 2022025154 (print) | LCCN 2022025155 (ebook) | ISBN 9780310134626 (paperback) |
    ISBN 9780310134633 (ebook)
Subjects: LCSH: Bible. New Testament--Language, style. | Greek language, Biblical--Grammar. | BISAC:
    RELIGION / Biblical Criticism & Interpretation / New Testament | RELIGION / Christian Ministry
    / Preaching
Classification: LCC PA817 .M655 2022 (print) | LCC PA817 (ebook) | DDC 487/.4--dc23/eng/20220720
LC record available at https://lccn.loc.gov/2022025154
LC ebook record available at https://lccn.loc.gov/2022025155

Cover design: LUCAS Art & Design
Typeset by Teknia Software

Printed in the United States of America

24 25 26 27 28 29 30 31 32 33 34 /TRM/ 15 14 13 12 11 10 9 8 7 6 5 4 3 2

for Big Terry

who deeply desires to know God's Word better
but who does not have the time to learn traditional Greek

Codex Sinaiticus is an important majuscule manuscript from the fourth century. The images posted here are from the full-sized black and white facsimile of the manuscript produced in 1911 by Kirsopp Lake and Clarendon Press. The Codex Sinaiticus Project website (codexsinaiticus.org/en) has new images and information about this manuscript. Image courtesy of the Center for the Study of New Testament Manuscripts (csntm.org).

TABLE OF CONTENTS

PREFACE

When people learn that I'm a Greek teacher, one of the more common responses is, "I've always wanted to learn Greek." I always ask them why they want to learn Greek. To date, only one person has said he wanted to actually learn the language. Everyone else wanted to understand the Bible better, and especially to know the meaning of the Greek words behind the English translation.

In a perfect world, we would have studied Greek for years and be able to understand the Bible better. But the world is not perfect, and many people are not able to spend the years required to fully learn Greek, even those who have a seminary education.

As I thought about how I might help the situation, I came to the conclusion that if people knew a little about Greek and a lot about how to use good biblical study tools, they could in fact glean much from the Greek Bible and from other resources that are otherwise beyond their grasp. This includes:

- making sense of the information that Bible software shows;
- finding what the Greek words behind the English translation mean;
- seeing the author's flow of thought and his central message;
- understanding why translations are different;
- reading good commentaries and using other biblical tools that make use of Greek.

Several years ago I wrote *The Interlinear for the Rest of Us: The Reverse Interlinear*, and *The Zondervan Greek and English Interlinear New Testament*. These two interlinears help people get to the Greek behind the English, and the data I created to make these interlinears is also used by some Bible software programs. I am now writing this book to help you learn how to use interlinears and other such tools.

There are, of course, many dangers in relying on tools rather than fully learning Greek, and I expressed those concerns in the preface to the interlinears. My fear is that people will think they know Greek well enough to come up with their own interpretations without commentary support. However, this is the same concern I have for all my first-year Greek students who are learning Greek in the traditional manner.

Alexander Pope once said, "A little knowledge is a dangerous thing." But as I indicated in *The Interlinear for the Rest of Us*, I think it's a little bit of arrogance that is dangerous. So I offer this book, trusting that you will recognize the limits of the approach.

Greek for the Rest of Us is divided into two sections.

- **Foundational Greek** teaches you enough Greek so you can use Bible study software, understand a Strong's Bible and a reverse interlinear, and do Greek word studies.

- **Church Greek** teaches you more Greek so you can understand Greek-English interlinears, use better reference works, especially commentaries, and learn my exegetical method, "phrasing."

The greatest challenge of the book was to find good examples of what I am teaching, especially for the homework assignments. I have relied quite heavily on the work of my friend Daniel Wallace and his grammar (with permission), *The Basics of New Testament Syntax*. Many of the grammatical categories and examples I use are from his work, and this should prove an easy transition for you to move from *Greek for the Rest of Us* to his book. If you are especially adventurous, you should use his full grammar, *Greek Grammar Beyond the Basics*.

Be sure to get the accompanying workbook so you can take the theoretical teachings in this book and apply them practically. Keep an eye on my online class, www.billmounce.com/biblestudygreek/class. Go to the lesson you are currently studying to see what is available. You will find encouraging blogs, downloads, and helps for memorizing vocabulary. Also, please subscribe to my YouTube channel (www.youtube.com/billmounce) for videos in the playlists Greek Word of the Day, Greek Verse of the Week, and The Professor Says, where you can learn fun things to say in Greek.

My experience in teaching this class over the past thirty years is that the biggest challenge students face is to realize this is an academic endeavor. Some people think that because it's not the traditional method for learning Greek, it will be easy. To be sure, it will be *easier*, but this is still an academic topic and requires academic rigor. Don't let that scare you, but you should be prepared for real work.

I primarily use the Mounce translation and Accordance to illustrate Bible software, but you can also use Logos, The Bible Study App (from OliveTree), and others. Tutorials on how to use the apps are in the online course in the relevant lessons. If you use Accordance, be sure to purchase the Mounce Study Bundle.

Of the many people I would like to thank, most goes to my Greek assistant Matt Smith for his many hours of help, to my colleagues Lynn Losie, Doug Stuart, and Daniel Wallace for their help, to my editors Verlyn Verbrugge and Chris Beetham, and to the many students who patiently endured while I changed my mind on how to teach this material, especially Lew Dawson.

I am also thankful that Lee Fields has written the Hebrew counterpart, *Hebrew for the Rest of Us*. My old appendix on Hebrew can still be downloaded from the last lesson in the online class, but I encourage you to study his book. I trust that you will find this a valuable resource as you work to understand the Word of God better.

Bill Mounce
Washougal, Washington
February, 2022

ABBREVIATIONS

BIBLE VERSIONS

CSB	Christian Standard Bible
CEB	Common English Bible
ESV	English Standard Version
KJV	King James Version
NAB	New American Bible
NASB	New American Standard Bible (2020)
NEB	New English Bible
NET	New English Translation
NIV	New International Version (2011 edition)
NIV (1984)	New International Version (1984 edition)
NIrV	New International Reader's Version
NKJV	New King James Version
NLT	New Living Translation
NRSV	New Revised Standard Version
RSV	Revised Standard Version
TEV	Today's English Version
TNIV	Today's New International Version

BOOK ABBREVIATIONS

BBG	*The Basics of Biblical Greek* (William Mounce, Zondervan)
BNTS	*The Basics of New Testament Syntax* (Daniel Wallace, Zondervan)
BDAG	*A Greek-English Lexicon of the New Testament and Other Early Christian Literature* (3rd ed.; revised and edited by Frederick Danker, University of Chicago)
GGBB	*Greek Grammar Beyond the Basics* (Daniel Wallace, Zondervan)
IRU	*Interlinear for the Rest of Us: A Reverse Interlinear for New Testament Word Studies* (William Mounce, Zondervan)

OTHER ABBREVIATIONS

cf.	compare
e.g.	for example
i.e.	that is (used for a restatement)
p.	page
pp.	pages

WHAT WOULD IT LOOK LIKE IF YOU KNEW A LITTLE GREEK?

What will you be able to do when you are done working through this book that, perhaps, you cannot do now?

1. You will learn to use your Bible software and my interlinears. Software can be a significant tool in your Bible study. You can call up a verse and mouse over an English word, and the software will show you all sorts of dazzling information. But what does it all mean? (The illustrations in this book use the Mounce translation and Accordance.)

If you check out John 3:16, you might see something unusual, not "For God so loved the world" but "For this is how God loved the world" followed by a colon.

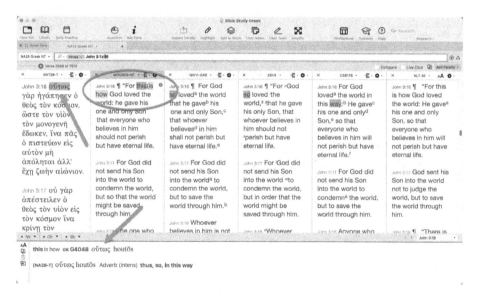

You can look over at your Greek text and see what Greek word is being translated by "this is how" (οὕτως), but if you don't know Greek that doesn't help.

If you look in the Instant Details window at the bottom of the screen, it gives you some more information about this Greek word. But what does "Adverb (intens)" mean, and why does my translation treat οὕτως so differently than other translations (except the CSB and NET)?

If you have a fuller Greek dictionary, you could triple click οὕτως and see a fuller definition of the word, but can you understand it?

οὕτω/οὕτως adv. of οὗτος (Hom.+ gener. 'so'); the form οὕτως is most used, before consonants as well as before vowels; the form οὕτω (En 98:3 before a vowel; EpArist only before consonants) in the NT only Ac 23:11; Phil 3:17; Hb 12:21; Rv 16:18 w. really outstanding attestation and taken into the text by most edd.; by others, with t.r., also Mt 3:15; 7:17; Mk 2:7; Ac 13:47; Ro 1:15; 6:19 (B-D-F §21; W-S. §5, 28b; Mlt-H. 112f; W-H. appendix 146f. Also in ins [s. Nachmanson 112], pap [Mayser 242f; Crönert 142] and LXX [Thackeray p. 136] οὕτως predominates)

1. referring to what precedes, *in this manner, thus, so*
a. w. a correlative word καθάπερ . . . οὕτως (s. καθάπερ) *(just) as . . . so* Ro 12:4f; 1 Cor 12:12; 2 Cor 8:11. καθὼς . . . οὕτως *(just) as . . . so* Lk 11:30; 17:26; J 3:14; 12:50; 14:31; 15:4; 2 Cor 1:5; 10:7; Col 3:13; 1 Th 2:4. ὡς . . . οὕτως *as . . . so* Ac 8:32 (Is 53:7); 23:11

By the time you are done with *Greek for the Rest of Us*, all these mysteries and many more will be made clear!

You can download samples of my two interlinears in the Orientation lesson in the online class. Years ago I came up with the idea of a "reverse interlinear," which keeps English word order and alters the order of the Greek words.

For	God		so	loved	the	world	that	he	gave	his	one		and only
γὰρ	ὁ	θεὸς	οὕτως	ἠγάπησεν	τὸν	κόσμον	ὥστε	→	ἔδωκεν	τὸν	μονογενῆ	←	←
cj	d.nsm	n.nsm	adv	v.aai.3s	d.asm	n.asm	cj		v.aai.3s	d.asm	a.asm		
1142	3836	2536	4048	26		3836	3180	6063		1443	3836	3666	

Son,		that	whoever	believes	in	him	shall	not	perish	but	have	eternal	life.
τὸν	υἱὸν,	ἵνα	πᾶς ὁ,	πιστεύων	εἰς	αὐτὸν	→	μὴ	ἀπόληται	ἀλλ᾽	ἔχῃ	αἰώνιον	ζωήν.
d.asm	n.asm	cj	a.nsm	d.nsm	pt.pa.nsm	p.a	r.asm.3		pl	v.ams.3s	cj	v.pas.3s	a.asf	n.asf
3836	5626	2671	4246	3836	4409	1650	899	660	3590	660	247	2400	173	2437

When I was done with that project, I did a more traditional Greek-English interlinear that keeps the Greek order and alters the English.

16	οὕτως		γὰρ		ἠγάπησεν	ὁ	θεὸς	τὸν	κόσμον,	ὥστε				τὸν
	"For this is how	For	God	loved	*{the}*	*God*	the	world:	*{that}*	he	gave	his
1142	4048		1142	2536	26		3836	2536	3836	3180	6063	1443	1443	3836
	adv		cj		v.aai.3s		d.nsm	n.nsm	d.asm	n.asm	cj			d.asm

		υἱὸν	τὸν	μονογενῆ	ἔδωκεν,	ἵνα	πᾶς	ὁ	πιστεύων	εἰς	αὐτὸν
one	and only	Son	*{the}*	*one and only*	*he gave*	that	everyone	who	believes	in	him
3666	3666	3666	5626	3836	3666	1443	2671	4246	3836	4409	1650	899
n.asm	d.asm	a.asm	n.asm	d.asm	a.asm	v.aai.3s	cj	a.nsm	d.nsm	pt.pa.nsm	p.a	r.asm.3

→	μὴ	ἀπόληται	ἀλλ᾽	ἔχῃ		ζωὴν	αἰώνιον.
should	not	perish	but	have	eternal	life.	*eternal*
660	3590	660	247	2400	173	2437	173
	pl	v.ams.3s	cj	v.pas.3s		n.asf	a.asf

2. You will discover the meaning of the Greek words that lie behind the English. This is called doing "word studies." Without learning how to use the Greek study tools, the best you can do is study what the English word means. But an English word rarely, if ever, has the same meaning as the Greek word it is translating. A word as simple as "a" or "the" does not have an exact counterpart in Greek; there isn't even a word in Greek for "a."

Words have what is called a "semantic range." This means a word doesn't have just one meaning, but a range of meanings. Think through all the ways we use the words "can" and "run." The range of meaning of a Greek word will almost never be the same as the range of meaning for the English word used to translate it. So just because an English word can have a certain meaning, it's by no means certain that the Greek behind it has that same meaning.

A good example of this is the Greek word σάρξ, *sarx*. This word can be translated many different ways because English has no exact counterpart to it. In as short a book as Galatians, *sarx* is translated by the NIV (1984) as "flesh," "human effort," "illness," "man," "no one," "ordinary way," "outwardly," "sinful nature," and "that nature." All these English words partially overlap in meaning with *sarx*, but none is an exact equivalent.

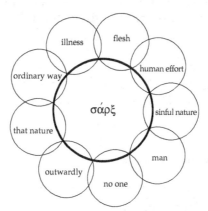

So when you study Galatians 5:16, "Walk by the Spirit, and you will not gratify the desires of the flesh," you don't want to study the English word "flesh"; you want to study the Greek word it translates, σάρξ.

In 1 Corinthians 7:1 the RSV translates, "It is well for a man not to *touch* a woman." Lots of good youth-group talks on dating come out of the word "touch." But guess what? The NIV (1984) translates the verse as, "It is good for a man not to *marry*," and the 2011 version reads, "It is good for a man not to *have sexual relations* with a woman." Wait a minute! Are we talking about dating or are we talking about marriage? The fact of the matter is that ἅπτεσθαι, *haptesthai*, can mean "to touch," or it can be speaking of marriage or even sexual relations. Translators have to pick one meaning or the other.

Another example is John 3:16, the verse I talked about earlier.

> For God so loved the world that he gave his one and only Son,
> that whoever believes in him shall not perish but have eternal
> life. (NIV)

What does "so" mean? Most readers think it means "a lot." That's about
the only way someone would read the English. But did you know that
the Greek word behind "so" most likely means, "in this way"? "For
God loved the world *in this way:* he gave...." The giving of his Son
shows *how* God loved the world, *not how much.* (This is why the footnote in the ESV reads, "Or *For this is how God loved the world.*")

3. *You will learn the basics of exegesis.* "Exegesis" is a fancy word for
Bible study. What meaning did the author intend to convey? The RSV
translates 1 Corinthians 7:36 as,

> If any one thinks that he is not behaving properly toward his
> betrothed, if his passions are strong, and it has to be, let him do
> as he wishes: let them marry—it is no sin.

Paul has been encouraging people not to marry in order to be more
involved in gospel ministry, but then he says that if that's not your gift,
if your passions are strong, then there is nothing wrong with getting
married. Go ahead and marry your "betrothed." "Any one" refers to the
fiancé.

However, when you read the same verse in the NASB (1995) it says,

> But if any man thinks that he is acting unbecomingly toward
> his virgin *daughter,* if she is past her youth, and if it must be so,
> let him do what he wishes, he does not sin; let her marry.

The italics in the NASB's translation indicate that it has added a word,
but the difference is more than that. The question is, who is the "man"?
In the NASB, Paul is thinking of a father/guardian who believes his
daughter's fiancé is acting improperly. Either way you look at this
verse, it can be confusing, and requires exegesis.

Part of helping you learn exegesis is to teach you a methodology I
call "phrasing." You will learn to divide a biblical story into smaller,
more manageable, units, locate the main thought, and see how the other
statements in the passage relate to the main point. You will then lay the
passage out visually in a way that helps you see the author's flow of

thought. This is the best way to help you learn what good commentary writers are doing.

For example, below is the salutation from Jude. How many main thoughts are there, and how many descriptions of the recipients does the author include?

> 1:1   Jude,
>   a servant of Jesus Christ and
>   a brother of James,
>
>   To those
>   who have been   called,
>   who are   loved by God the Father and
>   kept by Jesus Christ:
>
> 1:2   Mercy, peace and love be yours in abundance.

The salutation breaks down into three sections: author; recipients; greeting. Jude tells us three things about the recipients: they have been called; they are loved by God; they are kept by Jesus.

4. *You will often be able to understand why translations are different.* How many times have you been in a Bible study where the leader is discussing a verse, but your Bible appears to say something considerably different? How can the translations be so different? What does the verse really mean? Let me give you a few examples.

When Jesus instituted what we call the "Lord's Supper," he instructed his disciples concerning the cup: "Drink ye all of it" (Matt 26:27 KJV). My dad tells the story of how, when he was young, he made sure he drank every last little bit of grape juice in the communion cup. He would shake it until every drop was gone; he was going to obey Scripture and drink "all of it." Only one problem: that's not what the verse means. The "all" means "all of you," not "all the liquid." The CSB translates, "Drink from it, all of you."

Luke 2:14 is one of the better-known verses in the Bible. In the KJV it reads,

> Glory to God in the highest, and on earth peace, good will toward men.

Is there anything in this verse that bothers you? It's a statement of blessing, but does God's peace really extend to all people? "Peace" is a marvelous biblical concept that designates the cessation of hostility between God and us; it's the result of justification (Rom 5:1). If you are not justified, you are not at peace. How can God's peace be extended to all people?

The ESV says,

> Glory to God in the highest, and on earth peace among those with whom he is pleased!

Here, peace isn't extended to all people, but only to those who are the recipients of God's pleasure. Why are the KJV and the ESV different? The answer is that the Greek manuscripts are different at this verse. Some have *eudokias* with the "*s*" (the Greek sigma), which is followed by the ESV; others have *eudokia*, which is followed by the KJV. The "*s*" completely changes the meaning of the blessing.

Another example is Mark 16. If you are reading the chapter in the RSV, after the women see that the tomb is empty, the Bible says,

> And they went out and fled from the tomb; for trembling and astonishment had come upon them; and they said nothing to any one, for they were afraid.

The gospel ends at verse 8 on a note of fear. But let me tell you a story that is related, although it won't sound like it at first. Have you ever seen those movies they often show in high school sociology class about the snake people of the Appalachians? They handle rattlesnakes as part of their church worship, and they don't die (usually). They also drink poison, and they don't die (sometimes). Why are these people doing this? Why are some of my distant cousins doing this? (Some actually are my cousins, by the way. My family is from Gravel Switch, Kentucky.) "Because the Bible says so," they might respond. If you are reading the KJV, it doesn't stop at verse 8 but goes on to verse 20. Verses 17–18 say,

> And these signs shall follow them that believe; In my name shall they cast out devils; they shall speak with new tongues; They shall take up serpents; and if they drink any deadly thing, it shall not hurt them; they shall lay hands on the sick, and they shall recover.

Wouldn't you like to know whether these verses truly belong in the Bible or not?

Here is a more subtle example. In 2 Corinthians 1:15 the ESV reads,

> Because I was sure of this, I wanted to come to you first, so that you may have a second experience of grace.

Sounds as if Paul is talking about a second work of grace subsequent to conversion. But see how other translations handle the passage.

> In this confidence I intended at first to come to you, so that you might twice receive a blessing (NASB).

> Because I was sure of this, I wanted to come to you first, so that you might have a double pleasure (RSV).

> Because I was confident of this, I wanted to visit you first so that you might benefit twice (NIV).

Since none of the other translations give any suggestion of a second work of grace, it's doubtful that the ESV means to suggest this. (I can say this with full certainty, since I was one of the twelve translators of the ESV.)

So what are we going to do with these differences? First of all, we'll work to understand why they are different. Second, we'll learn to see how different translations actually agree (for the most part), but are trying to convey different nuances, or one translation is more general and the other is more specific. So often in Bible study when the translations are different, we seem content to let them say different things, but we need to see how they actually agree.

5. *The final thing that I am going to help you learn is how to read good commentaries.* Let's say you're going to have a Sunday School lesson on Romans 1:17 and you need the help of a commentary. (A commentary is a book that explains what each verse means.) One of the best commentaries on Romans is by C. E. B. Cranfield, so let's say you pick it up and try to read his discussion of the verse. Here is a small part of his discussion (pp. 95–96).

> The other main disagreement concerns the question whether in the phrase δικαιοσύνη θεοῦ in 1.17; 3.21, 22 (cf. 10.3) θεοῦ is to be understood as a subjective genitive or as a genitive of origin, or—to put it differently—whether δικαιοσύνη refers to an activity of God or to a status of man resulting from God's action, righteousness as a gift from God. In support of the view

that θεοῦ is a subjective genitive and δικαιοσύνη refers to God's activity, a number of arguments have been advanced: (i) That in 3.5 (θεοῦ δικαιοσύνη) θεοῦ must be a subjective genitive (cf. also 3.25, 26) ....

Does this make sense? Probably not right now. But by the end of this book you will know know what a genitive is. You'll know what a subjective genitive and a genitive of origin are. I want you to know enough about English and Greek grammar so that you can pick up an excellent commentary and be able to follow the discussion.

Stated in reverse, I don't want you to make silly mistakes that come from misreading commentaries or misapplying Greek grammar. For example, you probably know the passage, "Are all apostles? Are all prophets? Are all teachers? Do all work miracles? Do all speak in tongues?" (1 Cor 12:29). Have you ever heard anyone claim the answer is "Yes," and insist that a "real" Christian must have spoken in tongues once? I have. But when you get your commentary on 1 Corinthians out, you will read something like this: "Questions preceded by μή expect a negative answer." What does that mean? It means that Greek can indicate whether the person asking the question expects the answer "Yes" or "No." (We do this in English by adding a phrase, like: "All don't speak in tongues, do they?") In 1 Corinthians 12:29, the Greek indicates that Paul's expected answer is, "No." The NLT has an elegant way of expressing this. At the end of the list of questions they have, "Of course not!" The answer to all the questions is, "No."

LIMITATIONS

There are limitations to our approach, and they are the same limitations placed on any first-year Greek student. You are at the beginning stages of learning Greek, and my concern is that you will forget that you know only a little. I'm going to give you the ability to sound authoritative by citing Greek words and grammar, and perhaps be completely wrong. I actually put off writing this book for several years because of this concern, but I finally came to the conclusion, as I've said, that it's not a little Greek that proves dangerous. It's a little bit of pride that proves dangerous.

If you don't respect the fact that you are only starting to learn Greek, then these tools can become just another way you can be wrong. I know a well-known speaker who was talking about how a Christian should not incur debt. I believe in debt-free living (for the most part), so don't misunderstand me at this point, but the problem was in how he used Romans 13:8: "Owe no one anything, except to love each other, for the one who loves another has fulfilled the law" (ESV). He claimed something like the following.

> Now what's really important in Romans 13:8 is that there are three negations. Unlike in English, where if you have two negations they cancel each other out, in Greek when you have double negations they pile up on each other making the statement stronger. Paul has three negations in Romans 13:8 and he's making the point that it's really a sin ever to go into debt.

But the fact of the matter is that there are no negatives in this verse in the sense this author speaks of negatives. You'll find μή used once in the idiom εἰ μή, *except,* and twice as parts of words meaning *to no one* and *nothing.* In none of these situations do the rules the speaker was citing apply. He is teaching thousands of people, and he's completely and totally wrong. So I say as a gentle warning: please remember what we're doing and what we're not doing. We're learning to use the tools; we're trying to follow good commentaries; we're trying to understand what words mean. We're not learning enough Greek to make complicated grammatical pronouncements that aren't supported by the commentaries.

I remember when I was in seminary sitting in the balcony of a large and well-known church, listening to the preacher say, "The Greek says this and the Greek says that." I'm looking at the Greek and I say (I hope to myself), "You're wrong, you're wrong, you're wrong." He didn't really know Greek, but he was using it—it seemed to me—to elevate himself in a position of authority over his people. He should have been more careful, and more humble.

Jehovah's Witnesses are another good example of misusing Greek. They will cite John 1:1—"In the beginning was the Word and the Word was with God and the Word was *a god*"—and argue that there is no word "the" before "God." Jesus is not "the" God but "a" god, a created god. But if they really knew Greek, they wouldn't make such a horrible and obvious mistake, for two reasons. (1) There's technically no such thing as the word "the" in Greek. There is a word, ὁ, that can be translated as "the," but it can also be translated as "my," as "your," or as many other words. There is no exact equivalent for the word "the" in Greek. (2) Grammatically the Greek explicitly states that Jesus is, in our language, "the God" (cf. *GGBB*, pp. 266–69).

One last illustration. Last year I was sitting at my desk grading papers, minding my own business, and I received a phone call from an elderly gentleman. He started talking and was evidently lonely so I listened, and within ten minutes he had accused every translator of being intentionally deceitful, of not knowing what they were doing, of mistranslating God's Word, and God was going to curse them. I said,

Sir, do you know any translators?

No, I've never met any of them.

Well, I know a lot of them, and they are godly men and women who would never mistranslate anything on purpose, and they know a lot more Greek than you.

But they don't translate 2 Peter 3:5 properly. The Greek says God created "die-uh" [his mispronunciation of the Greek preposition] "water." The earth is formed *through* water. "Die-uh" means "through" and so in this verse Peter is saying that God created the world "through" water, and they are translating it "out of" water.

He was absolutely insistent that *dia* meant "through," and he went through a fifteen-minute discussion in physics. (I didn't have any idea what he was talking about.) When he finally paused for a breath, I said, "First of all, it's pronounced 'dia.' There's a good chance that if you can't pronounce it, then you probably don't know what it means." (I was a little frustrated.) Then I tried to explain that all words have a range of meaning. *Dia* can mean "through," but it can also mean "out of" or "by," and the translators must make an interpretive decision as to which word they use. (By the way, the ESV did agree on "through," so he should be happy.) I tried to impress on him the fact of how dangerous it was to slander Christian brothers and sisters and to accuse them of intentionally doing things wrong when he didn't know what he was talking about.

So why should you learn a little Greek, if it's possible to make these types of errors? Because the personal rewards of deepening your biblical study are so great that it's worth the effort. Just remember the importance of humility (Phil 2:1–13) and meekness (Matt 5:5), and that while knowledge puffs up, love builds up (1 Cor 8:1).

Be sure to check out all the free resources for this textbook, especially the online class, at BillMounce.com/biblestudygreek

Bill Mounce
For an informed Love of God

Home » Bible Study Greek

4. English Nouns

After the alphabet, inflection is what makes Greek the most different from English and hard for us to understand. Inflection just means that words change their form because of differences in meaning and function, much like the same pronoun can be "he" (masculine), "she" (feminine), or "they" (plural). In this chapter we will focus on the inflection of English nouns.

Downloads

Slides (Keynote | PowerPoint)

Doxology (sheet music)

Doxology (mp3)

You can also purchase Bill's video lectures that cover the book and homework exercises. Tell your discipleship pastor that this is the tool for learning Greek and deepening Bible study in the church!

PART I

FOUNDATIONAL GREEK

This is your first of two passes through the greek language. This is the easiest of the two sections of the book, although it may be more challenging if you have never learned a foreign language. In foundational greek we'll be meeting the basic concepts that make up the greek language:

- Greek alphabet and transliteration

- How to pronounce greek

- What "inflection" and strong's numbers are

- Basics of the greek noun and verbal system

- How to do greek word studies

CHAPTER 1

THE GREEK LANGUAGE

The Greek language has a long and rich history stretching all the way from the fourteenth century BC to the present. The earliest form of the language is Mycenaean Greek that used a script called "Linear B." The form of Greek used by writers from Homer (eighth century BC) through Plato (fourth century BC) is called "Classical Greek." It was a marvelous form of the language, capable of exact expression and subtle nuances. Its alphabet was derived from the Phoenicians as was that of Hebrew. Classical Greek existed in many dialects, of which three were primary: Doric, Aeolic, and Ionic. Attic was a branch of Ionic.

Athens was conquered in the fourth century BC by King Philip of Macedonia. Alexander the Great, Philip's son, was tutored by the Greek philosopher Aristotle. Alexander set out to conquer the world and spread Greek culture and language. Because he spoke Attic Greek, it was this dialect that was spread. It was also the dialect spoken by the famous Athenian writers. This was the beginning of the Hellenistic Age.

As the Greek language spread across the world and met other languages, it was altered (which is true of any language). The dialects also interacted with each other. Eventually this adaptation resulted in what today we call Koine Greek. "Koine" means "common" (from the phrase κοινὴ διάλεκτος, the "common language") and describes the common, everyday form of the language used by everyday people. It was not a polished literary form of the language, and in fact some writers of this era purposefully imitated the older style of Greek (which is like someone today writing in Elizabethan English).

Because Koine was a simplified form of Classical Greek, many of the subtleties of Classical Greek were lost. For example, in Classical Greek ἄλλος meant "other" of the same kind, while ἕτερος meant "other" of a different kind. If you had an apple and you asked for ἄλλος, you would receive another apple. But if you asked for ἕτερος, you would be given perhaps an orange. But in the Koine, ἄλλος and ἕτερος were interchangeable. It is this common Koine Greek that is used in the Septuagint, the New Testament, the Apostolic Fathers, the New Testament Apocrypha, Josephus, Plutarch, and to some degree Philo.

The Koine period lasted until the fourth century, which saw the rise of Byzantium, whose name was changed to Constantinople and eventually Istanbul. Byzantium Greek describes the language until 1453 when Constantinople was conquered by the Ottoman Turks, and from that date until now we call the language Modern Greek.

For a long time Koine Greek confused scholars because it was significantly different from Classical Greek. Some hypothesized that it was a combination of Greek, Hebrew, and Aramaic. Others attempted to explain it as a "Holy Ghost language," meaning that God created a special language just for the Bible. But discoveries of Greek papyri found in Egypt over the past one hundred years have shown that this language was the language of the everyday people, used in the writings of wills, private letters, receipts, shopping lists, etc.

There are two lessons we can learn from this. As Paul says, "In the fullness of time God sent his Son" (Gal 4:4), and part of that fullness was a universal language. No matter where Paul traveled, he could be understood.

But there is another lesson that is a little closer to the pastor's heart. God used the common language to communicate the gospel. The gospel does not belong to the erudite alone, to the scholars and the clergy; it belongs to all people. It now becomes your task to learn this marvelous language so that you can more effectively make known the grace of God to all people.

By the way, I often hear that we should learn Latin because it is the basis of English. Not true. English is a Germanic language, and Latin is a Romance language.

Languages can be grouped into families. There is a hypothetical base language we call "Proto-Indo-European." It developed into four language groups.

- Romance languages (Latin, French, Italian, Portuguese, Romanian, Spanish, and others)

- Germanic languages (English, German, Danish, Dutch, Norwegian, Swedish, and others). Technically the base language for this group is called "Proto-Germanic."

- Greek languages (Linear B, Classical, Koine, Byzantine, Modern Greek)

- Indo-Iranian (Iranian, Sanskrit)

There was a lot of borrowing between Romance and Germanic languages (think where the countries are located), and both of these language groups borrowed from Greek. English especially was heavily influenced by other languages. This can be illustrated by words they have in common.

- From Greek (didactic, apostle, theology)
- From Latin (aquarium, name, volcano)
- From French (closet, resume, prestige)

On the other hand, Hebrew and Aramaic come from another family called the Semitic languages, and there was little borrowing between them and the Proto-Indo-European languages. Almost every Aramaic word would sound strange to you (and English to them).

So why learn Greek rather than Latin? I learned Latin and read Caesar's *Gallic Wars*; it was interesting. I learned Greek and read the Bible; it was life changing.

CHAPTER 2

THE GREEK ALPHABET

In this chapter we'll learn the twenty-four letters of the Greek alphabet and the transliteration of each.

INTRODUCTION

2.1   A transliteration is the equivalent of a letter in another language based on its sound. For example, the English "b" is the transliteration of the Greek "beta" (β) because they have the same sound.

This does not mean that a similar combination of letters in one language has the same meaning as the same combination in another. kappa + alpha + tau (κατ) does not mean "cat."

Some word-study books and commentaries avoid the Greek form and give only the transliteration. It's common in modern texts to set off a transliterated word in italics. "Jesus's last word from the cross was *tetelestai.*"

ALPHABET CHART

2.2   The following chart lists the letter's name, its transliteration, the small and capital Greek form, and its pronunciation. The online class (billmounce.com/biblestudygreek/2) will help you with the pronunciation of the alphabet.

letter	translit- eration	lower case	upper case	pronunciation	
Alpha	*a*	α	A	a	as in father
Beta	*b*	β	B	b	as in Bible
Gamma	*g*	γ	Γ	g	as in gone
Delta	*d*	δ	Δ	d	as in dog
Epsilon	*e*	ε	E	e	as in met
Zeta	*z*	ζ	Z	z	as in daze
Eta	*ē*	η	H	e	as in obey
Theta	*th*	θ	Θ	th	as in thing
Iota	*i*	ι	I	i	as in intrigue
Kappa	*k*	κ	K	k	as in kitchen
Lambda	*l*	λ	Λ	l	as in law
Mu	*m*	μ	M	m	as in mother
Nu	*n*	ν	N	n	as in new
Xi	*x*	ξ	Ξ	x	as in axiom
Omicron	*o*	ο	O	o	as in not
Pi	*p*	π	Π	p	as in peach
Rho	*r*	ρ	P	r	as in rod
Sigma	*s*	σ/ς	Σ	s	as in sit
Tau	*t*	τ	T	t	as in talk
Upsilon	*u/y*	υ	Υ	u	as the German ü
Phi	*ph*	φ	Φ	ph	as in phone
Chi	*ch*	χ	X	ch	as in loch
Psi	*ps*	ψ	Ψ	ps	as in lips
Omega	*ō*	ω	Ω	o	as in tone

Learning the capital letters is not as critical right now, but they are easy and you might as well learn it all now.

Different books follow slightly different transliteration schemes. Be sure to check the book's scheme before looking up a word. If you would rather learn modern Greek pronunciation, see this lesson in the online class.

HELPS

2.3   The vowels are α, ε, η, ι, ο, υ, ω. The rest are consonants.

2.4   Sigma is written as ς when it occurs at the end of the word, and as σ when it occurs elsewhere: ἀπόστολος.

2.5   Upsilon is transliterated as "*u*" if it's preceded by a vowel (εὐαγγέλιον → *euangelion*), and "*y*" if it occurs as a single vowel (μυστήριον → *mystērion*).

2.6   There are five letters that are easily confused.

Greek	English
η	n
ν	v
ρ	p
χ	x
ω	w

2.7   Notice the many similarities among the Greek and English letters, not only in shape and sound but also in their respective order in the alphabet. The Greek alphabet can be broken down into sections. It will parallel the English for a while,[1] differ, and then begin to parallel again. Here are those natural divisions.

α	*a*	ζ	*z*	ι	*i*	ο	*o*	φ	*ph*
β	*b*	η	*ē*	κ	*k*	π	*p*	χ	*ch*
γ	*g*	θ	*th*	λ	*l*	ρ	*r*	ψ	*ps*
δ	*d*			μ	*m*	σ ς	*s*	ω	*ō*
ε	*e*			ν	*n*	τ	*t*		
				ξ	*x*	υ	*u/y*		

---

[1]   Of course, Greek isn't actually following English since Greek was created before English; it just looks that way to us.

PRONOUNCING THE ALPHABET

2.8   In pronouncing the Greek letters, use the first sound of the name of the letter. Alpha is an "a" sound (there is no "pha" sound); lambda is an "l" sound (there is no "ambda" sound).

2.9   There is some disagreement among scholars on the pronunciation of a few letters, but I have chosen the most common, called "Erasmian" pronunciation. This is a different pronunciation scheme than is used by modern Greek, which is a much more beautiful pronunciation than the Erasmian suggests.

> You can download a chart from the online class that lists both the Erasmian and modern pronunciations. You can also listen to me and a modern Greek speaker work through the alphabet; all the vocabulary in the online class has both pronunciations.

2.10   The letter γ usually has a hard "g" sound, as in "get." However, when it's immediately followed by γ, κ, χ, or ξ, it's pronounced as "n." The word ἄγγελος is pronounced "angelos" (from which we get our word "angel"). The γ pronounced like an "n" is called a "**gamma nasal**" and is transliterated as "n" (*angelos*).

2.11   The ι can be either short or long, like the two i's in the English "intrigue." When you are memorizing vocabulary and not sure how to pronounce an ι, just listen to how your teacher pronounces the words (or to me on the website).

MISCELLANEOUS

2.12   **Iota subscript**. Sometimes an iota is written under the vowels α, η, or ω (ᾳ, ῃ, ῳ). This iota is not pronounced, but it does affect the word's meaning. It normally is not transliterated. The vowel combination is called an "improper diphthong."

2.13   **Capitals**. The Greek Testament was originally written in all capital letters without punctuation or spaces between the words. For example, John 1:1 began,

ΕΝΑΡΧΗΗΝΟΛΟΓΟΣ

The cursive script was created before the time of Christ but became popular in the ninth century. In cursive, the letters are connected like our present-day handwriting. Spaces were also added between words. In Greek texts today, John 1:1 begins,

εν αρχῃ ην ο λογος

In our Greek texts today, capitals are generally used only for proper names, the first word in a quotation, and the first word in the paragraph.

> The first capital letters were written with straight lines, which were easier to carve into a writing material like rock. In the first century AD, a modified style of capital letters was created called "uncial." These letters had more curves so they could be more easily written on the newer writing materials such as papyrus and parchment. The earliest New Testament documents are called uncials because of the style of script. In the eighth to the ninth century, cursive script was written smaller and in a style that could be written faster, saving both time and parchment. This script is known as "minuscule"; there are currently 2,867 New Testament minuscule manuscripts.

CHAPTER 3

PRONUNCIATION

Just as it's important to learn how to pronounce the letters, it's also important to pronounce the words correctly. But in order to pronounce a Greek word you must be able to break it down into its syllables. This is called "syllabification." We'll also learn about accents and punctuation.

DIPHTHONGS

3.1   A **diphthong** is a combination of two vowels that produce one sound. The second vowel is always ι or υ. Be sure to listen to me pronounce the Greek words in the online class.

αι	as in aisle	αιρω
ει	as in eight	ει
οι	as in oil	οικια
αυ	as in sauerkraut	αυτος
ου	as in soup	ουδε
υι	as in suite	υιος
ευ, ηυ	as in feud	ευθυς / ηυξανεν

BREATHING MARKS

3.2   Greek has two **breathing marks**, "rough" and "smooth." Every word beginning with a vowel or ρ has a breathing mark. I omitted the breathing marks in the previous chapter.

The **rough breathing mark** is a ʽ placed over the first vowel in a word or an initial rho. It adds an "h" sound to the word.

ὑπερ	→	*hyper*
ῥαββι	→	*rhabbi*

As you can see, the rough breathing mark is transliterated as an *h* and is placed before the transliterated vowel but after the initial ρ.

The **smooth breathing mark** is a ʼ placed over the first vowel in a word and is not pronounced or transliterated.

ἀποστολος	→	*apostolos*
αὐτος	→	*autos*

Either breathing mark is placed before an initial capital letter.

Ἰσραηλ	→	*Israēl*
Ἰεροσόλυμα	→	*Hierosolyma*

Either breathing mark is placed over the second vowel of an initial diphthong.

αἰτεω	→	*aiteō*
Αἰτεω	→	*Aiteō*
Αἱ	→	*Hai*

Here is the first part of John 1:1 with breathing marks.

ἐν ἀρχῃ ἡν ὁ λογος

SYLLABIFICATION

3.3　Greek words syllabify basically the same way as English words do. Therefore, if you "go with your feelings" (and you are a native English speaker), you will syllabify Greek words almost automatically. If you practice reading the examples below and listen to the reading exercises in the online class, you should pick it up. I will mark the syllables below with a space. The two most basic rules are:

■ There is one vowel or diphthong per syllable (just like in English).

■ A single consonant goes with the following vowel (e.g., αὐ τός, not αὐτ ός).

I included the interlinear translation for the fun of it.

John 3:16	οὕ τως	γαρ	ἠ γα πη σεν	ὁ	θε ος	τον	κο σμον,	ὥ στε[1]
	so	for	he loved	the	God	the	world	so that

τον	υἱ ον	τον	μο νο γε νη	ἐ δω κεν,	ἵ να	πας	ὁ	πι στευ ων
the	son	the	only	he gave	so that	each	the	one who believes

εἰς	αὐ τον	μη	ἀ πο λη ται	ἀλλ᾽	ἐ χη		ζω ην	αἰ ω νι ον.
in	him	not	he might perish	but	he might have		life	eternal

1 John 1:9	ἐ αν	ὁ μο λο γω μεν	τας	ἁ μαρ τι ας	ἡ μων,	πι στος
	if	we confess	the	sins	our	faithful

ἐ στιν	και	δι και ος,	ἵ να	ἀ φη		ἡ μιν	τας	ἁ μαρ τι ας
he is	and	just	so that	he might forgive		to us	the	sins

και	κα θα ρι ση	ἡ μας	ἀ πο	πα σης	ἀ δι κι ας.
and	he might cleanse	us	from	all	unrighteousness

Eph 2:8	τη	γαρ	χα ρι τι	ἐ στε	σε σω σμε νοι	δι α	πι στε ως·
	by the	for	grace	you are saved		through	faith

και	του το	οὐκ	ἐξ	ὑ μων,	θε ου	το	δω ρον.
and	this	not	of	you	of God	the	gift

ACCENTS

3.4 Almost every Greek word has an accent mark. It's placed over a vowel and shows which syllable receives the emphasis when you say the word.

name	*example*
acute	αἰτέω
grave	θεὸς
circumflex	Ἰησοῦς

Originally the accent was a pitch accent, the voice rising (αὐτός), falling (θεὸς), or rising and falling (Ἰησοῦς) on the accented

---

[1] σ goes with the following τ. See 3.11, rule 5.

syllable. A few centuries after the writing of the New Testament, most scholars believe the pitch accent was shifted to stress, as in English.

Here is John 1:1 as it is written with the breathing marks and accents.

ἐν ἀρχῇ ἦν ὁ λόγος

Be sure to consistently stress the accented syllable when saying the Greek word. Otherwise, other students will not know what Greek word you are saying.

3.5 Here are the verses we saw in 3.3 but now with accents. Read them, this time paying attention to which syllable receives the stress.

οὕτως γὰρ ἠγάπησεν ὁ θεὸς τὸν κόσμον, ὥστε τὸν υἱὸν τὸν μονογενῆ ἔδωκεν, ἵνα πᾶς ὁ πιστεύων εἰς αὐτὸν μὴ ἀπόληται ἀλλ᾽ ἔχῃ ζωὴν αἰώνιον (*John 3:16*).

ἐὰν ὁμολογῶμεν τὰς ἁμαρτίας ἡμῶν, πιστός ἐστιν καὶ δίκαιος, ἵνα ἀφῇ ἡμῖν τὰς ἁμαρτίας καὶ καθαρίσῃ ἡμᾶς ἀπὸ πάσης ἀδικίας (*1 John 1:9*).

τῇ γὰρ χάριτί ἐστε σεσῳσμένοι διὰ πίστεως· καὶ τοῦτο οὐκ ἐξ ὑμῶν, θεοῦ τὸ δῶρον (*Eph 2:8*).

> There is a true story about a cannibal tribe that killed the first two missionary couples who came to them. The couples had tried to learn their language, but could not. The third brave couple started experiencing the same problems with the language as had the two previous couples until the wife, who had been a music major in college, recognized that the tribe had a developed set of pitch accents that were essential in understanding the language. When they learned the significance these accents played in that language, they were able to learn the language and translate the Bible into that musically minded language. Luckily for us, while Greek accents were pitch, they are not that important.

3.6 **Acute to grave**. If the last syllable of a word has an acute accent and that word is *not* followed by a punctuation mark, the acute becomes a grave.

καί εἰρήνη → καὶ εἰρήνη

When we cite a single word that has a grave (e.g., καὶ), the grave is returned to the acute (καί).

DIACRITICALS

3.7 **Diaeresis**. There are some words in which we find two vowels that normally form a diphthong, but in the case of these words both vowels are pronounced. To show that these two vowels are pronounced as two separate sounds, a diaeresis (¨) is placed over the second vowel. This is like the French word *naïve* that was brought over into English. Ἡσαΐας (Ἡ σα ΐ ας) means "Isaiah" and has four syllables.

3.8 **Elision**. Sometimes the final vowel of a word drops off, and the word is marked for elision with an apostrophe (δέ → δ'; ἀλλα → ἀλλ'). English does something similar (e.g., "was not" → "wasn't").

PUNCTUATION

3.9 The comma and period are the same in Greek as they are in English. However, a dot above the line is the Greek semicolon, and an English semicolon is the Greek question mark.

Punctuation	Greek
θεός,	comma
θεός.	period
θεός·	semicolon
θεός;	question mark

VOCABULARY

3.10 You will be learning the 109 words that occur 150 times or more in the Greek Testament (including two other words). If you don't learn them, then you will not recognize anything when you look at a page of Greek. But these 109 words account for 92,696 of the 137,663 total word occurrences[2] in the Greek Testament (67%), and knowing the Greek words will make a verse or passage not look totally foreign. Knowing the vocabulary will also be important when we start phrasing a passage (chapter 21). Besides, it's fun to know some Greek words.

Remember, all these words are also in the free online class, at BillMounce.com/biblestudygreek. There you can see the Greek Word of the Day video for the word, hear its pronunciation, and see mnemonic devices for memorizing its definition. The number in parentheses is how many times it occurs in the Greek Testament; you don't have to memorize the number.

λόγος	word, Word; statement, message (329)
βασιλεία	kingdom (162)
ἄγγελος	angel; messenger (175)
κύριος	Lord; master, sir (713)
Ἰησοῦς	Jesus, Joshua (912)
Χριστός	Christ, Messiah (529)
θεός	God, god (1,316)
υἱός	son; descendant (377)
σωτήρ	savior (24)[3]
ὁ	the (19,822)

24,359 total word occurrences out of 137,663 (18%)

---

[2] All word counts are based on the Accordance text of Nestle/Aland edition 28. They do not include the longer ending of Mark (16:9–20) nor the story of the woman caught in adultery (John 7:53–8:11).

[3] Although σωτήρ occurs less than 150 times in the Greek Testament, I needed it for one of the exercises. It's a good word to know.

ADVANCED INFORMATION: SYLLABIFICATION RULES

3.11   Some people prefer to learn the actual rules for syllabification instead of trusting their instincts. Here are the basic rules.

   1.   *There is one vowel (or diphthong) per syllable.*

   ἀ κη κό α μεν   μαρ τυ ροῦ μεν

   There are as many syllables as there are vowels/diphthongs.

   2.   *A single consonant by itself (not a cluster[4]) goes with the following vowel.*

   ἐ ω ρά κα μεν   ἐ θε α σά με θα

   If the consonant is the final letter in the word, it goes with the preceding vowel.

   3.   *Two consecutive vowels that do not form a diphthong are divided.*

   ἐ θε α σά με θα   Ἠ σα ΐ ας

   4.   *A consonant cluster that cannot be pronounced[5] is divided, and the first consonant goes with the preceding vowel.*

   ἔμ προ σθεν   ἀρ χῆς

   5.   *A consonant cluster that can be pronounced together goes with the following vowel.*

   Χρι στός   γρα φή

   This includes a consonant cluster formed with μ or ν as the second letter, which is not natural for an English speaker.

   βρυ γμός   ἔ θνε σιν

   6.   *Double consonants[6] are divided.*

   ἀ παγ γέλ λο μεν   παρ ρη σί α

   7.   *Compound words[7] are divided where joined.*

   ἀντι χριστός   ἐκ βάλλω

---

[4]   A consonant cluster is two or more consonants in a row.

[5]   One way to check whether a consonant cluster can be pronounced together is to see whether those consonants ever begin a word. The cluster στ can be pronounced together because there is a word σταυρόω. Although the lexicon may not show all the possible clusters, it will show you many of them.

[6]   A double consonant is when the same consonant occurs twice in a row.

[7]   Compound words are words made up of two distinct words.

CHAPTER 4

ENGLISH NOUNS

W̲e will learn the causes of inflection in the English noun system: case, number, gender.

4.1 **Noun**. A noun is a word that stands for someone or something (i.e., a person, place, or thing).

Bill threw his big black *book* at the strange *teacher*.

4.2 **Inflection**. Sometimes the form of a word changes when it performs different *functions* in a sentence or when it changes its *meaning*. This is called "inflection."

For example, the personal pronoun is "he" if it refers to a male and "she" if it refers to a female. It's "she" when it's the subject of the sentence (e.g., "*She* is my wife"), but inflects to "her" when it's the direct object (e.g., "The teacher flunked *her*"). If the king and queen have one son, he is the "prince," but if they have two, they are "princes." If their child is a girl, she is a "princess." All these changes are examples of inflection.

The third-person pronoun is one of the most inflected words in English. (I will discuss the labels for the chart below later in the chapter.)

	masculine	*feminine*	*neuter*
subjective singular	he	she	it
possessive singular	his	her	its
objective singular	him	her	it
subjective plural	they	they	they
possessive plural	their	their	their
objective plural	them	them	them

INFLECTION DUE TO FUNCTION

4.3 The following grammatical concepts can affect the form of an English noun.

4.4 **Case.** Nouns perform different functions in a sentence. These different functions are categorized in "cases." In English there are three cases: subjective, possessive, and objective.

4.5 If a word is the *subject* of a verb, it's in the **subjective** case.

> *He* is my brother.

The subject is what does the action of an active verb and usually precedes the verb in word order.

> *Bill* ran to the store.

> The *ball* broke the window.

Word order shows that both "Bill" and "ball" are the subjects of their verbs. If it's difficult to determine the subject, ask the question "who?" or "what?" For example, Who ran to the store? Bill. What broke the window? The ball.

4.6 If a word shows *possession,* it's in the **possessive** case.

> *His* Greek Bible is always by *his* bed.

When showing possession, you can put "of" in front of the word, an apostrophe s after the word, or just an apostrophe if the word ends in "s."

> The Word *of God* is true.

> *God's* Word is true.

> The *apostles'* word was ignored.

4.7 If a word is the *direct object,* it's in the **objective** case. The direct object is the person or thing that is directly affected by the action of the verb. This means that whatever the verb does, it does it to the direct object. It usually follows the verb in word order.

Robin passed her *test*.

The waiter insulted *Hayden*.

Test and *Hayden* are the direct objects. You can usually determine the direct object by asking the question "what?" or "whom?" Robin passed what? Her test. The waiter insulted whom? Hayden.

case	function	example
Subjective	subject	*He* borrowed my computer.
Possessive	possession	He borrowed *my* computer.
Objective	direct object	He borrowed my *computer*.

Other than pronouns, most English nouns do not change their form when they perform different functions. For example, the word "teacher" stays the same whether it's the subject ("The *teacher* likes you") or the direct object ("You like the *teacher*"). However, to form the possessive, "teacher" adds apostrophe s ("She is the *teacher's* pet").

4.8   The **indirect object** is the person or thing that is indirectly affected by the action of the verb. This means that the indirect object is somehow involved in the action described by the verb, but not directly.

For example, "Karin threw Brad a ball." The direct object is "ball," since it's directly related to the action of the verb; it's what was thrown. But "Brad" is also related to the action of the verb, since the ball was thrown to him. "Brad" is the indirect object. If Karin threw Brad, then "Brad" would be the direct object.

One way to find the indirect object is to put the word "to" in front of the word and see if it makes sense.

"Karin threw Brad a ball."

"Karin threw to Brad a ball."

To whom did Karin throw the ball? To Brad. "Brad" is the indirect object.

English does not have a separate case for the indirect object. It uses the same form as the direct object (objective case).

4.9   **Word order.** English uses the order of words to determine which word is doing the action of the verb, receiving the action, etc. The subject is generally before the verb, and the direct object is generally after the verb. As we'll see in the next chapter, Greek uses a different linkage system to indicate which words are doing what, not word order.

INFLECTION DUE TO MEANING

4.10   **Number.** Inflection can also be caused by a word's number, which refers to whether a word is *singular* (referring to one thing) or *plural* (referring to more than one thing). English generally inflects a word relative to number in one of two ways. Most words add an "s" to make the word plural.

> *Students* should learn to study like this *student*.

Some words change an internal vowel or some other part of the word.

> The *woman* visited the *women*.

> The *child* joined in playing with the *children*.

4.11   **Gender.** Some words, mostly pronouns, inflect depending upon whether they are referring to a masculine, feminine, or neuter object. This is called "natural gender."

> *He* gave *it* to *her*.

"He," "it," and "her" are forms of the same pronoun. They are masculine, neuter, and feminine, respectively.

We refer to a man as "he" and a woman as "she." If a word refers to neither a masculine nor feminine thing, then it's neuter. We refer to a rock as an "it" because we do not regard the rock as male or female.

Another example is the word "prince." If the heir to the throne is male, then he is the "prince." If the child is female, she is the "princess."

Most English words do not change to indicate gender. "Teacher" refers to either a woman or a man.

VOCABULARY

ἀδελφός	brother (343)
ἀνήρ	male, husband; man (216)
ἄνθρωπος	man; person, human being; people, mankind (550)
γυνή	woman; wife (211)
πατήρ	father (413)
πνεῦμα	spirit, Spirit; wind, breath (379)
ἐγώ (ἡμεῖς)	I (we) (2,661)
σύ (ὑμεῖς)	you (2,903)
αὐτός	he, she, it (they, them) (5,577)

37,612 total word occurrences out of 137,663 (27%)

> You may be wondering why we are learning English grammar in a text on Greek. It is because, ultimately, you are learning Greek in order to better understand the biblical author's intended meaning. Meaning is conveyed with words and grammar. If we don't know Greek grammar, we will not be able to interpret the Greek text. And we can't understand Greek grammar if we don't understand English grammar.

CHAPTER 5

GREEK NOUNS

In Greek, we don't use word order to determine the
function of a word. Rather, the Greek words will
inflect to show their function, and they use something
called "case endings" to do so. The case ending is a
suffix attached to the end of the word. For example, if
you see the word θεοί, the ι tells you that the word is
plural and is functioning as the subject of a verb. There
are four cases: nominative (indicating subject), accusative (direct object), dative (indirect object), and genitive ("of").

GREEK INFLECTION

5.1   **Stem**. The basic form of a noun is called the "stem." For example,
the stem of the Greek word for "God" is θεο. The stem will inflect
due to two forces: function and meaning.

5.2   **Case endings**. Unlike English, most Greek nouns change their
form depending on their *function* in the sentence. They do this by
using case endings, which are suffixes added to the end of the
stem.

The Greek equivalent to the English subjective case is called the
nominative case. If a word is the subject of a verb, the writer will
put it into the nominative case by adding a nominative case ending onto the stem. The letter ς can be used as a nominative case
ending. In John 3:16, which word is the subject?

ἠγάπησεν   ὁ θεὸς   τὸν κόσμον
loved   *God*   the world
God loved the world (*John 3:16*).

23

Let me explain what I am doing in this illustration above, just to be clear.

The first line is the Greek. To save space, and because it's often not translated, I have usually kept ὁ (in all its forms) with the following word (e.g., ὁ is with θεός, and τόν is with κόσμον).

The second line is a word-for-word translation of the Greek. I have italicized the translation of the Greek word that illustrates the point I am making. For example, because I am talking about the subject, "God" is italicized in the translation above.

The third and following lines (if present) are normal translations of the verse. The first translation has been chosen to illustrate the point I am making. If there is only one translation, it's generally my own. If there are more than one, it means I am using multiple translations to illustrate a point, and I use the abbreviation of the translation to identify which translation I am using (see page xiii for a list of abbreviations). Usually the difference will be one of clarity; one translation will bring out the nuance of the construction and the other will leave it vague. Rarely do translations contradict each other.

In traditional approaches to Greek, we would see the ς case ending, recognize that this may indicate the word is in the nominative case (because we memorized it), and conclude that it's the subject of the verb. For our Bible Study Greek approach, we use the software or paper tools to tell us the word is in the nominative, but you still need to understand the concept of case endings.

5.3   The only way to determine the subject of a Greek sentence is by the case endings since the subject can occur before or after the verb.

Word order does not identify the subject. In our example θεός comes after the verb, but it's the case ending that tells us θεός is in the nominative and therefore is the subject of the verb.

Consider the following four sentences. How do we know that they are all saying that God loves the world, and not that the world loves God?

ἀγαπᾷ   ὁ Θεός   τὸν κόσμον
loves   the God   the world

ἀγαπᾷ   τὸν κόσμον   ὁ Θεός
loves   the world   the God

τὸν κόσμον   ὁ Θεὸς   ἀγαπᾷ
the world   the God   loves

ὁ Θεὸς   ἀγαπᾷ   τὸν κόσμον
the God   loves   the world

We know θεός is the subject in all four sentences because ς is a case ending indicating the nominative case and hence the subject of the verb. Although the order of the words is different, each example has the same basic meaning.

5.4   **Number**. Along with function, the *meaning* of a word can cause inflection. The main example is whether a word is singular or plural.

Instead of adding an "s" to a word, Greek indicates singular or plural by using different case endings. The difference between the singular and plural here is indicated by the case endings ς and ι.

> ἀπόστολος → apostle
>
> ἀπόστολοι → apostles

ἀπόστολος is nominative singular, and ἀπόστολοι is nominative plural.

5.5   **Gender**. A noun is either masculine, feminine, or neuter. It has only one gender and it never varies.

Most Greek nouns do not follow natural gender. In other words, the gender of a word has no necessary connection to the meaning of the word. This is called "grammatical gender."

- ἁμαρτία is a feminine noun meaning "sin," although "sin" is not a female concept.

- ἁμαρτωλός is a masculine noun meaning "sinner," although "sinner" is not a masculine concept.

- πνεῦμα is a neuter word meaning "spirit," but the Holy Spirit is not a thing; he is a "person."

However, you will see natural gender in pronouns (αὐτός, "he"; αὐτή, "she") and words like "brother" (ἀδελφός, masculine) and "sister" (ἀδελφή, feminine).

PARSING

5.6 **Lexical form.** The lexical form of a noun is the form it is listed as in the lexicon. ("Lexicon" is just a fancy term for a dictionary.) This is the vocabulary form you are memorizing. The **inflected form** is the form as it appears in the actual text. For example, the lexical form of the word meaning "world" is κόσμος. If it occurs as a direct object, the inflected form will be κόσμον.

5.7 **GK Numbers.** For many years we have used what are called "Strong's numbers." Each Greek and Hebrew word was tagged with a unique number by Dr. James Strong. This way, no matter what inflected form a word took, it could always be identified by the same number. The words κόσμον and κόσμος are both #3180.

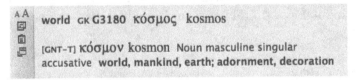

world GK G3180 κόσμος kosmos

[GNT–T] κόσμον kosmon Noun masculine singular accusative world, mankind, earth; adornment, decoration

Because Strong's numbers originally omitted many Greek and Hebrew words, Zondervan introduced a new set of numbers (done by Ed Goodrick and John Kohlenberger; hence, "GK"), and it's these numbers that I am using in this book and my databases. At the online class at chapter 5, you can download a conversion chart to move between the two numbering systems. The word κόσμος in the Strong system is #2889.

world G2889 κόσμος kosmos

[GNT–T] κόσμον kosmon Noun masculine singular accusative world, mankind, earth; adornment, decoration

However, if you are using my translation (*MOUNCE-NT*), it will show the GK number (#3180).

> **AA**
>
> **world** GK **G3180** κόσμος kosmos
>
> [GNT-T] κόσμον kosmon Noun masculine singular accusative **world, mankind, earth; adornment, decoration**

For all other translations and resources, Accordance shows the Strong's number. Logos uses the Strong's numbers for everything. The "G" in front of the number means it is a Greek word.

5.8 **Gloss**. When a tool like Accordance gives you a short definition of a word, it's the word's gloss. This is not meant to be used in translation and Bible study. A gloss is simply one of the main meanings the Greek word has. When I talk about what a word "means," I am not talking about its gloss but about its fuller and more complete meaning.

5.9 **Parsing**. Your Bible study tools will parse the noun for you. This means they will tell you its case, number, gender, lexical form, and perhaps other pieces of information such as its gloss. Different tools follow different patterns; they will not necessarily be case, number, gender.

On the next page is John 3:16 in Accordance and Logos. What do they tell you about the word κόσμον?

5.10 There are basically four cases in Greek: nominative, accusative, dative, and genitive.

NOMINATIVE

> When a discussion of a noun (and eventually a verb) is preceded with a grammatical term such as "subject," "direct object," "descriptive," "possessive," etc. (as below), these are the technical names of the grammatical category. These are the terms commentaries use to discuss grammar.

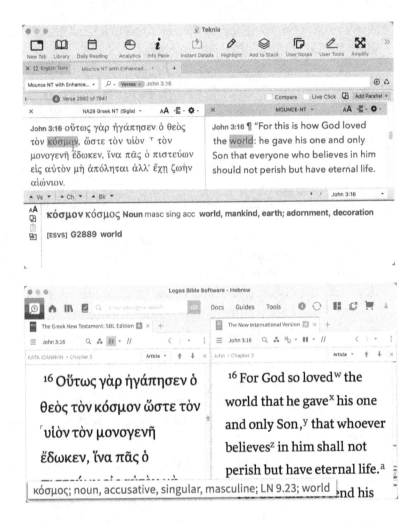

5.11 Subject. The normal use of the nominative case is to designate the subject of a verb.

ὁ θεὸς   αὐτὸν   ἤγειρεν ἐκ   νεκρῶν
God   *him*   *raised* *from dead*

God raised him from the dead (*Rom 10:9*).

Who raised him? God raised him. "God" is the subject.

You will come across words listed as nominative that will not be functioning as the subject of the verb. When this happens, tell yourself to have a little humility and realize that this is one of the grammatical constructions you haven't yet learned. This is also true of the other cases; I am only showing you the main uses of each case. There is much more to learn in Church Greek, the second part of this book.

5.12   **Lexical form**. The lexical form of a noun is its nominative singular form. If you see the inflected form ἀπόστολοι, which is nominative plural, the word would be listed in the lexicon under ἀπόστολος.

ACCUSATIVE

5.13   **Direct object**. A word functioning as a direct object is put into the accusative case.

ἠγάπησεν ὁ θεὸς τὸν κόσμον
loved   God   *the world*
God loved *the world* (John 3:16).

What did God love? He loved the world. "World" is the direct object.

DATIVE

5.14   **Indirect object**. The dative case is used to indicate the indirect object.

ὁ   πειράζων εἶπεν αὐτῷ· εἰ υἱὸς εἶ   τοῦ θεοῦ
the tempter   said *to him* if son you are of God

The tempter said *to him*, if you are the Son of God ... *(Matt 4:3)*.

"Him" (Jesus) is indirectly connected with the action of the verb "said."

GENITIVE

5.15   The Greek genitive case functions much like the English word "of" and the possessive case.

5.16   The **head noun** is the word that the word in the genitive is modifying. In the phrase "love of God," "love" would be the head noun and "God" would be in the genitive.

In English the possessive case can be indicated by the apostrophe. "Everyone breaks God's laws." Greek, however, does not have the apostrophe, and so all Greek constructions are in the form "of ...."

5.17 **Descriptive**. The most common use of the genitive is when the word in the genitive gives some description of the head noun. You will often find "of" used to translate this use.

ἐνδυσώμεθα τὰ ὅπλα τοῦ φωτός
Let us put on the armor of light
Let us put on the armor *of light* (Rom 13:12).

τοῦ φωτός is in the genitive, and ὅπλα is the head noun. "Light" is describing something about the head noun "armor."

5.18 **Possessive**. When personal pronouns are used to mean "my," "your," "his," etc., they will be in the genitive. However, in Greek they generally come after the head noun.

ἐξ Αἰγύπτου ἐκάλεσα τὸν υἱόν μου
out of Egypt I called son my
Out of Egypt I called *my* Son (Matt 2:15).

οἴνῳ ὀλίγῳ χρῶ διὰ ... τὰς πυκνάς σου ἀσθενείας.
wine little use because of frequent your illness
Use a little wine because of *your* frequent illnesses (1 Tim 5:23).

You will see this word order in a Greek-English interlinear, but the order is not visible in a reverse interlinear.

ἐξ Αἰγύπτου ἐκάλεσα μου τὸν υἱόν
out of Egypt I called my son

VOCATIVE

5.19 There technically is a fifth case, although it's so similar to the nominative in form (and in some ways, in function) that we still speak of the four cases in Greek. The vocative is the case of *direct address*. When speaking directly to a person, the word used is in the vocative.

ἔρχου κύριε Ἰησοῦ
come   Lord   Jesus
Come, Lord Jesus! (Rev 22:20)

κύριε represents one of the few forms in which the vocative is distinctly different from the nominative. Often, the vocative is identical in form to the nominative, but the software's parsing will still indicate that it is a vocative.

5.20   ὦ may be included if there is deep emotion or emphasis.

ὁ Ἰησοῦς εἶπεν αὐτῇ, ὦ γύναι, μεγάλη σου ἡ πίστις
Jesus   said   to her   O woman   great   your   the faith
ESV: Then Jesus answered her, "O woman, great is your faith!" (Matt 15:28)
NET: Then Jesus answered her, "Woman, your faith is great!"

Because "O" is archaic English, the NET doesn't explicitly translate it but allows "woman" to translate both words, ὦ γύναι.

VOCABULARY

γῆ	earth, land; region; humanity (248)
κόσμος	world (185)
οὐρανός	heaven; sky (272)
μαθητής	disciple (261)
πίστις	faith, belief; trust; teaching (243)
οὗτος	this (these) (1,383)
ἐκεῖνος	that (those) (260)
καί	and; even, also (9,139)
ἀλλά (ἀλλ᾽)	but (638)
δέ (δ᾽)	and; but (2,774)

53,015 total word occurrences out of 137,663 (39%)

CHAPTER 6

PREPOSITIONS

Prepositions and their objects form a prepositional phrase. Prepositions can have a wide range of meaning, and they control the case of their objects. Prepositional phrases can be adverbial or adjectival.

ENGLISH

6.1 A preposition is a word that indicates the relationship between a noun (or pronoun) and other words in the sentence.

> The book is *under* the table.

The preposition "under" describes the relationship between "book" and "table."

6.2 The noun that follows the preposition is called the **object of the preposition**.

> The flashlight is under the *bed.*
>
> She went through the *woods* to Grandma's house.

"Bed" is the object of the preposition "under," and "woods" is the object of "through."

6.3 English requires the object of all prepositions to be in the objective case. You would not say, "The book is under he." You say, "The book is under him." "He" is subjective and "him" is objective.

6.4   The preposition, its object, and any modifiers are together called the **prepositional phrase**.

> The flashlight is *under the bed.*

> She went *through the woods* to Grandma's house.

GREEK

6.5   **Elision**. Prepositions that end in a vowel may drop their final vowel when the following word begins with a vowel. The omission will be marked with an apostrophe. These changes were necessary in order to pronounce the combination of sounds more easily.

> μετὰ αὐτόν → μετ᾿ αὐτόν

6.6   When a preposition ends in a vowel and the following word begins with a vowel and a rough breathing, the consonant before the final vowel in the preposition often changes as well. In this example, the α drops out and τ becomes θ.

> μετὰ ἡμῶν → μετ᾿ ἡμῶν → μεθ᾿ ἡμῶν

You will see the various forms in the vocabulary section.

> ἀπό (ἀπ᾿, ἀφ᾿)

6.7   **Range of meaning**. Many Greek prepositions have a wide range of meanings. The preposition ἐν can mean "in," "among," "into," "with," "because," "while," etc. In many instances the meaning will be obvious from context, but in others the decision will be necessarily interpretive.

6.8   **Single case**. A preposition "governs" the case of its object. In other words, the case of the preposition's object is determined by the preposition.

Some prepositions like εἰς require their object to be in the accusative case.

ἐλθόντες εἰς τὴν οἰκίαν εἶδον τὸ παιδίον
going   into the *house* they saw the child
On coming to the *house*, they saw the child *(Matt 2:11)*.

οἰκίαν is accusative, and is the object of the preposition εἰς.

Some prepositions like ἐν take their objects in the dative case.

ἐβαπτίζοντο ἐν τῷ Ἰορδάνῃ ποταμῷ ὑπ' αὐτοῦ
they were baptized in the Jordan *river* by him
They were baptized by him in the *river* Jordan *(Matt 3:6)*.

ποταμῷ is dative, and is the object of the preposition ἐν. τῷ
Ἰορδάνῃ modifies ποταμῷ.

Some prepositions like ἀπό take their object in the genitive case.

νυνὶ δὲ κατηργήθημεν ἀπὸ τοῦ νόμου
now but we were released from the *law*
But now we have been released from the *Law* *(Rom 7:6)*.

νόμου is genitive, and is the object of ἀπό.

6.9   **Multiple cases.** Some prepositions are followed by an object that
      can be in two or even three cases. (The object of a preposition will
      never be in the nominative.) In this situation, the preposition has
      a different set of meanings depending on the case of its object.
      This is why a Greek lexicon divides its discussion of prepositions
      based on the case of its object. The translator must identify the
      case of the object before translating the preposition.

      For example, the preposition διά means "through" if its object is
      in the genitive case, but it means "on account of" if its object is in
      the accusative.

      οὕτως γὰρ γέγραπται διά τοῦ προφήτου
      in this way for it's written *through the* prophet
      for this is what has been written *through the prophet (Matt 2:5)*

      ἔσεσθε μισούμενοι ὑπὸ πάντων διά τὸ ὄνομά μου
      you will be hated   by all *on account of* the name my
      NIV: You will be hated by everyone *because of me (Matt 10:22)*.
      RSV: You will be hated by all *for my name's sake*.

PREPOSITIONAL PHRASES

6.10 As in English, the preposition, its object, and any modifiers are called a "prepositional phrase," which always begins with the preposition.

ὃ	προεπηγγείλατο	διὰ	τῶν προφητῶν	αὐτοῦ
which	he promised	*through*	*prophets*	*his*

which he promised *through his prophets (Rom 1:2).*

When doing Bible study, it's important to identify the end of the prepositional phrase.

6.11 In chapter 3 you learned the vocabulary word ὁ, which is the Greek definite article, "the." Because Greek does not have an indefinite article ("a"), we can simply call ὁ the "article."

- If a word or phrase is *not* preceded by the article, we say that it is **anarthrous**. In the sentence ὁ θεὸς ἀγαθός, the adjective ἀγαθός is anarthrous. "God is *good*."

- If a word or phrase *is* preceded by the article, we say that it is **articular**. In the sentence μὴ μιμοῦ τὸ κακὸν ἀλλὰ τὸ ἀγαθόν (3 John 11), κακὸν and ἀγαθόν are both articular, being preceded by the article in its form τό. "Do not imitate *the* evil but *the good*."

6.12 Greek regularly drops ὁ in a prepositional phrase. "In the world" could be written as ἐν τῷ κόσμῳ (τῷ is an inflected form of the article), or without the article as ἐν κόσμῳ. In this situation, and if it fits the context, the translator may put the article back in.

ἁμαρτία	ἦν	ἐν	κόσμῳ
sin	was	in	world

NIV: Sin was in *the* world *(Rom 5:13).*

6.13 **Adverbial**. Prepositional phrases are generally *adverbial*. In other words, the prepositional phrase will tell you something about the action of the verb. It will be anarthrous. The case of the object of the preposition will generally be dative or accusative.

δικαιούμενοι δωρεὰν τῇ αὐτοῦ χάριτι διὰ   τῆς ἀπολυτρώσεως
Being justified   freely   by   his   grace   *through* the   redemption

Being justified freely by his grace *through* the redemption
(Rom 3:24)

The prepositional phrase διὰ τῆς ἀπολυτρώσεως tells us the
means by which we are justified.

προέθετο ὁ θεὸς ἱλαστήριον   διὰ   τῆς πίστεως ἐν τῷ αὐτοῦ αἵματι
he set forth God as a propitiation *through the faith*   by the his   blood

CSB: God presented him as the mercy seat *by his blood, through
faith* (Rom 3:25).

"By his blood" is the means by which God accomplished the propitiation. "Through faith" is the means by which we receive the
benefits of Christ's sacrifice.

6.14   **Attributive**. When a prepositional phrase is articular, it can function as an adjective in that it modifies a noun. We call this the
adjectival or *attributive* use of the prepositional phrase. The case of
the object of the preposition will generally be genitive.

διὰ   τῆς ἀπολυτρώσεως τῆς ἐν Χριστῷ Ἰησοῦ
through the   redemption   *the   in Christ   Jesus*

Through the redemption *that is in Christ Jesus* (Rom 3:24)

The prepositional phrase "that is in Christ Jesus" tells us something about the "redemption," namely, how it is made available.
Because we do not have this construction in English, you will find
translators add words to make it acceptable English ("that is" in
the preceding translation).

If you are using a reverse interlinear, the verse will look like this:

through the   redemption   that came by Christ   Jesus
διὰ   τῆς ἀπολυτρώσεως τῆς   ἐν Χριστῷ Ἰησοῦ

6.15   When the prepositional phrase is functioning as an attributive, the word order will usually be article-noun-article-prepositional phrase. The second article is merely telling you that the following prepositional phrase is modifying the previous noun.

Usually the "article + prepositional phrase" is turned into a relative clause, which means a verb must be added.

οὕτως   γὰρ   ἐδίωξαν   τοὺς προφήτας τοὺς πρὸ ὑμῶν
in this way for   they persecuted the   prophets   the   before you

For that is how they persecuted the prophets *who were before you* (*Matt 5:12*).

The articular (τούς) prepositional phrase πρὸ ὑμῶν is modifying προφήτας.

Other times the article will not need to be translated, which is fine since all it's doing is showing that the following phrase is modifying the previous word.

τὴν   ἐξανάστασιν τὴν   ἐκ   νεκρῶν
the   resurrection   the   from dead

RSV: the resurrection *from the dead (Phil 3:11)*

The second τήν shows that ἐκ νεκρῶν modifies ἐξανάστασιν.

6.16   **Substantival**. Articular prepositional phrases can also function as a noun, what is called the substantival use.

ἔφαγεν καὶ ἔδωκεν τοῖς μετ᾿ αὐτοῦ
He ate   and   gave   to the   with   him

He ate and gave [the consecrated bread] *to those with him (Luke 6:4)*.

The prepositional phrase μετ᾿ αὐτοῦ is functioning as the indirect object of ἔδωκεν. Because we do not have this construction in English, translators will add words to this construction to make sensible English.

6.17   **Chart**. Perhaps this flow chart will help you remember the different functions of the prepositional phrase.

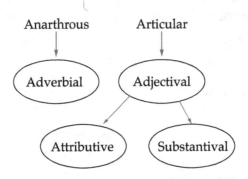

Anarthrous prepositional phrases tend to be adverbial. Articular prepositional phrases are adjectival, functioning either as an attributive or a substantive.

6.18   **Phrasing**. In chapter 14 you will learn an exegetical process I call "phrasing." It lays out the text graphically so you can see the main thoughts, the modifying thoughts, and the author's flow of thought.

In this example, the articular prepositional phrase ἐκ νεκρῶν modifes the noun ἐξανάστασιν (Phil 3:11) and so is indented under the word it modifies.

>   τὴν ἐξανάστασιν
>   τὴν ἐκ νεκρῶν

>   the resurrection
>   from the dead

Here is the phrasing of part of Romans 3:24.

>   δικαιούμενοι
>   δωρεὰν
>   τῇ αὐτοῦ χάριτι
>   διὰ τῆς ἀπολυτρώσεως
>   τῆς ἐν Χριστῷ Ἰησοῦ

being justified

> freely

> by his grace

> through the redemption

>> that is in Christ Jesus

Our being justified was done freely (i.e., at no cost to ourselves), it was done by God's grace (not our works), and it was accomplished through our redemption, which came from Christ Jesus. You can see how the prepositional phrase διὰ τῆς ἀπολυτρώσεως modifies the verbal form δικαιούμενοι, and how ἐν Χριστῷ Ἰησοῦ modifies ἀπολυτρώσεως.

In phrasing, I want to keep Greek word order as much as possible. But when I can't, I mark the original location of the moved word with an elipsis (see below).

Major conjunctions like γάρ go on their own line and the same distance in from the left side. This helps you see the overall flow of thought.

> γὰρ

οὕτως ... ἐδίωξαν τοὺς προφήτας

>> τοὺς πρὸ ὑμῶν.

> for

in this way ... they persecuted the prophets

>> before you.

I will be using bits and pieces of phrasing through the early chapters. Phrasing will also show you why we are learning grammar—not grammar for grammar's sake but so you can see the meaning of the verse.

VOCABULARY

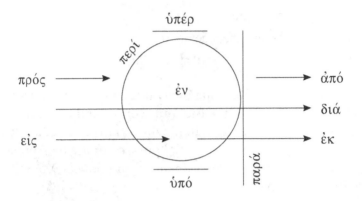

εἰς	acc: into; in (1,759)
ἐκ (ἐξ)	gen: from; out of (912)
πρός	acc: to ("towards"); with (699)
ἀπό (ἀπ᾽, ἀφ᾽)	gen: from ("away from") (644)
διά (δι᾽)	gen: through, by (666) acc: on account of
ἐν	dat: in; by; with (2,746)
παρά	gen: from (193) dat: with acc: beside
περί	gen: concerning (333) acc: around
ὑπέρ	gen: for ("in behalf of") (149)[1] acc: above
ὑπό (ὑπ᾽, ὑφ᾽)	gen: by (219) acc: under

61,335 total word occurrences out of 137,663 (45%)

---

[1] Although ὑπέρ occurs less than 150 times, it was necessary to complete the chart above.

CHAPTER 7

ENGLISH VERBS

English verbs have person and number, as well as tense, voice, and mood. You will also be introduced to the concept of "aspect."

7.1   **Verb**. A verb is a word that describes an action or a state of being.

Tom *hit* the ball.

Greek *is* the heavenly language.

7.2   **Person**. There are three persons: first, second, and third.

■ *First person* is the person speaking ("I," "we").

I am the teacher.

We are the students.

■ *Second person* is the person being spoken to ("you").

You are the student.

You are the best students.

■ *Third person* is everything else ("he," "she," "it," "they," "book"). You could also say that third person is that which is spoken about.

This *book* is wonderful.

7.3 **Number**. If the subject of a verb is third person singular (in the present active), English generally inflects the present active verb by adding "s."[1]

I kick the ball.	We kick the ball.
You kick the ball.	You kick the ball.
He kicks the ball.	They kick the ball.

There is no case or gender in verbs.

7.4 **Agreement**. Verbs must agree with their subject. You would not say "Bill *say* to the class that there *is* no tests."

- Since "Bill" is singular third person, you would say, "Bill *says* to the class."

- Because "tests" is plural, you would say, "There *are* no tests."

The presence or absence of the "s" at the end of the verb, and the difference between "is" and "are," are examples of agreement.

7.5 **Tense**. "Tense" in English refers to the *time* when the action of the verb takes place.

- If you study your Greek right now, the verb is in the present tense ("study").

- If you are planning on doing it tomorrow, the verb is in the future tense ("will study").

- If you did it last night, the verb is in the past tense ("studied").

In other words, in English the terms "tense" and "time" refer to the same thing.

7.6 **Principal parts**. English verbs divide into three forms: the present, past, and past participle. These are called the verb's "principal parts." Many verbs do not have three distinct forms.

---

[1] This is a characteristic of the present active. Other tenses are not affected. We say, "I loved," and, "He loved."

tense	"to swim"	"to eat"	"to walk"	"to read"
present	swim	eat	walk	read
past	swam	ate	walked	read
past participle	swum	eaten	walked	read

All other tenses are formed from one of these tenses with the aid of a helping word (e.g., "will swim," "have eaten").

7.7   **Voice**. The voice of a verb refers to the relationship between a verb and its subject.

- When a verb is **active**, the subject is *doing* the action of the verb.

  "I *walk* the dog."

  "They *called* the preacher."

  "I" is the subject of the verb "walk," which means it's doing the action of the verb.

- When a verb is **passive**, the subject of the verb is *receiving* the action. English forms the present passive by adding the helping verb "am/is/are" or "am/are being" to the past participle.

  Fido *is walked* by Tyler.

  They *are being called* by the preacher.

  "Fido" is the subject of the verb "is walked," but "Fido" is not doing the action of the verb "walked." The action of the verb is being performed by "Tyler," and it's being done to the subject, "Fido."

  You can often tell if a verb is passive by placing "by" after the verb and seeing if it makes sense. "I was hit." "I was hit by what?" "I was hit by the ball." "Was hit" is a passive verb.

  When you use a helping verb to form the passive voice, the time of the verbal construction is determined by the helping verb, not the main verb. For example, the active construction "I remember" shifts to "I am remembered" in the passive. Because "am" is present, the construction "am remembered" is present, even though "remembered" is a past participle.

MOOD

7.8   **Mood** refers to the relationship between the verb and reality.

7.9   **Indicative**. A verb in the indicative mood describes something that *is*, as opposed to something that may or might be. We say that the indicative is the mood of reality. The indicative includes statements and questions. For example, "I am rich." "Are you rich?" Most of the verbs we'll meet for some time are in the indicative mood.

> Greek *is* fun.

> Hebrew *requires* more study.

7.10   The **subjunctive** mood does not describe what is but what *may* or *might* be. In other words, it's the mood not of reality but of possibility or probability. In a sense, it describes an action that is one step removed from reality.

> I *might learn* Hebrew.

7.11   A common use of the subjunctive is in an "if" clause.

> If I *were* a rich man, I would hire a Greek tutor.

If in fact the speaker were rich, he would not have used the subjunctive "were" but the indicative: "I *am* rich and therefore I will hire a tutor." This would be a statement of fact, the mood being one of reality. However, if he were not rich, the speaker would use the subjunctive form "were": "If I *were* rich ...."

7.12   **Imperative**. The imperative mood is used to state a command. In English, the subject is always second person ("you"), whether implicit or expressed, sometimes with an exclamation mark as the sentence's punctuation.

> *Watch* the basketball game!

The English imperative is usually not inflected, but we do add words to strengthen or further define the intent of the imperative.

> Go *quickly*!

INFINITIVE

7.13 An **infinitive** is a verbal noun. It's most easily recognized as a verb preceded by the word "to."

> *To study* is my highest aspiration.

In this case, the infinitive "to study" is the subject of the verb "is."

Infinitives and participles (below) are technically not a mood, but it is normal to discuss them with moods.

PARTICIPLES

7.14 **Participles** are verbal adjectives. They can be formed by adding "-ing" to a verb.[2]

> The man, *eating* by the window, is my Greek teacher.

> After *eating*, I will go to bed.

7.15 **Participial phrase**. The participle and its accompanying elements form a participial phrase. Participial phrases generally begin with a participle and can include a direct object and other modifiers.

> After *eating the cake,* I refused to stand on the scale.

> The dog *sitting in the road* is in real trouble.

7.16 **Word order**. In a sentence like, "While eating, he saw her," English requires that "he" is the one who is eating, not "her," since "he" is closer in word order to the participle "eating." We will see that this is not the case in Greek, which uses inflection to link the participle to the word it modifies.

7.17 **Adverbial**. There are two types of participles. A participle can have an adverbial function.

> *After praying,* my Greek teacher gave us the final.

> After praying
> my Greek teacher gave us the final.

---

[2] There are other ways to form a participle. For example, in the following sentence, "eaten" is a past participle: "The food, eaten by the class, was delicious."

In this sentence, "praying" is a participle that tells us something relative to the verb "gave." The teacher gave us the final after he was done praying.

7.18 **Adjectival**. A participle can also have an adjectival function.

The woman, *sitting* by the window, is my Greek teacher.

The woman ... is my Greek teacher.
    sitting by the window

In this example, "sitting" tells us something about the noun "woman."

7.19 **Gerunds**. In English we also have gerunds. They are identical in form to a participle, but instead of functioning as an adjective they function as a noun.

Living well is a goal of our culture.

We'll see that Greek does not have gerunds because a Greek participle can function as a noun as well as an adjective.

7.20 **Phrasing**. In phrasing, it is important to identify the beginning and end of a participial phrase, much like you do with a prepositional phrase. The participial phrase is always dependent, so it is generally modifying something. Put the participial phrase under (or above) the word that it modifies.

After eating the cake,
    I started doing the dishes.

"After" is an adverb that emphasizes when the action of the participle occurred.

ASPECT

7.21 Aspect is perhaps the most difficult concept to grasp in Greek verbs, and yet it's the most important and most misunderstood. The basic genius of the Greek verb is not its ability to indicate *when* the action of the verb occurs (time), but what *type of action* it describes, or what we call "aspect." So let's first learn about aspect in English.

7.22 What is the difference between saying "I studied last night" and "I was studying last night"? The first merely says that an event occurred last night; it describes a simple event. It does not give you a clue as to the precise nature of your study time. The second pictures the action of studying as an ongoing action, a process, something that took place over a period of time. This difference between a simple event ("studied") and a process ("was studying") is what I mean by "aspect."

In Galatians 2:12 the RSV reads,

For before certain men came from James, he *ate* with the Gentiles; but when they came he drew back and separated himself, fearing the circumcision party.

What does Paul mean by "ate"? Did Peter eat one meal or did he eat often with the Gentiles? Is Paul confronting Peter for doing just one thing wrong? I always thought so, until I learned that this particular Greek verb indicates an ongoing action. Peter *often ate* with the Gentiles before he pulled back under pressure from some of the Jewish Christians. This is why the NIV uses "used to" in their translation.

Before certain men came from James, he *used to eat* with the Gentiles. But when they arrived, he began to draw back and separate himself from the Gentiles because he was afraid of those who belonged to the circumcision group.

7.23 There are three aspects. The **undefined** (or "perfective") aspect means that the action of the verb is thought of as a simple event, without commenting on whether or not it's a process or a completed action.

For God so *loved* the world that he *gave* his only Son, that whoever believes in him should not perish but have eternal life. (John 3:16 RSV)

This is the "default" form of the verb. If you just want to say something happened, and you don't want to say anything else about the nature of the action, you use the simple, undefined form of the word: "I studied."

7.24 The **continuous** (or "imperfective") aspect means that the action of the verb is thought of as an ongoing process.

> In pointing out these things to the brothers *and sisters*, you will be a good servant of Christ Jesus, *constantly* nourished on the words of the faith and of the good doctrine which you have been following *(1 Tim 4:6; NASB)*.

When you want to emphasize that the action of the verb is continuous, that it is an ongoing process, you use the continuous form of the verb: "I was studying."

7.25 The **perfective** (or "combinative") aspect describes an action that was brought to completion and its results are felt in the present. Of course, the time of the verb is from the viewpoint of the writer/speaker, not the reader. In one sense, the perfective aspect is the combination of the undefined (completed act in the past) and the continuous (ongoing effects of that act), hence the term "combinative."

> For the one who *has died* has been set free from sin (Rom 6:7).

> For *it's written* that Abraham had two sons (Gal 4:22).

> That which *is born* of the flesh is flesh, and that which *is born* of the Spirit is spirit (John 3:6).

7.26 **Portrayal of reality**. Language does not describe what necessarily is. Language is used to describe an event in the way in which the speaker wants you to understand. The same event could be accurately described as a simple, continuous, or perfected event. There is not a necessary link between reality and my description of that reality.

If I chose to use a continuous verbal form, it's saying that I want to emphasize the continuous nature of the event. I want to look at the action from the inside as it were, as if we were part of the action itself.

πολλοὶ πλούσιοι ἔβαλλον   πολλά
Many   rich   *were putting in*   much.

NET: Many rich people *were throwing in* large amounts
(Mark 12:41).

ESV: Many rich people *put in* large sums.

ἔβαλλον is an imperfect, emphasizing the continual action of putting money in.

What is interesting is that a few verses later, Jesus will use the aorist to describe the same event because in that context he was looking at the action as a whole, from the outside as it were, not wanting to emphasize some particular nature of the action.

πάντες γὰρ ἐκ   τοῦ περισσεύοντος αὐτοῖς ἔβαλον
all   for   out of   abundance   to them   *they put*

NRSV: For all of them *have contributed* out of their abundance
(Mark 12:44).

Jesus says they "put" (ἔβαλον is an aorist), summing up all their actions.

It's not that one aspect is right and one is wrong; it's a matter of what the speaker wants to express. You can describe the same event with both an undefined aspect and a continuous aspect. Language is a portrayal of reality.

VOCABULARY

ἐπί (ἐπ᾿, ἐφ᾿)	gen: on, when (886) dat: on the basis of, at acc: on, to, against
κατά (κατ᾿, καθ᾿)	gen: against; (472) acc: according to; throughout
μετά (μετ᾿, μεθ᾿)	gen: with (466) acc: after
οὐ (οὐκ, οὐχ)	not (1,646)
μή	not, lest (1,041)
ἵνα	in order that; so that; that (662)
ὅτι	that; because (1,291)
γάρ	for (1,041)
οὖν	therefore; so (496)

69,336 total word occurrences out of 137,663 (50%). Congratulations. On average, you now know half of the words you will come across on any page in the Greek Testament.

CHAPTER 8

GREEK VERBS (INDICATIVE)

Greek verbs link to their subject not by word order but because the verb agrees with its subject in person and number (along with the subject being in the nominative). There are, for the most part, four Greek tenses, and they convey a mixture of time and aspect.

INFLECTION

8.1   **Agreement**. A Greek verb must agree with its subject in person and number. If the subject is singular, the verb must be singular. If the subject is first, second, or third person, so must the verb.

8.2   **Personal endings**. Greek verbs indicate their person and number by adding different suffixes to the end of the word. These suffixes are called *personal endings*. This is somewhat like adding an "s" to an English verb when its subject is third person singular present. "I walk Archer," becomes, "She walks Archer." (Archer is my German Shepherd.)

8.3   **Paradigm**. On the next page is a Greek paradigm of the verb ἀκούω, which means "I hear." Notice how the personal endings change depending on the subject's person and number. You do not have to memorize these endings; just be aware of how they function. (However, it is kind of fun to be able to recite this paradigm when your friends ask you to say something in Greek.)

person and number	Greek	Translation
first person singular	ἀκούω	I hear
second person singular	ἀκούεις	You hear
third person singular	ἀκούει	He/she/it hears
first person plural	ἀκούομεν	We hear
second person plural	ἀκούετε	You hear
third person plural	ἀκούουσι	They hear

"Morphology" is the study of how a language uses small pieces of information (called "morphemes") to construct a word.

The stem of a word is a morpheme; it carries the basic meaning of the word. A personal ending is also a morpheme. You can form a verb by combining its stem, adding what is called a "connecting vowel" (to help pronounce the verb), and then adding the personal ending.

So, for example, if you want to say "we hear," you join three parts: ἀκου (stem) + ο (connecting vowel) + μεν (personal ending) → ἀκούομεν. For more on morphology see 25.26–32.

8.4 **Parsing**. The software will simply parse this information for you, that is, tell you the verb's person, number, tense, voice, mood, and lexical form. Here is an example from Accordance when I hover the mouse over ἠγάπησεν in John 3:16.

ἠγάπησεν ēgapēsen ἀγαπάω (ἀγάπη) agapaō (agapē) **Verb third singular aorist active indicative to love** (Predicate)

8.5   **Nominative**. Verbs have double links with their subject. The personal ending on the verb points to its subject, and the case of the subject points to the verb. This is the primary function of the nominative case.

Χριστὸς Ἰησοῦς ἦλθεν εἰς τὸν κόσμον ἁμαρτωλοὺς σῶσαι
Christ   Jesus   came   into the   world   sinners   to save
Christ Jesus came into the world to save sinners *(1 Tim 1:15)*.

8.6   **Accusative**. Direct objects link to their verb through their case ending. This is the primary function of the accusative case.

παράγγελλε ταῦτα   καὶ δίδασκε
Command   *these things* and   teach
Command and teach *these things (1 Tim 4:11)*.

8.7   **Predicate nominative**. In this chapter you will learn two verbs, εἰμί and γίνομαι. The peculiarity of these verbs is that they are not followed by a direct object. Much like we say in English "It is I" and not "It is me" (if you speak correctly), εἰμί and γίνομαι are followed by a word in the nominative. It is called a "predicate nominative."

τὸ δὲ τέλος τῆς   παραγγελίας ἐστὶν ἀγάπη
the and goal   of this   command   is   *love*
And the goal of this command is *love (1 Tim 1:5)*.

The word ἀγάπη is nominative.

8.8   **Unexpressed subject**. Because the verb's personal ending indicates the person and number of its subject, Greek often does not include an explicit subject.

οὐδὲ καίουσιν λύχνον καὶ τιθέασιν αὐτὸν ὑπὸ τὸν μόδιον
Neither *they* light   lamp   and put   it   under the   bowl
NIV: Neither do *people* light a lamp and put it under a bowl
(Matt 5:15).
NASB: nor do people light a lamp and put it under a basket
CSB: No one lights a lamp and puts it under a basket

8.9   **Lexical form**. The lexical form of a verb is the first person singular, present indicative. In the traditional language approach, you would have to be able to figure out the lexical form from an inflected form. But in our approach, the tools will tell you the lexical form. If you moused over the inflected form ἠγάπησεν ("he loved"), you would see that the lexical form is ἀγαπάω.[1]

> A A **ἠγάπησεν** ēgapēsen ἀγαπάω (ἀγάπη) agapaō
> (agapē) **Verb** third singular aorist active indicative **to love**
> (Predicate)

ASPECT

8.10   In 7.21–26 I introduced the topic of aspect in the English verbal system. In English, time is more important than aspect. It's just the reverse in Greek; aspect is more important than time.

In other words, what is at the heart of the Greek verbal system is not so much telling the reader *when* something happens but rather what *kind of action* occurs. I wish we could put off discussing aspect until Church Greek, but you need to have some basic idea of what is going on in order to achieve our goals for Foundational Greek.

Let's review the three aspects, but this time in Greek.

8.11   The **undefined** ("perfective"[2]) aspect tell us nothing about the kind of action. It is the default aspect.

χάριν ἔχω τῷ ἐνδυναμώσαντί με Χριστῷ Ἰησοῦ τῷ κυρίῳ ἡμῶν
thanks I have to the *one who strengthens* me Christ Jesus Lord   our
I thank Christ Jesus our Lord, who *has given* me *strength (1 Tim 1:12).*

Paul isn't telling Timothy anything more other than that Jesus strengthened him. He doesn't comment about this being a one-time enablement, or a daily strengthening. For whatever reason,

---

[1]   Some of the older grammars and some modern commentaries list the infinitive form (λέγειν, "to say") as the lexical form, but lexicons are consistent now in listing verbs in the first person singular, present indicative (λέγω, "I say").

[2]   The name "perfect" comes from the Latin *perfectivum* meaning "completed."

it was not important for Paul to be more specific, so he uses the undefined aspect.

8.12 The **continuous** ("imperfective"[3]) aspect describes an action as ongoing.

πάντας ἀνθρώπους θέλει   σωθῆναι
all   people   *he wishes* to be saved

He [God] ... *wishes* all people to be saved *(1 Tim 2:4)*.

God's salvific plans are not a one-time thought but his ongoing preoccupation.

8.13 The **perfective** ("combinative") aspect describes an action that was brought to completion (and hence is in the past) but has effects felt in the speaker's present.

ψευδολόγων,   κεκαυστηριασμένων   τὴν   ἰδίαν   συνείδησιν
of liars   *having been seared*   their   own   conscience

NIV: liars, whose consciences *have been seared (1 Tim 4:2)*.

Because the opponents' consciences have been seared (completed past event), they are liars (present effects).

8.14 A good example is Jesus's words to his disciples in Mark 8:34:

If anyone wishes to come after me, let him *deny* himself and *take up* his cross and *follow* me.

"Deny" and "take up" in the Greek are described as simple events, while the aspect of the verb "follow" is a process. The aspect of "deny" and "take up" does not tell us anything about the nature of those actions. They do not tell us whether the "deny and take up" occur only once in your life, or if you are to do this every day. But the aspect of "follow" emphasizes that the commitment to discipleship involves a day-to-day following, as you would expect from the meaning of the word.

Interestingly, we learn in Luke's parallel, 9:23, that "take up" is actually a daily spiritual exercise. This isn't a contradiction with

---

[3] The name "imperfect" comes from the Latin *imperfectivum* meaning "not complete."

Mark, who doesn't tell us anything about the action of "take up." Luke is more specific, using the same form of the verb but adding the adverbial construction, "daily."

TENSE

8.15   In Greek, a tense carries two connotations: aspect and time. For example, the aorist (tense) describes an undefined action (aspect) that normally occurs in the past (time). In this book, I use the term "tense" to refer only to the *form* of a verb (e.g., present tense, future tense, aorist tense); I do not use "tense" to designate *when* an action of a verb occurs. I always use the term "time" to describe *when* the action of that verb occurs. Please do not confuse "tense" and "time."

8.16   There are five tenses in Greek. The key is to remember the combination of time and aspect conveyed by each tense.

tense	*time (normally)*	*aspect*
present	present	continuous
future	future	undefined
aorist	past	undefined
imperfect	past	continuous
perfect	completed, effects felt in present	perfective (undefined and continuous)

PRESENT INDICATIVE

8.17   The present indicative describes an action that generally occurs in the present. The word "generally" is important. As we learn more about Greek verbs, you will discover that they are not tied to time as closely as they are in English. For example, a present tense Greek verb can describe a past action or a timeless action. But more about that later.

The present tense can convey any form of undefined or continuous action, which at times can make translation hard and interpretive. For example, a translator can choose either "I preach" or "I am preaching" based on which fits the context best.

τινὲς δὲ καὶ δι᾽ εὐδοκίαν τὸν Χριστὸν κηρύσσουσιν
some but indeed through goodwill the Christ *preach*
ESV: Some indeed *preach* Christ ... from good will *(Phil 1:15).*
NASB: Some ... *are preaching* Christ ... from good will.

FUTURE INDICATIVE

8.18 **Predictive**. The future indicative describes an action that will occur in the future.

τὸ δὲ πνεῦμα ῥητῶς λέγει ὅτι ἐν ὑστέροις καιροῖς
the but Spirit expressly he says that in later times
ἀποστήσονταί τινες
will fall away some
ESV: Now the Spirit expressly says that in later times some *will depart* from the faith *(1 Tim 4:1).*

Futures are generally translated with a simple form (i.e., undefined aspect), "will fall away," rather than "will be falling away."

TWO PAST TENSES (AORIST AND IMPERFECT INDICATIVE)

8.19 Greek has two tenses that indicate past time. The difference between the two is aspect.

8.20 **Aorist**. The aorist tense describes an *undefined* action that normally occurs in the past. It is the default past tense.[4]

ἐγένετο Ἰωάννης ὁ βαπτίζων ἐν τῇ ἐρήμῳ
he appeared John the Baptizer in the desert
John the baptizer *appeared* in the desert *(Mark 1:4).*

---

[4] The name "aorist" comes from the Greek ἀόριστος meaning "undefined."

8.21   **Imperfect**. The imperfect tense describes a *continuous* action that normally occurs in the past.

εἰσελθὼν   εἰς   τὴν   συναγωγὴν   ἐδίδασκεν
after entering   into   the   synagogue   *he was teaching*

He entered the synagogue and *was teaching* (Mark 1:21).

8.22   This distinction between the aorist and imperfect can be important for exegesis. John 19:3 reads,

ἤρχοντο   πρὸς αὐτὸν καὶ   ἔλεγον, χαῖρε ὁ βασιλεὺς
they were coming up to   him   and   said   Hail   King

τῶν   Ἰουδαίων καὶ   ἐδίδοσαν   αὐτῷ   ῥαπίσματα
of the   Jews   and   they were striking   him   hands

ESV: They came up to him, saying, "Hail, King of the Jews!" and struck him with their hands *(John 19:3).*

But how often did the soldiers approach Jesus, and how often did they strike him? Only once? The NET and NRSV make the English as clear as the Greek, which uses imperfect verbal forms (ἤρχοντο, ἔλεγον, ἐδίδοσαν).

NET: They came up to him *again and again* and said, "Hail, King of the Jews!" And they *struck* him *repeatedly* in the face.

NRSV: They *kept coming up* to him, saying, "Hail, King of the Jews!" and *striking* him on the face.

PERFECT INDICATIVE

8.23   The Greek perfect describes an action that was brought to completion and whose effects are felt in the present from the standpoint of the speaker. Because it describes a completed action, the action described by the perfect verb occurred in the past.

For example, "Jesus died" is a simple statement of an event that happened in the past. In Greek this would be in the aorist. But if we used the Greek perfect to say, "Jesus has died," then we would expect the verse to continue by spelling out the present significance of that past action. "Jesus has died *for my sins.*"

Another example is the verb "to write." When the Bible says, "It is written," it's usually in the perfect tense. Scripture was written in the past but is applicable in the present. That is why translations can write either "It is written" or "It has been written." Their decision will depend on the context, and whether the emphasis is on the completion of the event or its ongoing implications.

ἐποίησαν αὐτῷ ὅσα   ἤθελον,   καθὼς γέγραπται   ἐπ᾽   αὐτόν
they did   to him whatever they wished just as   *it had been written* about him

NRSV: They did to him whatever they pleased, as *it is written* about him *(Mark 9:13).*

NLT: They chose to abuse him, just as the Scriptures *predicted.*

8.24   In English, using "have" or "has" has somewhat the same meaning as the Greek perfect. They describe an action that was completed in the recent past but has implications in the immediate present.

> I *wrote* last night.

> I *have written* and am still not done.

> It *has been written.*

The English present tense can also describe a past action with current consequences.

> It is *written.*

I know. It's confusing to have "perfect" used in two different ways, but scholars are starting to use the terms "perfective," "imperfective," and "combinative" for the three aspects. I will always refer to the "imperfective aspect" or the "imperfect tense," the "perfective aspect" or the "perfect tense."

VOICE

8.25 As in English, voice in a Greek verb indicates the relationship between the verb and its subject.

ACTIVE

8.26 The active voice means the subject does the action of the verb. This is the normal use of the active voice and is called the **simple active**.

Χριστὸς	Ἰησοῦς	ἦλθεν	εἰς	τὸν κόσμον	ἁμαρτωλοὺς	σῶσαι
Christ	Jesus	came	into	the world	sinners	to save

Christ Jesus *came* into the world to save sinners *(1 Tim 1:15)*.

PASSIVE

8.27 The passive voice means the subject receives the action of the verb. This is the normal use of the passive voice and is called the **simple passive**.

ἁγιάζεται	γὰρ	διὰ	λόγου	θεοῦ	καὶ	ἐντεύξεως
it is consecrated	because	by	the word	of God	and	prayer.

because it *is consecrated* by the word of God and prayer *(1 Tim 4:5)*

MIDDLE

8.28 Greek has active and passive voices. It also has a third voice called the "middle." It's a tad complicated to understand at first, but if we are going to understand our Strong's Bibles, this needs to be learned.

8.29 If a verb is in the middle voice, it means the subject still does the action of the verb but in some way in which the subject is emphasized in the action of the verb. I know; it's complicated and nuanced. In a sense, the verb in the middle voice is pointing a finger back at the subject and saying that the subject has some special interest in the action of the verb other than just doing the action of the verb. The technical name for this is "subject affectedness."

ἐξελέξατο ἡμᾶς ἐν αὐτῷ πρὸ καταβολῆς κόσμου
He chose   us   in him   before foundation of world

He chose us in him before the foundation of the world (*Eph 1:4*).

God's election of his children was done, among other reasons, for himself, for his glory (Eph 1:6).

8.30 **Reflexive**. There are a few cases where the middle approaches the idea of a reflexive construction where the subject performs the action of the verb on himself or herself. You may see it with verbs that are reflexive in meaning, such as "clothing yourself."

καὶ ἀπελθὼν   ἀπήγξατο
and going away   he hanged for himself

And going away, *he hanged himself* (*Matt 27:5*).

Judas did the action to himself.

While common in Classical Greek, this use of the middle is rare in Koine Greek and was replaced by the active and the reflexive pronoun (e.g., σεαυτόν).

εἰ υἱὸς εἶ   τοῦ θεοῦ, βάλε σεαυτὸν κάτω
if son you are of God   throw yourself down

If you are the Son of God, *throw yourself* down (*Matt 4:6*).

8.31 There are two things that make understanding the middle difficult. One is that it is a matter of nuance that can't be replicated in English. The other is that scholarship is right in the middle of changing its mind about the precise meaning of the middle voice. But here is what you need to know right now.

- The middle often has a meaning that sounds active to us. When you mouse over a verb, don't be surprised to see the software parse the verb as a middle even though the translation is active. Most middles are translated as actives.

For example, ἔρχομαι is middle in the present. It always has an active meaning, "to come."

> ἔρχονται erchontai ἔρχομαι erchomai **Verb** third plural present middle indicative **to come, go** (Predicate)
>
> [ESVS] G2064 come

- In the present, imperfect, and perfect tenses, the middle is identical in form to the passive. The verb λύομαι could be either passive ("I am loosed") or middle ("I am loosed for myself"). The "for myself" is a standard way grammars identify the middle voice, even though it sounds strange. Most software programs don't differentiate middle from passive since they are telling you the form, not the meaning. They will say that the verb is either middle or passive, and sometimes it gives both parsings.

- In the future and aorist tenses, the middle is distinctly different from the passive. The verb ἐλύθην means "I was loosed" (aorist passive), and ἐλυσάμην means "I loosed for myself" (aorist middle). Software will parse these forms as explicitly middle or passive.

DEPONENT VERBS

8.32 Greek has a category of verbs called "deponent" verbs. A deponent verb is one that is middle or passive in its *form* but active in its *meaning*; its form is always middle or passive but its meaning is always active. It can never have a passive meaning. For example, the aorist deponent ἐπορεύθησαν means "they went."

8.33 With the new understanding of the middle, deponents are simply classified as middle. However, many commentaries and grammars will still talk about deponent verbs.

8.34 Most tools will list these forms as "middle" or "passive" and not "deponent." In Matthew 2:9, ἐπορεύθησαν is translated, "they continued their journey"; the verb is deponent.

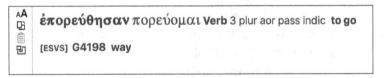

ἐπορεύθησαν πορεύομαι Verb 3 plur aor pass indic **to go**

[ESVS] G4198 **way**

8.35 How then will you know how these deponents are to be translated?

- The translators know which verbs are deponent, and they have translated these words with active meanings.

- If the lexical form of the verb ends in ομαι, it's deponent in the present tense (e.g., πορεύομαι). Nondeponent verbs have lexical forms ending in ω or μι (λύω, δίδωμι).

INDICATIVE MOOD

8.36 In the next chapter you are going to learn the different moods. However, you already know one, the indicative mood. Most of the examples we have seen so far are indicative verbs.

8.37 A verb in the indicative describes something that *is*, as opposed to something that *may* or *might* be, or something that *ought* to be. Statements, questions, and even lies are in the indicative. This is called the **declarative indicative**.

ἀλήθειαν λέγω   οὐ ψεύδομαι
truth   *I speak*   not *I lie*
I am speaking the truth; *I am* not *lying (1 Tim 2:7).*

νόμον οὖν   καταργοῦμεν διὰ   τῆς πίστεως;
law   therefore *we nullify*   through   the   faith
Do we therefore *nullify* the law through faith? *(Rom 3:31)*

GREEK WORD ORDER

8.34 A **postpositive** is a word that cannot occur as the first word in the Greek clause. They usually are the second word, sometimes third, and rarely fourth (or more). We usually translate these words as the first word in the English clause.

You will not see this word order issue in the Reverse Interlinear since it follows English word order, but you will see it in the Greek-English interlinear.

The postpositives you have learned are δέ (chapter 5) and γάρ and οὖν (chapter 7).

Οἱ   δὲ   παραπορευόμενοι ἐβλασφήμουν αὐτὸν
those *and* passing by   derided   him
And those who passed by derided him *(Matt 27:39).*

ἕκαστος γὰρ τὸ ἴδιον φορτίον βαστάσει
each   *for*   his own   load   will carry

For each one will bear his own load *(Gal 6:5).*

δεῖ   οὖν   τὸν ἐπίσκοπον ἀνεπίλημπτον εἶναι
it's necessary *therefore* the overseer   above reproach   to be

Therefore, it's necessary for the overseer to be above reproach
(1 Tim 3:2).

VOCABULARY

λέγω	I say, tell (2,345)
λαλέω	I speak (294)
ἀποκρίνομαι	I answer (231)
ἔρχομαι	I come (631)
εἰσέρχομαι	I come in(to), enter (194)
ἐξέρχομαι	I come out (216)
ὁράω	I see (454)
ἀκούω	I hear; understand, obey (426)
εἰμί	I am (is, are; was, were) (2,460)
γίνομαι	I become; am (668)

77,408 total word occurrences out of 137,663 (56%)

CHAPTER 9

GREEK VERBS (NONINDICATIVE)

In this chapter we'll see a quick overview of the different moods, and focus a little on the various uses of the infinitive and the participle.

ASPECT

9.1 Once you are out of the indicative, the Greek verbal system has no time significance; it's all about aspect.[1] Let's review.

- Verbal forms built on an *aorist* tense stem indicate an *undefined* action

- Verbal forms built on a *present* tense stem indicate a *continuous* action.

- Verbal forms built on a *perfect* tense stem indicate a *completed* action with *ongoing effects*.

This is a significant difference from English. Just because a nonindicative verb is formed from the present tense doesn't mean it describes an event happening in the present; it only means it's continuous.

9.2 You remember that "mood" is the verb's relationship to reality. The **indicative** mood is the mood of reality, used when the speaker/writer wants to portray something as fact (including questions).

---

[1] There is something called "relative time," and we'll discuss that in Church Greek. Technically, there is no *absolute* time outside of the indicative.

SUBJUNCTIVE MOOD

9.3   **Purpose**. Because the subjunctive mood is one step removed from reality, it's appropriate for purpose statements. Whenever you see ἵνα, you can expect the following verb to be a subjunctive.

ταῦτα   παράγγελλε,   ἵνα   ἀνεπίλημπτοι   ὦσιν
these things   command   so that above reproach   *they might be*
Command these things so that *they may be* above reproach
(*1 Tim 5:7*).

9.4   **Conditional**. The subjunctive can also be used in the "if" clause ("protasis") of a conditional sentence (an "if … then …" sentence).

ἐὰν   οὖν   τις   ἐκκαθάρῃ   ἑαυτὸν ἀπὸ τούτων,
if   therefore someone *might cleanse* himself from these things

ἔσται   σκεῦος εἰς τιμήν
he will be vessel   for honor

ESV: Therefore, if anyone *cleanses* himself from what is dishonorable, he will be a vessel for honorable use (*2 Tim 2:21*).

IMPERATIVE MOOD

9.5   **Command**. The basic function of the imperative mood is to state a command.

γύμναζε δὲ   σεαυτὸν πρὸς εὐσέβειαν
train   but yourself   for   godliness
Rather, *train* yourself for godliness (*1 Tim 4:7*).

9.6   **Person**. In English all imperatives are second person; in Greek there are second and third person imperatives. Because there is no English equivalent to a third person imperative, the translation must be a little idiomatic. βλέπε (second person singular) means "(You) look!" The imperative βλεπέτω (third person singular) means "Let him look!" or "He must look!" The words "let" or "must," and a pronoun supplied from the person of the verb ("him"), can be added to convey the meaning of the Greek.

πορεύου εἰς γῆν   Ἰσραήλ
go   to   land   of Israel

Go to the land of Israel *(Matt 2:20)*.

πορεύου is second person. φευγέτωσαν in the example below is third person.

τότε οἱ ἐν τῇ Ἰουδαίᾳ φευγέτωσαν εἰς τὰ ὄρη
then those in Judea   *let them flee*   into the mountains

NIV: Then *let those* who are in Judea *flee* to the mountains *(Matt 24:16)*.

CSB: Then those in Judea must flee to the mountains.

9.7   It's difficult to bring out the significance of the present continuous imperative. The aspect must generally be expressed by the meaning of the word.

οὗτοι δὲ δοκιμαζέσθωσαν πρῶτον, εἶτα διακονείτωσαν
they   but *let them be tested*   first   then *let them serve*

ἀνέγκλητοι ὄντες
blameless   being

NIV: They *must* first *be tested*; and then if there is nothing against them, *let them serve as deacons* (1 Tim 3:10).

INFINITIVE

9.8   **Complementary.** The infinitive can complete the thought of the verb.

ἤρξατο ὁ Ἰησοῦς κηρύσσειν καὶ λέγειν, μετανοεῖτε
began   Jesus   *to preach*   and *to say*   repent.

NASB: Jesus began *to preach* and *say*, "Repent" *(Matt 4:17)*.

ESV: Jesus began to preach, saying, "Repent."

Began to do what? Began to preach.

9.9   **Purpose**. The infinitive can also indicate purpose.

Χριστὸς Ἰησοῦς ἦλθεν εἰς τὸν κόσμον ἁμαρτωλοὺς σῶσαι
Christ   Jesus   he came into the   world   sinners   *to save*
Christ Jesus came into the world *to save* sinners (*1 Tim 1:15*).

PARTICIPLE

9.10   As in English, a Greek participle is a verbal adjective. This means a participle can function adverbially (*adverbial*) or adjectivally. As an adjective, it can function both as a normal adjective (*attributive*) and as a noun (*substantival*). This gives us three basic uses.

ADVERBIAL PARTICIPLE

9.11   Adverbial participles emphasize the verbal nature of the participle and modify a verb, usually the main verb of the clause. Because of this, most adverbial participles are nominative because the subject of the verb is doing the action of the participle.

ἠλεήθην,   ὅτι   ἀγνοῶν   ἐποίησα ἐν   ἀπιστίᾳ
I was shown mercy because *being ignorant* I acted   in   unbelief
NIV: I was shown mercy because I acted *in ignorance* and unbelief (*1 Tim 1:13*).

> ἠλεήθην, ὅτι ... ἐποίησα
> ⠀⠀⠀⠀ἀγνοῶν
> ⠀⠀⠀⠀ἐν ἀπιστίᾳ

> I was shown mercy because ... I acted
> ⠀⠀⠀⠀being ignorant
> ⠀⠀⠀⠀in unbelief

The participle "being ignorant" is telling us something about the action of the verb "I acted." Because he was ignorant, he acted in unbelief.

ἐλθόντες εἰς τὴν οἰκίαν εἶδον τὸ παιδίον μετὰ Μαρίας
coming into the house they saw the child with Mary
Coming into the house, they saw the child with Mary *(Matt 2:11)*.

ἐλθόντες εἰς τὴν οἰκίαν
εἶδον τὸ παιδίον μετὰ Μαρίας

coming into the house
they saw the child with Mary

"Coming" tells you something about when they "saw" Jesus.

9.12 **Anarthrous.** Adverbial participles will always be anarthrous; they will never be preceded by the article. If Matthew had written ὁ ἐλθόντες, the participle could not have been adverbial.

9.13 **Temporal participle.** One of the most common uses of adverbial participles is to indicate relative time. The time indicated by the participle is relative to the time of a finite verb. The **aorist** participle can describe an action occurring *before* the time of the finite verb. "After" is often added to this type of participle. At other times, the translator lets the sequence of verbal forms indicate the time relative to the main verb.

νηστεύσας ... ὕστερον ἐπείνασεν
fasting then he was hungry
ESV: *After fasting* ... he was hungry *(Matt 4:2)*.
NRSV: He fasted ... and afterwards he was famished.

The **present** participle can describe something happening *at the same time* as the action of the main verb. "When" or "while" is often added to this type of participle.

συναλιζόμενος παρήγγειλεν αὐτοῖς
staying with he charged them
RSV: *While staying with* them he charged them *(Acts 1:4)*.

ἐνήργησεν ἐν τῷ Χριστῷ ἐγείρας αὐτὸν ἐκ νεκρῶν
he worked in Christ *raising* him from dead
NIV: [which] he exerted in Christ *when he raised* him from the dead *(Eph 1:20)*.

9.14 This is called **relative time**. In other words, the time of the participle is relative to the time of the main verb.

- The aorist participle indicates an action occurring *prior* to the time of the verb ("after").

- The present participle indicates an action occurring at the same time as the verb ("when"/"while").

ATTRIBUTIVE PARTICIPLE

9.15 The adjectival participle can modify a noun or pronoun. We call these attributive participles. (Some people will call them adjectical participles.) There are two keys to identifying an attributive participle.

- It is generally preceded by the article ("articular").

- Both the article and the participle will agree in case, number, and gender with the word it modifies ("agreement"). Greek can't use word order like English does because the Greek participle doesn't necessarily immediately follow the word it modifies, although it normally does.

ἥτις ἐστὶν ἐκκλησία θεοῦ ζῶντος
which is   church   of God living
which is the church of the *living* God *(1 Tim 3:15)*

       ἥτις ἐστὶν ἐκκλησία θεοῦ
                       ζῶντος

       which is the church of the ... God
                           living

The participle "living" is modifying the noun "God" (both are genitive singular masculine).

ὁ   λαὸς ὁ   καθήμενος ἐν σκότει φῶς εἶδεν μέγα
the people *the sitting*   in darkness light saw   great
The people *living in darkness* have seen a great light *(Matt 4:16)*.

ὁ λαὸς ... φῶς εἶδεν μέγα

ὁ καθήμενος ἐν σκότει

the people ... light saw great

the sitting in darkness

The words λαός and καθήμενος are both nominative masculine singular. This agreement is the linkage between the participle and the word it modifies.

9.16 When used with ὁ, the participial phrase will normally follow the noun in the order "article-noun-article-modifier." This is called the "second attributive position" (11.21).

ὁ   θεὸς ὁ   ποιήσας τὸν   κόσμον καὶ   πάντα τὰ   ἐν   αὐτῷ
the God the making   the   world   and   all   the   in   it
The God *who made* the world and everything in it *(Acts 17:24)*.

9.17 The translator may need to add the appropriate pronoun to make better English sense. Which pronoun is used is determined by the word the participle is modifying.

καὶ   παράγων ὁ Ἰησοῦς ἐκεῖθεν εἶδεν ἄνθρωπον
And *going along* Jesus   from there he saw man
And Jesus, as *he was passing on* from there, saw a man *(Matt 9:9)*.

To show that it was Jesus who was passing on, I added "he."

9.18 **Form.** There is no difference in form between a participle functioning adjectivally or one functioning adverbially. The participle καθήμενος is καθήμενος whether it is adverbial or adjectival. The clue is the article.

9.19 Relative time does not apply to the adjectival participle, only the adverbial.

9.20   A participle can also function as a noun.[2] It will generally be articular. The key difference in distinguishing an attributive from a substantival participle is that the latter will *not* have a word to modify.

πάντα   δυνατὰ τῷ   πιστεύοντι
all things   possible   for the *believing*
All things are possible for *the one who believes* (Mark 9:23).

Notice that once again I had to add words —"the one who"—to say the same thing in English as is said in Greek. The translation of the Greek participle is often idiomatic, i.e., not word-for-word.

προσεύχεσθε ὑπὲρ τῶν διωκόντων ὑμᾶς
pray   for   *the persecuting you*
Pray for *those persecuting you* (Matt 5:44).
The participial phrase is acting as a noun, in this case the object of the preposition ὑπέρ.

9.21   **Summary**

- An adverbial participle is anarthrous and indicates an action occurring before (aorist) or simultaneous with (present) the verb.

- An adjectival participle is generally articular and can function either as an attributive or a substantive.

- An attributive participle agrees with the word it modifies in case, number, and gender.

- A substantival participle gets its number and gender from the implied word it's referring to. Its case is determined by its function in the sentence.

---

2   Technically, when an "-ing" word is used as a noun, in English it's called a "gerund." We don't use "gerund" in Greek grammar.

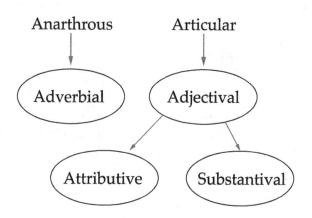

VOCABULARY

οἶδα	I know; understand (318)
γινώσκω	I know; understand (222)
πιστεύω	I believe, trust (237)
θέλω	I want (208)
δίδωμι	I give (415)
δύναμαι	I am able (210)
ἐσθίω	I eat (158)
ἔχω	I have (706)
λαμβάνω	I take; receive (258)
ποιέω	I do; make (568)

80,708 total word occurrences out of 137,663 (59%)

WORD STUDIES

Words have a "semantic range." "Semantic" refers to a word's meaning; "semantic range" refers to the range of possible meanings a word possesses. Think of all the ways we use the word "run."

I scored six runs today.

Could you run that by me again?

My computer runs faster than yours!

He runs off at the mouth.

I left the water running all night.

He ran to the store.

The car ran out of gas.

The clock ran down.

Duane ran for senate.

Her nose ran.

I ran up the bill.

I prefer the phrase "bundle of meanings." Think of a bundle of sticks. A word usually does not possess just one meaning; a word has different meanings, hence "bundle." One of the sticks in the bundle may be larger than the others—the word may have one dominant meaning—but nevertheless every word has a bundle of meanings. This is true in any language.

For example, the semantic range of the preposition ἐν is quite large. Look at how it's used in the following verses. (All translations are from the ESV.)

τὸ γὰρ ἐν αὐτῇ γεννηθὲν ἐκ πνεύματός ἐστιν ἁγίου
the for *in* her conceived of spirit is holy
for that which is conceived *in* her is from the Holy Spirit (*Matt 1:20*).

τοῦ ... Ἰησοῦ γεννηθέντος ἐν Βηθλέεμ ... ἐν ἡμέραις Ἡρῴδου
the Jesus was born *in* Bethlehem *in* days of Herod
Jesus was born *in* Bethlehem ... *in* the days of Herod (*Matt 2:1*).

καὶ μὴ δόξητε λέγειν ἐν ἑαυτοῖς
and not presume to say *in* yourselves
and do not presume to say *to* yourselves (*Matt 3:9*)

Ἐγὼ ... ὑμᾶς βαπτίζω ἐν ὕδατι
I you baptize *in* water
I baptize you *with* water (*Matt 3:11*).

θεραπεύων πᾶσαν νόσον καὶ πᾶσαν μαλακίαν ἐν τῷ λαῷ.
healing every disease and every infirmity *in* the people
healing every disease and every affliction *among* the people
(*Matt 4:23*)

μὴ ὀμόσαι ὅλως· μήτε ἐν τῷ οὐρανῷ, ὅτι θρόνος ἐστὶν τοῦ θεοῦ
not swear at all either *in* the heaven for throne it is of God
Do not take an oath at all, either *by* heaven, for it is the throne of
God (*Matt 5:34*).

Also, languages are not codes. There is not a one-to-one correspon-
dence between languages, especially vocabulary. Rarely if ever can you
find one word in one language that corresponds exactly to another
word in another language, especially in its semantic range. English has
no single word that matches the range of meanings for ἐν. The semantic
range of a Greek and English word may overlap, but they are not
identical.

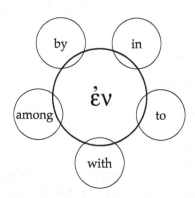

So how do we translate when we do not have English words that correspond exactly to the Greek? We have to interpret, and this happens in a two-step process.

1. See what the Greek word meant.
2. Determine how to convey its meaning into English.

All translation is interpretive. For example, in 1 Timothy 6:13–14 Paul writes,

> In the presence of God who gives life to all things, and of Christ Jesus who in his testimony before Pontius Pilate made the good confession, I *charge* you to keep the commandment unstained and free from reproach until the appearing of our Lord Jesus Christ. *(RSV)*

The Greek word behind "charge" is παραγγέλλω, which means "to command, insist, instruct, urge," a wide range of meanings for which there is no single counterpart in English. The translator must decide whether Paul is "commanding" Timothy (who is a member of his inner circle, fully trusted, and probably his best friend) or "urging" him. This is an interpretive decision that must be made by the translator. The RSV chose "charge," and the NKJV rightly (in my opinion) selected "urge." All translation is interpretive.

Let's say that you want to discover for yourself what Paul means when he "charges" Timothy to keep the commandment unstained. It makes no sense to look up the English word "charge," because "charge" can't mean "urge," and "urge" can't mean "charge." If you want to decide for yourself what Paul is saying, you have to know the Greek word behind the English, learn its semantic range, and then make an interpretive decision.

How do you do this? There are four steps.

■ Decide what word to study.

■ Identify the Greek word.

■ Discover its semantic range.

■ Look for something in the context that helps determine what the biblical author meant by this word in this particular verse.

STEP 1. CHOOSE THE ENGLISH WORD

I annoyed many people for many years asking what I think is an extremely important question: "What is the minimum it takes to become a Christian?" You are at a bus stop, and a university freshman walks up to you and says, "You're a graduate student in divinity, aren't you?" ("Divinity" is the word they use in Scotland for biblical studies.) You say, "Yes." She says, "What is a Christian anyway?" Go! You have two minutes to tell her before the bus comes. What are you going to say? You want to tell her enough of the gospel so that if she responds, she will truly have become a Christian. However, if you don't tell her enough and she responds, will she really have become a Christian? Or if you add to the basic gospel message, will you drive her away unnecessarily?

Sound hypothetical? No, it happened to me, and I didn't have an answer. I promised myself that would never happen again, so I started searching out all the short and succinct statements about becoming a Christian because I wanted to have a two-minute answer the next time I was asked that question.

Romans 10:9–10 is one of those succinct and crucial passages on the nature of salvation.

> If you declare with your mouth, "Jesus is Lord," and believe in your heart that God raised him from the dead, you will be saved. For it is with your heart that you believe and are justified, and it is with your mouth that you profess your faith and are saved.

The key term in the entire passage is what? It's "Lord," isn't it? The essence of salvation is the confession, "Jesus is Lord," accompanied with the acceptance of the resurrection. So what does "Lord" mean? Its meaning is crucial to our salvation, and hers.

This is actually the first step in doing a Greek word study: you've decided on a significant word. If you try to do word studies on every word you read, not only will you run out of time but you'll get bored. So how do you pick the right word? There is not a clear-cut answer to this question, but here are some suggestions.

A. LOOK FOR THE HUB

Think of a paragraph or verse as a bicycle wheel. If you pull one spoke off here and another off there, the wheel still functions. However, if you remove the hub, the entire wheel falls apart. Likewise, there are words you could omit from your study, and the passage would still hold together—these are the spokes. The most important words to study are the ones that form the hub, the center of a paragraph or verse; these are the words that, if removed, cause the passage to fall apart. Let me give a few examples.

In the Beatitudes Jesus pronounces a blessing on the "poor" (which means, those who know they have nothing and therefore turn to God), the "hungry" (whose spiritual appetites are satisfied only by God), and those who "weep" (over their spiritual bankruptcy). If any of those words are removed from their verse—poor, hungry, weep—the passage falls apart and loses its meaning.

Jesus's answers to Satan's temptations are built around the words "bread" (all that sustains us, physically and spiritually), "worship" (offering all that we are before God), and "test" (unnecessarily questioning God's promise to care). These words form the hub of the passage.

When Jesus called Levi as a disciple, he says, "I have not come to call the righteous but sinners to repentance" (Luke 5:32). The "righteous" are those who mistakenly think they are right with God, and the "sinners" are those who perhaps do not follow Jewish ritual but understand their lack of righteousness before God. These words form the hub of their passage.

To say it another way, does a verse "hang" on a word? It will be a word that is central to the meaning of the verse, and without it the sentence will not make sense. These are the words worth studying.

B. DOES A WORD SOUND LIKE A THEOLOGICAL TERM?

You cannot get far especially in Paul's letters without coming across terms that describe theological truths. These words often carry the weight of the passage. Consider Romans 3:22–24, one of the most condensed theological passages in the Bible. (The italicized words in parentheses are my explanatory additions.)

> This righteousness (*being declared innocent of sin*) from God comes through faith (*trusting that God did on the cross for us what we could not do for ourselves*) in Jesus Christ to all (*Jew and Gentile*

alike) who believe. There is no difference, for all have sinned (*broken the rules that govern our relationship with God*) and fall short of the glory of God (*the praise and honor God intended for his creation*), and are justified (*made righteous; same word group as the previous "righteousness"*) freely by his grace (*God's goodness extended to those who do not deserve it*) through the redemption (*the freedom from sin gained through Christ's work on the cross*) that came by Christ Jesus.

You can see that every word I explained is a key theological term and worthy of a word study.

C. IS THE WORD REPEATED?

When a word weaves its way through a paragraph, it may be an important word. In the prologue to John (1:1–18), "grace" plays an important role. Jesus was full of grace and truth (vv 14, 16b), and we have received from him "grace upon grace" (v 16).

Sometimes a theme may weave its way through the passage but uses different words. Again, in John's prologue, many words are used to describe Jesus: word; life; light; flesh; only Son; only God. All would make for good word studies.

D. SOMETIMES PASSAGES CONTAIN WORDS THAT DON'T MAKE SENSE

These may even be common English words, but the common meaning doesn't seem to fit in a particular verse. This may be a clue that the word is worth investigating. What is an "unclean" spirit? One that doesn't bathe properly? No. In this context, "unclean" means that which cannot be brought into contact with what is holy, and carries the idea of moral and spiritual corruptness.

What does it mean for the "word" to become "flesh"? (John 1:14). In everyday discourse we do not speak of a "word" becoming "flesh." "Word" in this passage has Old Testament and philosophical roots that John adapts to define Jesus; "flesh" doesn't mean something sinful but that Jesus, the Word, actually became a human being.

What does it mean that the Word "dwelt among us?" (John 1:14). In what sense? The Greek σκηνόω means "to pitch, live in a tent." The related noun (σκηνή) was used of the tabernacle in the wilderness. So the idea of Jesus's incarnation reflects the Old Testament concept of the dwelling of God with his people.

E. COMPARE TRANSLATIONS

Sometimes a word or phrase will be translated quite differently from translation to translation. The translators may be struggling with what is probably an important word. This is worth studying.

Matthew 6:13 contains the most difficult phrase in the Lord's Prayer to understand. The NIV writes, "And *lead us not* into temptation," but the NLT says, "And *don't let us yield* to temptation." Which is it? Don't "lead" or don't "let us yield"?

In the heart of Paul's letter to the Romans, he says that sinners "are justified freely by his grace through the redemption that is in Christ Jesus, whom God set forth as a ἱλαστήριον by his blood" (3:24b–25a). ἱλαστήριον describes the heart of what happened on the cross, but look at how the translators struggle to translate this important word:

- "sacrifice of atonement" (NIV, NRSV)

- "propitiation" (NASB, ESV, KJV, NKJV)

- "expiation" (RSV, NAB)

- "the mercy seat" (CSB, NET)

- "the place of sacrifice" (CEB)

- "the sacrifice for sin" (NLT)

- "sacrifice for reconciliation" (NJB)

- "the means by which people's sins are forgiven" (TEV)

- "the means by which people's sins are forgiven" (Good News Bible)

Word studies are generally fun and informative. They give us good preaching and teaching illustrations, and help us to fill out the meaning of a passage. But most importantly, these are God's words and it's worth hanging on to them.

What do you think "Lord" means in Romans 10:9 (our example above)? Let's find out.

STEP 2. IDENTIFY THE GREEK WORD

Your next step is to find the Greek word behind the English.

PAPER INTERLINEAR

You can use one of my interlinears. Here is the phrase in *IRU*.

Jesus	is	Lord
Ἰησοῦν		κύριον
n.asm		*n.asm*
2652		*3261*

> Since this is the first time I have used the *IRU* format for showing you a verse, I need to stop and explain it for you.
>
> The first line is the English (in English word order).
>
> The second line is the Greek, with the word order altered to match the English.
>
> The third is the parsing. Ἰησοῦν is a noun, accusative singular masculine. There is a key in the front of *IRU* as to what the codes mean.
>
> The fourth is the word's GK number. There is a conversion guide to Strong's numbers in lesson 5 in the online class.

The inflected form of the word translated "Lord" is κύριον. It's a noun, accusative singular masculine, and its GK number is #3261. The conversion chart tells you its Strong's number is #2962.

If you are using my Greek-English interlinear that keeps the Greek word order, then here is the information. Be sure to read the explanation of the layout in the preface.

ὁ	κηρύσσομεν.	⁹ ὅτι	ἐὰν	ὁμολογήσῃς	ἐν	τῷ		στόματί	σου			κύριον
that	we proclaim:	that	if	you confess	with	*{the}*	your	mouth,	*your*	"Jesus is		Lord,"
4005	3062	4022	1569	3933	1877	3836	5148	5125	5148	2652		3261
r.asn	v.pai.1p	cj	cj	v.aas.2s	p.d	d.dsn		n.dsn	r.gs.2			n.asm

Ἰησοῦν	καὶ	πιστεύσῃς	ἐν	τῇ		καρδίᾳ	σου	ὅτι	ὁ	θεὸς		αὐτὸν	ἤγειρεν
Jesus	and	believe	in	*{the}*	your	heart	*your*	that	*{the}*	God	raised	him	*raised*
2652	2779	4409	1877	3836	5148	2840	5148	4022	3836	2536	1586	899	1586
n.asm	cj	v.aas.2s	p.d	d.dsf		n.dsf	r.gs.2	cj	d.nsm	n.nsm		r.asm.3	v.aai.3s

ἐκ		νεκρῶν,	σωθήσῃ·	¹⁰	→			καρδίᾳ	γὰρ			πιστεύεται	
from	the	dead,	ˏyou will be saved.ˌ		For	with	the	heart	*For*	a	person	believes	and
1666		3738	5392					2840	1142			4409	
p.g		a.gpm	v.fpi.2s					n.dsf	cj			v.ppi.3s	

SOFTWARE (FREE)

Go to my site, BillMounce.com, and from the main menu select Greek-English Interlinear Bible. I am just starting to develop this site, so don't be surprised to find a lot more information and features.

Select the book, enter a chapter and verse, and press the "Lookup verse" button. It shows the English word from my translation, and the Greek word behind it — inflected form, lexical form (Greek and transliteration), its parsing, and its Strong's and GK number. The full verse is listed. If you click on any line in the list, you will see a fuller definition of the Greek word.

	English	Inflected	Lexical	Transliteration	Parsing	Strong	GK
Romans ▼	that	ὅτι	ὅτι	hoti	conj	3754	4022
Chapter: 10	if	ἐάν	ἐάν	ean	conj	1437	1569
Verse: 9	confess	ὁμολογήσῃς	ὁμολογέω	homologeō	aor act subj 2 sg	3670	3933
Lookup verse	with	ἐν	ἐν	en	prep-dat	1722	1877
that if you confess with your mouth, "Jesus is Lord," and believe in your heart that God raised him from the dead, you will be saved.		τῷ	ὁ	ho	dat sg neut	3588	3836
	mouth,	στόματι	στόμα	stoma	dat sg neut	4750	5125
	your	σου	σύ	sy	gen sg 2nd	4571	5148
	Lord,"	κύριον	κύριος	kyrios	acc sg masc	2962	3261
	"Jesus	Ἰησοῦν	Ἰησοῦς	Iēsous	acc sg masc	2424	2652
	and	καί	καί	kai	conj	2532	2779

Concordance	**Word:** Ἰησοῦς occurs 917x
	Definition: *a Savior, Jesus*, Mt. 1:21, 25; 2:1, et al. freq.; *Joshua*, Acts 7:45; Heb. 4:8; *Jesus*, a Jewish Christian, Col. 4:11

To learn enough Greek to go deeper in your Bible study, check out BillMounce.com/gru

SOFTWARE (PUCHASE REQUIRED)

If you prefer to work with software, finding the Greek behind the English is easy. Because software is always changing, I hesitate to show you how to do this, so I will keep the videos on the class's website updated.

Accordance. Be sure you are using an English text that is connected to the Greek (called "Strong's Bibles"), and be sure to have the Instant Details window showing. Go to Romans 10:9 and mouse over the word "Lord."

Bible Study (OliveTree). The Greek appears in the Quick Details box when you mouse over "Lord" (currently the Macintosh version only). You can also click on the word, Mac and Windows versions.

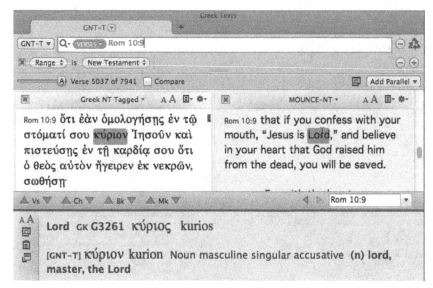

Accordance

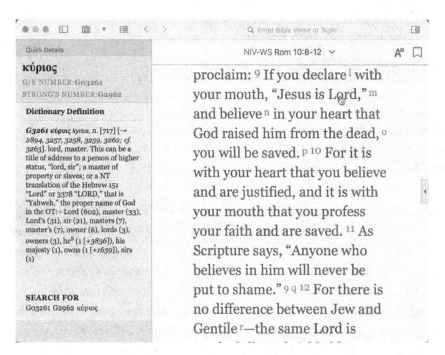

Bible Study App (OliveTree)

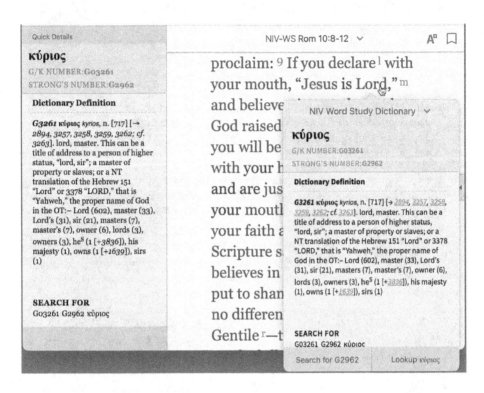

Logos. When you do a mouse over on Logos, it shows the pertinent information along the bottom. If you have Logos set up properly, you can also select the word and the Greek word in the secondary text is selected.

we proclaim: 9 If you declare[g] with your mouth, "Jesus is Lord,"[h] and believe[i] in your heart that God raised him from the dead,[j] you will be saved.[k] 10 For it is with your heart that you believe and are justified, and it is with your mouth that you profess your faith and are saved. 11 As Scripture says, "Anyone who believes in him will never be put to shame."[e] 12 For there is no difference between Jew and Gentile[m]—the same Lord is Lord of all[n]	κηρύσσομεν. 9 ὅτι ἐὰν ὁμολογήσῃς ἐν τῷ στόματί σου **κύριον** Ἰησοῦν καὶ πιστεύσῃς ἐν τῇ καρδίᾳ σου ὅτι ὁ θεὸς αὐτὸν ἤγειρεν ἐκ νεκρῶν, σωθήσῃ 10 καρδίᾳ γὰρ πιστεύεται εἰς δικαιοσύνην, στόματι δὲ ὁμολογεῖται εἰς σωτηρίαν. 11 λέγει γὰρ ἡ γραφή, **Πᾶς ὁ πιστεύων ἐπ' αὐτῷ οὐ καταισχυνθήσεται.** 12 οὐ γάρ ἐστιν διαστολὴ Ἰουδαίου τε καὶ Ἕλληνος, ὁ γὰρ αὐτὸς **κύριος πάντων**, πλουτῶν εἰς πάντας τοὺς ἐπικαλουμένους αὐτόν 13 **Πᾶς** γὰρ **ἔσηται τὸ ὄνομα κυρίου**

κύριος; noun, accusative, singular, masculine; Strong's Greek #2962; LN 12.9

Be sure to check out the smart-phone apps from the three companies listed above.

STEP 3. DISCOVER ITS SEMANTIC RANGE

Before you can discover what the word means in a particular context, you have to learn its range of meaning, its semantic range. As I have been saying, we are looking for the semantic range of the Greek, not the English, since they are almost always (if not always) different. So we are going to learn the semantic range of the Greek word κύριος.

DICTIONARIES

The easiest way to do this is to triple-click on "Lord" and the default Greek dictionary shows. It will give you a feel for the semantic range. If you've set the default Greek lexicon to Mounce Greek Dictionary, this is what you will see.

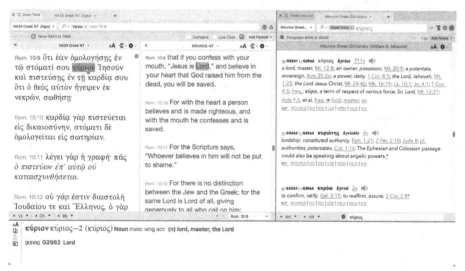

If you use my *Mounce's Complete Expository Dictionary of Old and New Testament Words*, you will get a much fuller discussion. On the next page is a quick summary, and the full article (with the related Hebrew and Greek words) is at the end of this chapter.

Noun: κύριος (*kyrios*), GK G3261 (S G2962), 717x. *kyrios* means "master, lord, sir" as well as "Lord." Most of its occurrences are in Luke's two works (210x) and Paul's letters (275x). The most plausible reason for this is that Luke wrote for, and Paul wrote to, people whose lives were dominated by Greek culture and language. *kyrios* occurs over 9,000x in the LXX, 6,000 of which replace the Hebrew proper name for God, Yahweh.

There are more advanced dictionaries that eventually you want to use. A two-volume set that is quite affordable is *The Greek-English Lexicon of the New Testament Based on Semantic Domains* by Louw and Nida (United Bible Society).

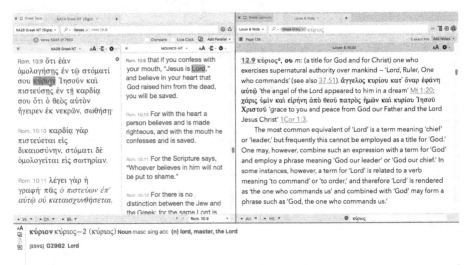

If you use their paper version, look up your word in their index first. The words are not listed alphabetically but by their basic meanings.

The standard Greek dictionary is *A Greek-English Lexicon of the New Testament and Other Early Christian Literature,* third edition edited by Frederick Danker (University of Chicago Press, 2000). On the next page is how it is seen inside Accordance, followed by a summary of its sections.

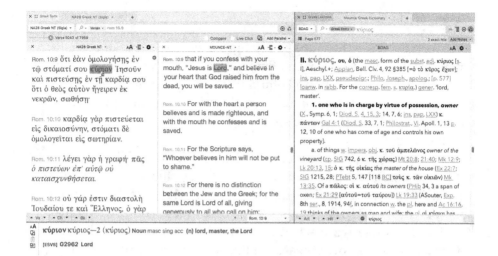

1. one who is in charge by virtue of possession, *owner*
2. one who is in a position of authority, *lord, master*
   a. of earthly beings, as a designation of any pers. of high position
   b. of transcendent beings
      α. as a designation of God
      β. Closely connected w. the custom of applying the term κ. to deities is that of honoring (deified) rulers with the same title
      γ. κύριος is also used in ref. to Jesus:
         א in OT quotations, where it is understood of the Lord of the new community
         ב Apart from OT quots., Matt and Mk speak of Jesus as κύριος only in one pass.... but they record that he was addressed as 'Lord' (κύριε), once in Mk (7:28) and more oft. in Matt.... Luke refers to Jesus much more frequently as ὁ κ.
         ל Even in the passages already mentioned the use of the word κ. raises Jesus above the human level
      δ. In some places it is not clear whether God or Christ is meant
      ε. of other transcendent beings

There are some older Greek lexicons that, in their day, were helpful and often groundbreaking, but because of their age you should not use them now. *The Vocabulary of the Greek New Testament,* by Moulton & Milligan (Eerdmans); *Biblico-Theological Lexicon of New Testament Greek,* by Cremer (T. & T. Clark); *A Greek-English Lexicon of the New Testament,* by Thayer (Harper).

CONCORDANCE

Another way to see the word's semantic range is to see all the verses
where that Greek word is used. Remember, don't search for the English
word but for the Greek word behind it. There may be several different
Greek words that are translated "Lord," and κύριος may not always be
translated with "Lord"; these are the limitations of an English
concordance.

For example, σάρξ is translated in Galatians by the NIV (1984) as
"body" (1 time), "flesh" (1), "human effort" (1), "illness" (2), "man" (1),
"no one" (1), "ordinary way" (2), "outwardly" (1), "sinful nature" (7),
and "that nature" (1). (In some of these occurrences, σάρξ was com-
bined with another word when translated.) But with a Greek-English
concordance, you know you are looking at every place the same Greek
word occurs, regardless of how it's translated.

If you want to use computers, then the simplest way to see a Greek-
English concordance is to use my free Greek dictionary, at
billmounce.com/greek-dictionary.

1. Enter the word's GK number, Strong's number, the word in
    Greek script, or the word in transliteration. Press Search.

Search the Greek Dictionary

kyrios

Search

2. Click on the correct word. In this case there is only one.

Search results

κύριος

... Greek transliteration: **kyrios** 26179 reads
Testament: ...

3. Scroll down to see the entries. You will notice that the word
    translating κύριος is listed in transliteration, Greek, and then
    parsed.

Greek-English Concordance for κύριος

Matthew 1:20	But as he pondered this, behold, an angel of the Lord (*kyriou* | κυρίου | gen sg masc) appeared to him in a dream, saying, "Joseph, son of David, do not be afraid to take Mary as your wife; for that which has been conceived in her is by the Holy Spirit.
Matthew 1:22	All this took place so that what was spoken by the Lord (*kyriou* | κυρίου | gen sg masc) through the prophet might be fulfilled:
Matthew 1:24	When Joseph arose from sleep, he did what the angel of (*kyriou* | κυρίου | gen sg masc) the Lord (*kyriou* | κυρίου | gen sg masc) had told him, he took her as his wife,
Matthew 2:13	After they had gone, an angel of the Lord (*kyriou* | κυρίου | gen sg masc) appeared in a dream to Joseph, saying, "Rise, take the child and his mother, flee to Egypt, and stay there until I tell you; for Herod is going to search for the child to destroy him."
Matthew 2:15	and was there until the death of Herod. This was to fulfill what was spoken by the Lord (*kyriou* | κυρίου | gen sg masc) through the prophet: "Out of Egypt I have called my son."
Matthew 2:19	But when Herod died, an angel of the Lord (*kyriou* | κυρίου | gen sg masc) appeared in a dream to Joseph in Egypt,
Matthew 3:3	For this is he who was spoken of by Isaiah the prophet when he said, 'The voice of one crying out in the wilderness: Prepare the way of the Lord (*kyriou* | κυρίου | gen sg masc); make his paths straight.'"
Matthew 4:7	Jesus said to him, "It also stands written: 'You shall not put the Lord (*kyrion* | κύριον | acc sg masc) your God to the test.'"
Matthew	Then Jesus said to him, "Away with you, Satan! For it stands written, 'You shall worship the Lord

If you are studying a verse (and not just the word), you can also use my Greek–English Interlinear Bible (discussed above). When you click on a word, the Concordance button becomes active and you can see the same concordance as above.

Biblical concordance for the Greek word κύριος { GK: 3261; Strongs: 2962; 660x)

Matthew 1:20	But as he pondered this, behold, an angel of the Lord { *kyriou* | gen sg masc } appeared to him in a dream, saying, "Joseph, son of David, do not be afraid to take Mary as your wife; for that which has been conceived in her is by the Holy Spirit.
Matthew 1:22	All this took place so that what was spoken by the Lord { *kyriou* | gen sg masc } through the prophet might be fulfilled:
Matthew 1:24	When Joseph arose from sleep, he did what the angel of { *kyriou* | gen sg masc } the Lord { *kyriou* | gen sg masc } had told him, he took her as his wife,
Matthew 2:13	After they had gone, an angel of the Lord { *kyriou* | gen sg masc } appeared in a dream to Joseph, saying, "Rise, take the child and his mother, flee to Egypt, and stay there until I tell you; for Herod is going to search for the child to destroy him."
Matthew 2:15	and was there until the death of Herod. This was to fulfill what was spoken by the Lord { *kyriou* | gen sg masc } through the prophet: "Out of Egypt I have called my son."
Matthew 2:19	But when Herod died, an angel of the Lord { *kyriou* | gen sg masc } appeared in a dream to Joseph in Egypt,
Matthew 3:3	For this is he who was spoken of by Isaiah the prophet when he said, 'The voice of one crying out in the wilderness: Prepare the way of the Lord { *kyriou* | gen sg masc }; make his paths straight.'"
Matthew 4:7	Jesus said to him, "It also stands written: 'You shall not put the Lord { *kyrion* | acc sg masc } your God to the test.'"
Matthew 4:10	Then Jesus said to him, "Away with you, Satan! For it stands written, 'You shall worship the Lord { *kyrion* | acc sg masc } your God and serve him alone.'"
Matthew 5:33	"Again, you have heard that it was said to those of old, 'You shall not break an oath, but carry out the vows you made to the Lord.' { *kyriō* | dat sg masc }
Matthew 6:24	"No one can serve two masters { *kyriois* | dat pl masc }, for either he will hate the one and love the other, or he will be devoted to the one and despise the other. You cannot serve God and possessions.
Matthew 7:21	"Not everyone who says to me, 'Lord { *kyrie* | voc sg masc }, Lord,' { *kyrie* | voc sg masc } will enter the kingdom of heaven, but the one who does the will of my Father in heaven.
Matthew 7:22	On that day many will say to me, 'Lord { *kyrie* | voc sg masc }, Lord { *kyrie* | voc sg masc }, did we not prophesy in your name, and in your name cast out demons, and in your name do many mighty works?'
Matthew 8:2	A leper came up to him, knelt down, and said, "Lord { *kyrie* | voc sg masc }, if you are willing, you can make me clean."
Matthew 8:6	saying, "Lord { *kyrie* | voc sg masc }, my servant is lying at home paralyzed, suffering terribly."
Matthew 8:8	But the centurion replied, "Lord { *kyrie* | voc sg masc }, I am not worthy for you to come under my roof, but just say the word and my servant will be healed.
Matthew 8:21	Another of his disciples said to him, "Lord { *kyrie* | voc sg masc }, permit me first to go and bury my father."
Matthew 8:25	The disciples went to him and woke him, crying out, "Lord { *kyrie* | voc sg masc }, save us! We are perishing!"
Matthew 9:28	When he had gone into the house, the blind men came to him; and Jesus said to them, "Do you believe that I am able to do this?" They said him, "Yes, Lord." { *kyrie* | voc sg masc } to
Matthew 9:38	so pray the Lord { *kyriou* | gen sg masc } of the harvest to send out workers into his harvest." to
Matthew 10:24	"A disciple is not above his teacher, nor a servant above his master { *kyrion* | acc sg masc }.
Matthew 10:25	It is enough for the disciple that he be as his teacher, and the servant as his master { *kyrios* | nom sg masc }. If they have called the head of the house 'Beelzebul,' how much more will

Close Concordance

There are several ways to do this in Accordance. Go to my dictionary and click on the link to your favorite translation (See the magnifying glass cursor at the bottom of the screenshot.) If you want to see how the NIV translates all the verses where κύριος occurs, click on NIV. Clicking on the frequency at the top (e.g., 717x) will also display a Greek-English concordance listing.

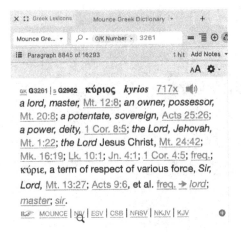

Another way is to right-click on "Lord," and choose Search for Key Number.

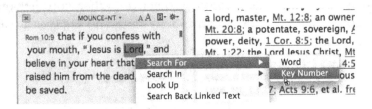

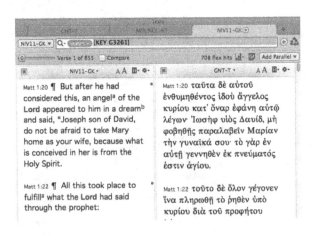

Once you have done a Key number search, you can have the Analysis function show you what words were used to translate κύριος.

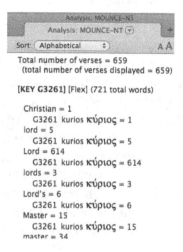

COMPARE TRANSLATIONS

You can also check other translations to see how they translate the term. For our case, they all use "Lord." But if we were looking up another word, you might see more variety.

For example, as mentioned earlier, the RSV translates 1 Corinthians 7:1 as, "It is well for a man not to *touch* a woman." (The Greek word behind "touch" is ἅπτω, #721.) But the NIV (1984) translates, "It is good for a man not *to marry*," and the NLT writes, "Yes, it's good *to abstain from sexual relations*" (and most translations). The point is that you can

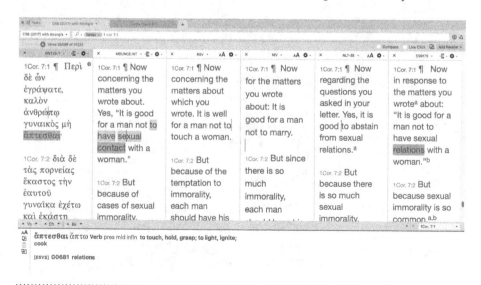

see the range of the word's meaning. If you use different translations to discover the word's semantic range, be sure to choose different types of translations, both formal and dynamic.

WORD-STUDY BOOKS

There are specific books that help you see the semantic range of a word and, to a greater or lesser degree, will tell you more about the word, especially its usage throughout the Bible and other ancient writings. But be careful when using these books. Up to this point you have been reading and studying the Bible and learning for yourself what the word means. It's a lot more fun and rewarding to discover this information for yourself. The minute you turn to one of these books, much of the joy of self-exploration is gone; but more importantly, realize that you are reading a person's opinion about the word. The word-study books, while good, are not inspired like Scripture. However, they are good to check your own work.

You will excuse me, but my favorite is my own, *Mounce's Complete Expository Dictionary of Old and New Testament Words*. I included the entry on κύριος at the end of this chapter. This book was specifically written for people who haven't learned Greek in the traditional way (or forgot what they had learned) and yet want to know what the Greek and Hebrew words of the Bible mean. It avoids many of the pitfalls and limitations of previous word-study books. The electronic version is especially easy to use. Just right-click on the word in Accordance and choose Look Up>>Dictionary.

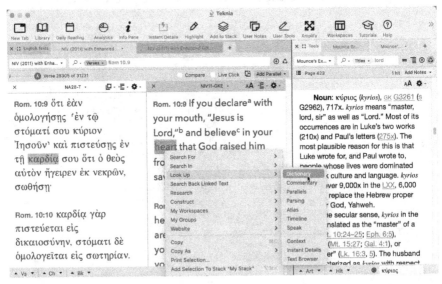

My second favorite one-volume word-study book is Chris Beetham's *Concise New International Dictionary of New Testament Theology and Exegesis*. It lists words alphabetically and by their GK number, and the discussion is excellent. You can download Beetham's article on κύριος in lesson 10 in the online class.

Beetham's work is an abridgment of the five-volume set, *New International Dictionary of New Testament Theology*, edited by Colin Brown, updated by Moisés Silva. This too is an excellent discussion of the words in the New Testament that often moves, as the name implies, into the word's theological significance; however, it's generally too advanced for most people at the Foundational Greek level. You will want to locate the word in the Greek Word Index because cognate words are often discussed under just one of the words. For example, under the entry for ἀδελφός ("brother") are the entries for ἀδελφή ("sister"), ἀδελφότης ("brotherhood"), φιλάδελφος ("loving one's brother [or sister]"), φιλαδελφία ("love for brother [or sister]"), and ψευδάδελφος ("false brother"). You can download Silva's article on κύριος in lesson 10 in the online class.

Geoffrey W. Bromiley's one volume *Theological Dictionary of the New Testament: Abridged in One Volume* (Eerdmans) is, as the name says, an abridgment of the multivolume *Theological Dictionary of the New Testament*, edited by G. Kittel and G. Friedrich (Eerdmans). Some of us affectionately call Bromiley's abridgment *Little Kittel* or *Kittelbits*. Whatever its name, Bromiley did a masterful job of cutting out discussion that is mostly irrelevant for you at the Foundational level. It lists words alphabetically based on their transliteration. But be sure to use the index; it doesn't discuss every Greek word, and you could spend a long time looking for an entry that isn't included. The full multivolume series of *TDNT*, while looking good on your shelf, is of little value for you at your stage.

I cannot recommend *Vine's Expository Dictionary of Old and New Testament Words*. There have been many advances in our understanding of Greek words since its publication, and I know of no Greek teacher who will recommend this work. Nor would I recommend the multivolume word studies by Wuest (*Word Studies from the Greek New Testament*), Vincent (*Word Studies in the New Testament*), and Robertson (*Word Pictures in the New Testament*).

You could look up your passage in a good commentary, and it might discuss the word's meaning. In my own commentary on the Pastoral Epistles,[1] I placed a heavy emphasis on word studies. Here is a simplified entry of "mercy."

> ἔλεος, "mercy," describes acts of pity and help that are appropriate within a relationship between two people. In classical Greek, mercy was the response when something unfortunate and undeserved happened to someone. It was an emotional response to a bad situation. But in the LXX it translates חֶסֶד *hesed*, and this association governs its meaning in the NT. N. Glueck argues that חֶסֶד *hesed* indicates not so much love and faithfulness as it does the conduct proper to the covenantal relationship between God and Israel. Mercy therefore primarily defines a relationship and secondarily elicits a response of pity to those within the relationship. Mercy is not a subjective emotion but an objective act appropriate for this relationship. This is why חֶסֶד *hesed* can also be translated by δικαιοσύνη, "righteousness," another term describing conduct appropriate to a certain relationship (cf. Ladd, Theology, 440; cf. Gen 19:19; 20:13; 21:23; 24:27; Prov 20:28). From this would naturally develop the association between God's mercy and his faithfulness, loyalty, and love. This also holds true when a person has mercy for another. It is not just that one should have mercy, but that one should act in a manner appropriate to the relationship and within that context have mercy (examples in E. R. Achtemeier, IDB 3:352–54; cf. Luke 1:58; 1 Pet 1:3). Because the biblical concept of mercy was governed by that of covenant, the concept of mercy developed the connotation of help or kindness that could be asked or requested of a superior, but never demanded (P. C. Craigie, EDT, 708). This accounts for the similarity between the biblical concepts of grace and mercy; both are gifts of God to an undeserving people.
>
> Paul uses ἔλεος, "mercy," and ἐλεεῖν "to be merciful," twenty-four times (Rom 12:8; 15:9; 1 Cor 7:25; 2 Cor 4:1; Gal 6:16; Eph 2:4; Phil 2:27), twelve in Rom 9–11 (Rom 9:15 [2x], 16, 18, 23; 11:30, 31 [2x], 32) and seven in the PE. Both sides of the theological coin evident in the OT are also found in Paul. On the one side, people cannot demand God's mercy (Rom 9–11); he is free to grant it as he wills. On the other, God's mercy will come to those who are in relationship with him. Thus letters can be started (1 Tim 1:2; 2 Tim 1:2; v.l. in Titus 1:4; cf. 1 Pet 1:3; 2 John 3; Jude 2) and ended (Gal 6:16) with a pronouncement of God's mercy. Since mercy is the appropriate conduct of God toward Christians, Paul says it is the basis of his own salvation

---

[1] *Pastoral Epistles*, in Word Biblical Commentary (Grand Rapids: Zondervan, 2000), 10–11.

(1 Tim 1:13, 16; cf. 1 Cor 7:25) and of others (Titus 3:5; cf. Eph 2:4; 1 Pet 1:3; especially Rom 11:32). It is both a present reality (2 Tim 1:16; cf. Phil 2:27) and a future hope (2 Tim 1:18; cf. Jas 2:13; Jude 21–23; summary in H.-H. Esser, NIDNTT 2:597).

OTHER BOOKS

If the word is an important theological term, it may be discussed in reference works like the *Evangelical Dictionary of Theology*, edited by Walter A. Elwell and Daniel J. Treier. This is a marvelous book, and everyone ought to have a copy of it for their study. (I don't often say that.)

STEP 4. EXPLORE THE CONTEXT

It's time to make a decision. Once you have located the Greek word and learned its semantic range, it's time to decide what it means in the particular verse you are studying. The question is, how do you decide?

In short, the answer is "context." You look for something in the immediate context that gives a clue as to the precise meaning of the word. I like to think in terms of concentric circles. The word you are studying is the center of the circle. The next circle out is the verse, then the paragraph, the book, and so on.

The point is that you first look for something in the verse that will define the word. If there isn't anything, then look at the paragraph. If there is nothing to help you in the paragraph, go to the book as a whole. But

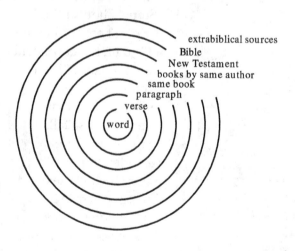

extrabiblical sources
Bible
New Testament
books by same author
same book
paragraph
verse
word

you want to stop as soon as you can. The further you go out from the center, the less assuredness you have that you are defining the word properly. But if you have to keep going out from the center, then you have to.

Why do you want to stop as soon as possible? Because different people can use the same word differently. Even the same person can use the same word differently in different contexts.

I saw this sign the other day: "GO CHILDREN SLOW." One of the sillier signs I have ever seen, it seemed to me. What does it mean? Does it mean, "Go, the children are slow," or, "Go children, but slowly," or, "Go slow, there are children." Obviously, it's the latter, but why is it obvious? Because we understand the sign within its *context* of being a road sign, and we probably notice that we are driving through a neighborhood full of children. And yet, in order to get to this understanding, we had to alter the word order and recognize that there

is a grammatical error in the sign ("slow" should be "slowly" since it's an adverb).

Another good one is, "Speed radar controlled." Silly sign #2. The radar doesn't control my speed. My foot does. (Of course, it could be argued that the threat of a ticket proven by a radar gun is the ultimate

cause of my speed.) How about these signs? "Stop." Shouldn't it be "Stop and then go"? "No parking here," when the sign is not in the parking lot but on the curb. And my other favorites from New England: "Lightly salted"; "Blind drive"; "Thickly settled."

The point is that common sense tells us these signs are to be understood within their context. The same is true for word studies. How does the context help us decide what a word means? Let's look at some examples as we move out from the center of the concentric circles.

VERSE

1 Thessalonians 4:3. "For this is the *will* of God, your sanctification." What is God's will for your life? To be sanctified; to be holy.

PARAGRAPH

1 Timothy 2:14–15. "And Adam was not deceived, but the woman was deceived and became a transgressor. Yet woman will be *saved* through bearing children, if she continues in faith and love and holiness, with modesty" (RSV). What does "saved" mean? Verse 14 suggests we are dealing with spiritual salvation ("transgression") and not physical safety.

BOOK

1 Timothy 1:10. At the end of a list of sins, Paul states that these are "contrary to *sound* doctrine." What is "*sound* doctrine"? Most translations miss the fact that the word is a medical metaphor meaning "healthy," and that it contrasts with the heresy being spread in Ephesus, which Paul elsewhere describes as sick and morbid (1 Tim 6:4), infectious abrasions (1 Tim 6:5) spreading like gangrene (2 Tim 2:17). Sound doctrine is that which is opposed to the infectious false teaching that damages people.

NEW TESTAMENT

In Romans 4:2–3 Paul says,

> If, in fact, Abraham was justified by works, he had something to boast about—but not before God. What does Scripture say? "Abraham believed God, and it was credited to him as righteousness."

("Justify" and "righteousness" are the same concept.) What does "justification" mean? How are we justified? If you look at James 2:21–24 you will see that James says,

> Was not our father Abraham considered righteous for what he did when he offered his son Isaac on the altar? You see that his faith and his actions were working together, and his faith was made complete by what he did. And the scripture was fulfilled that says, "Abraham believed God, and it was credited to him

as righteousness," and he was called God's friend. You see that a person is considered righteous by what they do and not by faith alone.

As you look at the whole of the New Testament, a fuller picture emerges as to the meaning of "justification." Paul is discussing how justification is granted; James is discussing how justification is shown to have occurred. A good word study shows that what at first appears to be contradictions are actually complementary teachings.

BIBLE

Acts 4:8 reads, "Then Peter, *filled* with the Holy Spirit, said to them, 'Rulers of the people and elders....'" But I thought Peter was filled at Pentecost (Acts 2:4)? What does "filled" mean in verse 8? If you look through Acts you will see this statement of "filling" repeated, always followed by mention of what the person said or did. But if you look at the book of Judges in the Old Testament, you will see the same metaphor used the same way for the Spirit possessing the person in a powerful but temporary way in order to accomplish a specific task. While the Holy Spirit comes in his fullness at a believer's conversion, Luke uses the terminology of Judges to describe a work of the Holy Spirit in which he grips a person in a special way to enable him or her to say or do something special.

EXTRABIBLICAL SOURCES

As you continue out to the outer circles, be careful. Once you get out of the Bible and are looking at how the word is used in secular thought, it becomes more and more possible that the words are being used differently. And especially if you are looking at how the word was used five hundred years before the writing of the New Testament, you must recognize that words can totally change their meaning over this time span. For example, a century ago, if you were to "skim" a book, this meant you would read it carefully. "To prevent" was "to go before," which today obscures Paul's meaning in the KJV of 1 Thessalonians 4:15.

> For this we say unto you by the word of the Lord, that we which are alive and remain unto the coming of the Lord shall not *prevent* them which are asleep.

The dead in Christ will go *first*.

These extrabiblical references can sometimes give us helpful *illustrations*. For example, Paul tells Timothy not to become "entangled" in civilian affairs (2 Tim 2:4). The verb ἐμπλέκω (GK G1861) can mean much more than "to be involved" (contra the NIV 1984; corrected to "entangled" in 2011), and this unfortunate translation has caused unnecessary grief for many pastors who were forced by their churches to have little or no contact with secular society, including a second job. (The blame for this does not lie with the NIV but with the unfortunate and unbiblical notion that a church must keep its pastor poor—but I digress.) The verb ἐμπλέκω means "to be involuntarily interlaced to the point of immobility, be entangled; to become involved in an activity to the point of interference with other activity or objective" (BDAG, 324). The word is used by the Shepherd of Hermas (*Similitudes*, 6.2.6–7) of a sheep, and by Aesop (74) of hares caught in thorns. Sheep and hares make great illustrations, but it's dangerous to define a biblical word based on them since they are so far removed from the biblical writer.

Frankly, for those pursuing Foundational Greek, it's probably too dangerous (exegetically) and too difficult to look at examples outside of the biblical canon. Extrabiblical texts may introduce problems with which you are not prepared to deal—best left alone at this stage I think.

So let's get back to our word study on "Lord" in Romans 10:9. Is there anything in the immediate context that will help us define the confession "Jesus is Lord" more precisely? The connection between the confession and belief in Jesus's resurrection suggests "Lord" means much more than "sir"; someone raised from the dead is more than a "sir."

As you move out into the paragraph, in verse 12 Paul says that Jesus is "Lord of all," asserting his universal lordship. It's especially significant that in verse 13 Paul quotes Joel 2:32, because in its Old Testament context Joel is speaking of Yahweh, God. Moo writes, "In the OT, of course, the one on whom people called for salvation was Yahweh; Paul reflects the high view of Christ common among the early church by identifying this one with Jesus Christ, the Lord."[2]

In Romans 1:4 Paul states that Jesus "was declared to be the Son of God in power according to the Spirit of holiness by his resurrection from the dead, Jesus Christ our Lord,"connecting Jesus's lordship with his resurrection as in 10:3, and with his identification as the Son of God. As we see who Jesus is as Lord, we see that he is also God's Son. As God's Son, the Old Testament references to God can be applied to Jesus.

---

[2] *The Epistle to the Romans* (Grand Rapids: Eerdmans, 1996), 660.

It's a small step from this to agreeing with Thomas's confession: "My Lord and my God!" (John 20:28).

As you expand further out into the New Testament, we find similar confessions: "At the name of Jesus every knee should bow, in heaven and on earth and under the earth, and every tongue confess that Jesus Christ is Lord, to the glory of God the Father" (Phil 2:10–11; cf. 1 Cor 12:3).

The answer to the question with which I started this word study is much clearer. What is the minimum it takes to get into heaven? You must have a correct understanding of who Jesus is, and that understanding causes you to submit to his lordship. We must believe that Jesus was raised from the dead, that he was raised to a position of lordship over all, and in his lordship we see that he is in fact the Son of God, Yahweh himself. Christianity is grounded in the historical event of the incarnation, death, and resurrection of Jesus Christ. Who we are as disciples is intimately tied up with who he is as Lord, our Lord and our God.

OTHER ISSUES

SEPTUAGINT

As you get further into word studies, you will often see writers paying special attention to how a word is used in the Septuagint, often abbreviated LXX. This is the Greek translation of the Hebrew Scriptures that was probably started about 250 BC and finished somewhere around the time of Christ. There are certain words that are important in the Hebrew Old Testament, especially theological words. When the Septuagint was translated, the translators chose a Greek word for each of these Hebrew words. When it comes to defining these same Greek words in the New Testament, it's the Hebrew word's background in the Old Testament via the Septuagint that may be the most important background in defining the Greek word, not its general usage in the first century.

For example, how did the LXX decide to translate the Hebrew word חֶסֶד (hesed, "steadfast love," ESV), which describes God's love for his covenantal people, when there is no such word in Greek? When the LXX translators finally settled on ἔλεος, generally translated as "mercy," ἔλεος automatically carried the specific meaning of חֶסֶד into the New Testament.

Given the fact that κύριος is used by the LXX to translate יהוה, "Yahweh," it is hard for me to imagine that the Jewish Paul meant anything less than confessing the deity of Christ in Romans 10:9.

COGNATES

A cognate is a word that is related to another and actually shares the same root. In English, the words "prince" and "princess" share the same root, although their specific forms are altered because they are masculine and feminine gender, respectively.

Most cognates have similar meanings. There may be differences in nuance, but for the most part cognates share the same basic meaning. The root ἀγαπ, "love," shows itself as a verb (ἀγαπάω), a noun (ἀγάπη), and an adjective (ἀγαπητός). Each of these words is called a "cognate," and each shares the same basic meaning.

However, other cognates do not share the same basic meaning, so be careful using a cognate to define another cognate.

COMMON MISTAKES

Before ending this discussion of word studies, I must cover common mistakes made in doing word studies. For a more detailed discussion of these issues you can read *Exegetical Fallacies* by D. A. Carson (Baker).

ANACHRONISM

The first is the bad habit of defining a Greek word using an English word derived from that Greek word. My favorite example is when someone talks about the "power" of God, and adds that this word "power" is δύναμις, from which we get our word "dynamite," and then conclude that God's power is dynamite.

This is totally backward and totally wrong. English wasn't a language until the second millennium A.D. Regardless of where our words came from, the English definitions don't work backward to the Greek definitions. Supposedly there was a reason why a specific Greek word was used as the basis of an English word, but especially as the years go by, that English word can take on a meaning different from its Greek origin. God's power is never pictured in Scripture as something that blows rocks apart or is loud.

ETYMOLOGICAL FALLACY

"Etymology" refers to how the word was originally created. What would you say if a pastor or Bible study leader told you that the "butterfly" is an animal made of butter that can fly? Or perhaps that a pineapple is a type of apple grown on pine trees? After the laughter died down, and if the speaker were serious, you would point out that this is not what the word means. The etymology, the pieces ("morphemes") that were originally used to make up the word, does not define the word today, any more than a butterfly is a milk by-product.

The worse example I know of is the Greek word for "repent," μετα- νοέω, which some people define as "to change your mind" but not necessarily your behavior. They often base their position on the meaning of the two morphemes that were used to create μετανοέω. "Repentance," they say, "involves an intellectual shift in understanding, but repentance does not require a change of action." This type of misuse of Greek etymology runs throughout Vine's *Expository Dictionary of Old and New Testament Words,* and why it's not recommended. Vine writes, "*meta,* 'after,' implying 'change,' ... *nous,* 'the mind,' ... hence signifies 'to change one's mind or purpose.'"[3] Certainly, the word can mean "to regret" (cf. Luke 17:3–4), but the New Testament's understanding of repentance is not drawn from the etymology of one morpheme but from the biblical concept of repentance, especially from the background of conversion in the Old Testament. See the article on *metanoeō* in Bromiley's *Theological Dictionary of the New Testament: Abridged,* where he writes, "The concept of conversion stresses positively the fact that real penitence involves a new relation to God that embraces all spheres of life and claims the will in a way that no external rites can replace.... It means turning aside from everything that is ungodly" (pp. 640–41). Besides, μετά does not mean "change," and you cannot move legitimately from "after" to "change."[4]

Is it ever the case that a word carries the meaning of its parts? Sure. The verb εἰσέρχομαι is made up of the preposition εἰς, meaning "into," and ἔρχομαι, meaning "to go." The verb εἰσέρχομαι means "to go into." But it's not the word's etymology that determines its current meaning.

---

[3] Nashville: Thomas Nelson, 1985, p. 525.

[4] BDAG lists a meaning of μετανοέω as, "change one's mind," but wisely does not list any biblical examples. The noun μετανοία also has a meaning, "a change of mind," but all biblical references are under the gloss, "with the nuance of 'remorse,' and later adds, "in our lit[erature] w[ith] focus on the need to change in view of responsibility to deity."

It's the use of this verb when Jesus and his disciples entered a house or a city. In other words, through its use we can see it has retained the meaning of its morphemes, but we don't assume its morphemes still define the word.

It's also true that some prepositions (ἐκ, κατά, ἀπό, διά, σύν) have what is called a "perfective" function. When added to a word they can intensify its meaning. The verb ἐσθίω means "I eat"; κατεσθίω means "I devour." Some perfective forms, however, have lost their intensified meaning, and the compound form has the same basic meaning as the simple word. For example, Paul tells Timothy in 1 Timothy 1:4 that the teaching of the opponents in Ephesus produce only "speculations," ἐκζήτησις. It's difficult to determine whether Paul intended the intensified "extreme speculations" (or perhaps "useless speculations"), or just "speculations," which is the meaning of the simple ζήτησις ("investigation, controversy, debate"). As always, context is the guide as to whether or not the intensified meaning is present.[5]

Connected to the etymological fallacy is the fact that words change their meaning over the years. Just think of the lyrics to the old song that ends, "We'll have a gay old time," or the KJV use of "prevent" in 1 Thessalonians 4:15 (cited above). What a word meant when it was first created, or what it meant five hundred years ago, may be at best irrelevant today. A word's meaning today is seen in how it's used today, not in how it used to be used.

- "Hussy" is from the Middle English word "huswife," meaning "housewife."

- "Enthusiasm" meant to be inspired or possessed by a god.

- "Nice" originally meant "foolish" in Middle English (from the Latin *nescire*, "to be ignorant").

- "Gossip" is from *godsib*, a word that referred to godparents, and came to be used of the type of chatter that stereotypically occurs at christenings.[6] Today, when I preach about gossip, christenings are nowhere in my mind, and its etymology is irrelevent in an attempt to define the Bible's prohibition of slander.

---

[5] Greek does have the "alpha privative," which is a way to negate a word much like the English "un-" or "ir-." These words always carry the meaning of the initial morpheme. The noun πίστις means "faithful"; ἀπιστία means "lack of belief, unbelief."

[6] See Moisés Silva, *God, Language, and Scripture* (Grand Rapids: Zondervan, 1991).

Words have a range of meaning, but that range is not determined by the morphemes that made up the word or by how it was used five hundred years earlier.

FOCUS ON THE LARGER UNIT

Even though this chapter has been on word studies, I need to emphasize that we can't put too much weight on a single word, thinking that the word, all by itself, is full of meaning. For the most part, we do not communicate with individual words but with phrases, sentences, and paragraphs. Focus your study on the larger unit, hesitating to place too much emphasis on an individual word.

Tied to this is the fact that theological concepts are larger than a word. Regardless of how many times you have heard the word ἀγάπη defined as the sacrificial love for the unlovely, the kind of love that is bestowed on the undeserving, that simply is not what the word in and of itself means. (I talk more about this on the lecture on this chapter in the online class.) It's not the word that conveys this meaning, but it's the concept of biblical love as illustrated by God that infuses ἀγάπη with this particular meaning in the biblical context.

On the next several pages is the article on "Lord" from my word-study book. You will notice that it contains references to all the Hebrew and Greek words that are translated as "Lord."

MOUNCE'S COMPLETE EXPOSITORY DICTIONARY OF OLD AND NEW TESTAMENT WORDS

Entry on "Lord" *(used with permission)*

OLD TESTAMENT

Noun: אָדוֹן (*'ādôn*), GK 123 (S 113), 773x. *'ādôn* is used with reference to "the Lord" and to people of high rank (especially superiors and persons of authority). *'ādôn* was commonly pronounced in place of the covenant name of Israel's God, Yahweh (יהוה [GK 3378]). The specific form of that vocalization is *'adōnāy* ("my Lord"), a plural noun with a first person singular suffix. This practice became so well established that the Greek translators of the Heb. Bible rendered "Yahweh" with the Greek equivalent of Lord (*kyrios*). English translations usually signify Yahweh as "Lord" by placing the letters "Lord" in small caps: "Lord."

The commandment not to take the Lord's name in vain, however, does not necessarily prohibit its pronunciation as Scripture is read, nor does the prohibition against blaspheming the name (Lev. 24:15–16) prevent any and every use of it.

(1) In addition to its use as the substitute pronunciation for the divine name Yahweh (GK 3378), *'adōnāy* also appears as a title for Yahweh approximately 442x (GK 151) in the Hebrew Bible. When it appears in this context, it's normally translated "Lord," but may also be understood as "Master" or "my Master."

(2) About 30x the word *'ādôn* addresses God as "Lord," as in Ps. 8:1, 9: "O LORD, our *Lord*, how majestic is your name in all the earth." Isaiah frequently calls God "The *Lord*, the LORD Almighty" (Isa. 3:1; 10:3). When Joshua sees the captain of the Lord's army, he addresses him as "my *Lord*" (Jos. 5:14; cf. Ps. 110:1).

(3) This word also refers to various human beings addressed as "lord" or "master." Joseph is the "master" of Pharaoh's household (Gen 45:8). A "husband" (even a wicked one) can be addressed with this word (Jdg. 19:26). Elijah the prophet is likewise called "lord" (1 Ki. 18:7). Uriah calls both King David and his army commander Joab *'ādôn* ("master" and "lord" in NIV of 2 Sam. 11:11). In fact, anyone with a position of leadership or authority can be addressed by this term. At the same time, to call someone "my lord" is sometimes merely a title of respect for someone (e.g., Gen. 24:18; 32:5; 1 Ki. 18:7).

(4) Similar to other biblical names, *'ādôn* appears in Heb. royal personal names: *Adoni*jah, *Adoni*kam, and *Adoni*ram; it also appears in the names of some pagan rulers, such as *Adoni*-Zedek (Jos. 10:1, 3) and *Adoni*-Bezek (Jdg. 1:5–7, "lord of Bezek," the Canaanite king of Bezek).

Noun: אֲדֹנָי (*'adōnāy*), GK 151 (S 136), 442x. *'adōnāy* means "Lord." In addition to its use as the substitute pronunciation for the divine name Yahweh (see discussion of GK 3378), *'adōnāy* also appears as an independent title for Israel's God. When it appears in this context, it's normally translated "Lord," but it may also be understood as "Master" or "my Master."

Proper Noun: יהוה (*yhwh*), GK 3378 (S 3068/3069), 6829x.

Proper Noun: יָהּ (*yāh*), GK 3363 (S 3050), 49x.The Hebrew name *yhwh* or "Yahweh," commonly translated into English as "the LORD," is the most frequently appearing name for God in the OT (almost 7000x). It appears in every OT book except Ecclesiastes, Song of Songs, and Esther. This name is often referred to as the Tetragrammaton because of the four (*tetra*) letters (*grammaton*) used in its Hebrew spelling. There is also an alternate, short form of the divine name (*yāh*) that appears nearly 50x, mostly in the book of Psalms (43x); it's best known from the Hebrew expression "Hallelu-*yah*" (translated, "Praise *the LORD*").

The modern spelling and pronunciation "Yahweh" merely represents our best, educated guess as to what the original pronunciation might have been. This is due to the fact that biblical Hebrew was originally written without vowels, and in Hebrew the vowels would show us the precise pronunciation and meaning of the name. The problem is compounded by the fact that the pronunciation of this name ceased from the Hebrew (Masoretic) reading tradition in order to avoid misuse in connection with the third commandment (Exod. 20:7; Deut. 5:11). That is, when the Jews were reading the Hebrew text and came to *yhwh*, instead of saying "Yahweh" they would say the Hebrew word "Adonai" (*'adōnāy*, GK 151, which means "Lord").

In terms of the origin and significance of the divine name, three texts from Exodus are especially important. (1) The first is Exod. 3:13–15. Here, the divine name is given for the first time in the context of Israel's imminent deliverance from Egypt. The revelation of the name is related to the statement, "I AM WHO I AM" (v. 14), where Moses is commanded to tell the Israelites that "I AM has sent me." Then, in verse 15, the divine name "Yahweh" is connected to the God of the patriarchs where it's stated that this name, "Yahweh," is his "eternal name." The connection between "I AM" and "Yahweh" is one of verbal person. "I AM" is the first person form of the verb "to be" (*hāyâ*; GK 2118; see *be*), while "Yahweh" represents the third person form of the same verb, perhaps "HE IS" or "HE WILL BE."

(2) In Exod. 6:2–8, the significance of the divine name resurfaces. In verses 2–3 it's stated, "God also said to Moses, 'I am the LORD [Yahweh], I appeared to Abraham, to Isaac and to Jacob as God Almighty, but by my name the LORD [Yahweh] I did not make myself known to them.'" This text also connects the fulfillment of the patriarchal promises (vv. 4, 7–8) with the deliverance of the nation of Israel from Egypt (vv. 5–6) and concludes with the statement, in verse 8, "I am the LORD" or "I am Yahweh."

(3) The texts from Exodus 3 and 6 record the origin of the divine name and locate its significance in the fulfillment of the patriarchal promises through Israel's deliverance from Egypt. The third text is Exod. 34:5–7. Here, in a remarkable display of the divine glory, God *himself* "proclaimed his name" while passing in front of Moses. This proclamation is to be understood as an exposition of the significance or character of the divine name. What does the divine name mean? It's written, "The LORD [Yahweh], the LORD [Yahweh], the compassionate and gracious God, slow to anger, abounding in love and faithfulness, maintaining love to thousands, and forgiving wickedness, rebellion and sin. Yet he does not leave the guilty unpunished; he punishes the children and their children for the sin of the fathers to the third and fourth generation." According to these verses, the divine name is God's covenant name and represents his steadfast determination to maintain the covenant relationship with his people.

In subsequent biblical history, the divine name, "Yahweh," is referred to as "the Name" (Lev. 24:11) or, more passionately, as "this glorious and awesome name" (Deut. 28:58). With reference to the eschatological city of God, the prophet Ezekiel records that its name will be, "THE LORD IS THERE" or "Yahweh is there." In light of the origin, significance, and use of the divine name in the OT, Jesus' statement in John. 8:58, "before Abraham was born, I am," clearly identifies Jesus as God, the God of the patriarchs and the deliverer of Israel, Yahweh himself (Exod. 3:14). See I (am).

NEW TESTAMENT

Noun: δεσπότης (*despotēs*), GK 1305 (S 1203), 10x. *despotēs* is similar in meaning to *kyrios* ("lord"), though it occurs far less often. The nuance of *despotēs* emphasizes the right and power to command. See *master*.

Noun: κύριος (*kyrios*), GK 3261 (S 2962), 717x. *kyrios* means "master, lord, sir" as well as "Lord." Most of its occurrences are in Luke's two works (210x) and Paul's letters (275x). The most plausible reason for this is that Luke wrote for, and Paul wrote to, people whose lives were dominated by Greek culture and language. *kyrios* occurs over 9,000x in the LXX, 6,000 of which replace the Hebrew proper name for God, Yahweh.

In the secular sense, *kyrios* in the NT is translated as the "master" of a slave (Matt. 10:24–25; Eph. 6:5), "owner" (Matt. 15:27; Ga. 4:1), or "employer" (Luke. 16:3, 5). The husband is characterized as *kyrios* with respect to his wife (1 Pet. 3:6; cf. Gen. 18:12, where "master" is *kyrios* in the LXX). By this Peter makes his point that Sarah thought of her husband respectfully. *kyrios* may also communicate politeness as in Matt. 18:21–22; 25:20–26; Acts 16:30, translated with the term of address "sirs." This word is also used to address heavenly beings such as angels (Rev. 7:14).

God is consistently depicted as *kyrios*, especially when the NT author is quoting an OT passage that uses *kyrios* for Yahweh (Rom. 4:8; 9:28–29; 10:16). Many OT formulas surface in the phrases "the hand of the Lord" (Luke. 1:66), "the angel of the Lord" (Matt. 1:20), "the name of the Lord" (Jas. 5:10), "the Spirit of the Lord" (Acts 5:9), and "the word of the Lord" (Acts 8:25). The prophetic formula, "says the Lord," also emerges from the OT (Rom. 14:11; 1 Cor. 14:21; 2 Cor. 6:17). Jesus also reflects his adoption of OT patterns when he refers to his Father as the "Lord of heaven and earth" (Matt. 11:25) and as "the Lord of the harvest" (Matt. 9:38).

The earliest Christian confession is that "Jesus is Lord." This was the climax of Peter's speech on Pentecost (Acts 2:36); by making this confession a person is saved (Rom. 10:9–10). Jesus is Lord whether he is on earth (Matt. 7:21; 21:29–30) or exalted in heaven (1 Cor. 16:22; Rev. 22:20). By confessing Jesus as *Lord*, the Christian community was also recognizing that he has dominion over the world. As a result of Jesus' sovereignty, one day every created being will acknowledge what the insignificant, persecuted community at Philippi confesses in its worship: "Jesus Christ is *Lord*" (Phil. 2:11).

Presently, all powers on earth and in heaven are subject to Jesus and must serve him, for he has been elevated to the position of *kyrios* (Eph. 1:20–21; 1 Pet. 3:22). John envisions him as the ruler over all the kings of the earth—"King of kings and *Lord* of lords" (Rev. 17:14; 19:15–16). The Roman emperor was called "king of kings" because he presided over the vassal kings of the empire, but how puny and conceited in light of the absolute sovereignty of the Lamb, the true *Lord* of lords. NT writers found their evidence for Jesus' lordship in Ps. 110:1, the most quoted psalm in the NT (see Matt. 22:44; 26:64; Acts 2:34; Eph. 1:20; Heb. 1:3, 13). This royal psalm speaks of the *kyrios* being seated at Yahweh's right hand in a rank of power, as demonstrated by the subjugation of his enemies. This is where Jesus currently abides, for the benefit of the church. See *NIDNTT–A*, 323–25.

PART II

CHURCH GREEK

In this section that I call "Church Greek," you will be delving into the Greek language and learning a wonderful method for studying the Bible I call "phrasing." You have seen bits and pieces of phrasing, and now you will learn the entire system. Phrasing will show you why you have been spending all this time learning grammar.

I call it "Church Greek" since this is the level of Greek that most people in chuch want to learn, and it is enough Greek to be able to use interlinears, read better commentaries, see why translations are different, and go deeper in your Bible study.

CHAPTER 11

MODIFIERS

There are many ways to modify an idea. In fact, if we only had subjects, verbs, and objects, communication would be more difficult and certainly less colorful. In this chapter we'll look at many different modifiers.

ARTICLE

11.1　The English **definite article** is the word "the." The **indefinite article** is the word "a." The definite article tends to be used to make a general idea more specific. In the sentence, "A book is about Greek," the identity of the book is not clear. If I said, "The book is about Greek," it would be clear I was speaking about a specific book.

11.2　The word ὁ is the single most important Greek word to memorize, often translated as "the." Not only does it occur 19,821 times in the New Testament, but it will give you significant clues as to the overall structure of a sentence.

	masculine	*feminine*	*neuter*
nom sg	ὁ	ἡ	τό
gen sg	τοῦ	τῆς	τοῦ
dat sg	τῷ	τῇ	τῷ
acc sg	τόν	τήν	τό
nom/voc pl	οἱ	αἱ	τά
gen pl	τῶν	τῶν	τῶν
dat pl	τοῖς	ταῖς	τοῖς
acc pl	τούς	τάς	τά

My recommendation is that you memorize the paradigm. It is that imporant of a word. If that is overwhelming, be sure at least to remember its number: GK #3836; Strong's #3588. When scanning a verse in Greek, you need to be able to quickly identify the article.

11.3   The word ὁ will be in the same case, number, and gender as the word it modifies ("agreement").

πιστὸς ὁ   λόγος   καὶ   πάσης   ἀποδοχῆς   ἄξιος
faithful *the word* and   all   acceptance   worthy
Trustworthy is *the word* and worthy of complete acceptance
(1 Tim 4:9).

λόγος is nominative singular masculine, so the article ὁ must be nominative singular masculine.

11.4   Nouns are only one gender (usually). Because words like ὁ can modify any noun regardless of its gender, and because they must be the same gender as the word they are modifying, they themselves must be able to be in any gender. That's why the paradigm for the article has twenty-four forms and not just eight.

11.5   The most common translation of ὁ is "the."

ἐγώ   εἰμι τὸ   ἄλφα καὶ τὸ ὦ,   λέγει κύριος ὁ θεός
I   am *the* Alpha and *the* Omega says   Lord   God
I am *the* Alpha and *the* Omega, says the Lord God *(Rev 1:8)*.

11.6   Greek uses ὁ when English does not use the definite article, such as before a personal name.

ὁ   Πέτρος εἶπεν αὐτῷ, φράσον ἡμῖν τὴν παραβολὴν ταύτην
the Peter   he said to him Explain   to us the parable   this
Peter said to him, "Explain this parable to us" *(Matt 15:15)*.

This includes the word for "God," θεός.

ἃ   ὁ θεὸς ἐκαθάρισεν, σὺ μὴ κοίνου
what *the* God   he cleansed   you not consider common

What *God* has made clean, you must not consider common (*Acts 10:15*).

11.7   The article ὁ is not always used when English requires the definite article, in which case the translator can add it back in. This is true especially in prepositional phrases.

ἐν   ἀρχῇ   ἦν   ὁ   λόγος
in   beginning   was   the   Word
In *the* beginning was the Word (*John 1:1*).

11.8   The article ὁ can function as a personal pronoun, especially in the ὁ δέ construction (οἱ δέ in the plural).

ὁ   δὲ   εἶπεν   αὐτοῖς,   οὐκ   ἀνέγνωτε   τί   ἐποίησεν   Δαυὶδ
the   but   said   to them   not   you read   what   did   David
But *he* said to them, "Have you not read what David did?" (*Matt 12:3*)

Οἱ   δὲ   εἶπαν   πρὸς   αὐτόν
they   and   said   to   him
And *they* said to Him (*Luke 5:33*)

11.9   The article ὁ can function as a possessive pronoun.

οἱ   ἄνδρες,   ἀγαπᾶτε   τὰς   γυναῖκας
the   men   love!   the   wives
NASB: Husbands, love *your* wives (*Eph 5:25*).

11.10 Sometimes ὁ functions with a word or phrase, in essence turning the construction into a substantive or a modifier.

μακάριοι   οἱ   πτωχοὶ   τῷ   πνεύματι
blessed   the   poor   in spirit
Blessed are *the poor* in spirit (*Matt 5:3*).
πτωχοί is an adjective functioning with οἱ as a noun.

ὅμοιοί εἰσιν παιδίοις τοῖς ἐν ἀγορᾷ   καθημένοις
like   they are children   who   in   marketplace sitting

NASB: They are like children *who sit in the marketplace* (Luke 7:32).

NIV: They are like children *sitting in the marketplace*.

τοῖς … καθημένοις is functioning as a noun, and is modified by the prepositional phrase ἐν ἀγορᾷ

Don't be surprised to find a lot of flexibility in translating ὁ.

ENGLISH ADJECTIVES

11.11 An **adjective** is a word that modifies a noun or pronoun (or another adjective).

> Bill threw his *big black* book at the *strange* teacher.

11.12 Adjectives can function *adjectivally* —like a regular adjective, also called an *attributive* adjective.

> She is a *good* student.

11.13 Adjectives can also function *substantivally* —as if they were a noun. In this case the adjective does not modify anything but performs a function in the sentence, such as the subject or the direct object.

> The *Good,* the *Bad,* and the *Ugly* are all welcome here.

> Out with the *old* and in with the *new.*

11.14 Adjectives can appear in the *predicate*, which means they occur after the verb "to be."[1]

> The Bible is *black.*

---

[1]   "To be" is the infinitive form of the verb, which in the indicative can be "is," "was," and so on.

GREEK ADJECTIVES

11.15 **Adjectival.** Greek adjectives can function *adjectivally* (also called an *attributive* adjective).

τότε παραλαμβάνει αὐτὸν ὁ   διάβολος εἰς τὴν ἁγίαν πόλιν
then he took   him   the devil   into the *holy* city
Then the devil took him into the *holy* city (*Matt 4:5*).

11.16 **Agreement.** An attributive adjective will agree with the word it modifies in case, number, and gender, just like the article. In other words, if the noun is genitive singular feminine, the modifying adjective will also be genitive singular feminine. This is why adjectives, like the article, have twenty-four forms, so they can modify words regardless of their case, number, or gender.

εἰσέλθατε διὰ   τῆς στενῆς πύλης
enter   through the *narrow* gate
Enter through the *narrow* gate (*Matt 7:13*).

πύλης is genitive singular feminine, and so the adjective στενῆς must also be genitive singular feminine.

11.17 **Substantival.** Greek adjectives can also function *substantivally*. Their gender and number are determined by the word they stand for; their case is determined by their function in the sentence.

οὗτός ἐστιν ὁ   υἱός μου ὁ   ἀγαπητός
This   is   the son my   the *beloved*
This is my Son, the *Beloved* (*Matt 3:17*).

ἀγαπητός is an adjective, and the verse can be translated with ἀγαπητός as an attributive adjective ("This is my beloved Son") or as a substantival adjective, as the example above shows.

It's often necessary to add a word to the translation in order to make sense of a substantival adjective. It's usually clear from context what word needs to be added. In Matthew 1:19, δίκαιος is an adjective meaning "righteous," and you need to add a word like "man" (since Joseph is male).

Ἰωσὴφ δὲ ὁ ἀνὴρ αὐτῆς, δίκαιος ὢν
Joseph but the husband of her righteous being

NIV (1984): Because Joseph her husband was a righteous *man* (Matt 1:19)

NLT: Joseph, her fiancé, was a good *man.*

The most famous example of a possible substantival adjective is from the Lord's Prayer. The question is, are we to pray that we be delivered from evil, or from the evil one, i.e., Satan? All translation is interpretive. πονηροῦ is an adjective meaning "evil."

ῥῦσαι ἡμᾶς ἀπὸ τοῦ πονηροῦ
deliver us from the *evil*

NASB: Deliver us from *evil* (Matt 6:13).

NIV: Deliver us from the *evil one.*

If all this is feeling familiar, it's because we saw the same things with participles, which are after all verbal *adjectives.*

11.18 **Predicate Position.** As in English, the Greek anarthrous adjective can also be in the predicate, and there does not have to be an explicit verb in the Greek sentence. The translator will have added the verb, normally a form of the verb "to be."

πλατεῖα ἡ πύλη καὶ εὐρύχωρος ἡ ὁδός
wide the gate and *easy* the way

The gate *is wide* and the way *is easy* (Matt 7:13).

GREEK–ENGLISH INTERLINEAR

> If you only want to learn how to use a reverse interlinear, the sections marked "Greek-English Interlinear" can be skipped.

11.19 **Position.** Greek adjectives are not always right before the noun as in English. Because reverse interlinears follow English order, you will not see this fact. But if you want to learn how to use a Greek-English interlinear, you need to understand the basics of what is happening with Greek adjectives.

11.20 **First Attributive Position.** Greek can use adjectives in the order article-adjective-substantive. Attributive adjectives tend to be articular.

ἀπὸ τῆς πρώτης ἡμέρας ἄχρι τοῦ νῦν
from the *first* day until the now
from the *first* day until now *(Phil 1:5)*

It's easy to see that τῆς πρώτης ἡμέρας means "the first day," with τῆς meaning "the," πρώτης being the adjective, and ἡμέρας the noun. It's easy because this is how English does it.

More accurately, I should say "article-modifier-noun." An adjective is only one possible modifier.

11.21 **Second Attributive Position.** Greek often lists the adjective in the order article-noun-article-modifier.

τὸ πνεῦμα τὸ ἅγιον
the spirit the *holy*
The *Holy* Spirit *(Eph 4:30)*

Greek could write "the Holy Spirit" or "the Spirit the Holy" with no significant difference in meaning. In the order article-noun-article-modifier, the second article is functioning as a grammatical marker, showing that the following word modifies the previous word. It does not need to be translated.

μετὰ τῶν ἀγγέλων τῶν ἁγίων
with the angels *the* holy
with the holy angels *(Mark 8:38)*

In the reverse interlinear, I kept the second article with its adjective.

the	Holy		Spirit
τὸ	τὸ	ἅγιον	πνεῦμα
d.asn	d.asn	a.asn	n.asn
3836	3836	41	4460

In my Greek-English interlinear, the same phrase will appear like this.

the	Spirit	the	holy
τὸ	πνεῦμα	τὸ	ἅγιον
n.asn	n.asn	n.asn	a.asn
3836	4460	3836	41

11.22 We have seen that when a prepositional phrase is modifying a word, it is generally in the second attributive position: article-noun-article-modifier (6.15).

αἱ δυνάμεις αἱ ἐν τοῖς οὐρανοῖς σαλευθήσονται
The powers   *the in the   heavens*   will be shaken

The powers *which are in heaven* will be shaken (Mark 13:25).

11.23 **First predicate position**. When the Greek has adjective-article-noun, we call it the first predicate position. The verb "to be" will generally need to be added.

μακάριοι οἱ εἰρηνοποιοί
blessed   the peacemakers
Blessed *are* the peacemakers (Matt 5:9).

The **second predicate position** is article-noun-adjective.

χαίρετε καὶ ἀγαλλιᾶσθε, ὅτι ὁ μισθὸς ὑμῶν πολὺς
rejoice   and be glad   for the reward your   great
Rejoice and be glad, for your reward *is* great (Matt 5:12).

In both these situations, the adjective must be anarthrous.

11.24 **Anarthrous**. Sometimes both the noun and the adjective will be anarthrous; there will be no article helping you see if the adjective is functioning as an attributive, substantive, or predicate. In this situation, let context be your guide. What fits the context?

πρέπον ἐστὶν ἡμῖν πληρῶσαι πᾶσαν δικαιοσύνην.
fitting it's for us to fulfill *all* righteousness
It's fitting for us to fulfill *all righteousness* (Matt 3:15).

πᾶσαν is giving an attribute of δικαιοσύνην.

ἐπὰν δὲ πονηρὸς ᾖ, καὶ τὸ σῶμά σου σκοτεινόν
when but bad is and the body your darkness
ESV: But when it's bad, your body *is full of darkness* (Luke 11:34).

Context shows that σκοτεινόν is in the predicate, with σῶμα as the subject.

11.25 The adjective πᾶς means "all," and oddly enough it occurs in the predicate position when functioning as an attributive.[2]

ὃς πάντας ἀνθρώπους θέλει σωθῆναι
who *all* people wishes to be saved

Who wishes *all* people to be saved (1 Tim 2:4)

11.26 **Adverb**. An adverb is a word (or phrase) that modifies a verb, or an adjective or another adverb. There are 277 adverbs in the Greek Testament occurring 3,644 times. Only three occur 150 times or more: καθώς; οὕτως; τότε. Accordance classifies καθώς as a conjunction, but the Greek lexicon lists it as an adverb. Resources often are not unified in how they classify adverbs, conjunctions, particles, and even some adjectives.

οὕτως ... προσεύχεσθε ὑμεῖς· Πάτερ ἡμῶν ὁ ἐν τοῖς οὐρανοῖς
in this way pray you Father our the in the heavens
Pray *this way*: Our Father who is in heaven *(Matt 6:9)*

The adverb οὕτως is modifying the verb προσεύχεσθε.

---

[2] The same is true of ὅλος, which means "whole," but this is not one of your vocabulary words.

τότε   παραγίνεται   ὁ Ἰησοῦς   ἀπὸ   τῆς Γαλιλαίας
then   he came   Jesus   from   Galilee

Then Jesus came from Galilee *(Matt 3:13)*

The adverb τότε tells us when Jesus came.

παραλαμβάνει αὐτὸν ὁ διάβολος εἰς ὄρος ὑψηλὸν λίαν
he took   him   the deil   to   mountain high   *very*

The devil took him to a *very* high mountain (Matt 4:8)

λίαν modifies the adjective ὑψηλὸν, saying it is "very" high. (λίαν occurs only 12 times in the Greek Testament.)

VOCABULARY

Modifiers you already know

ὁ	the

New vocabulary

ἅγιος	adjective: holy (233)
	plural noun: saints
ἄλλος	other, another (155)
εἷς	one (343)
μέγας	large, great (243)
πᾶς	singular: each, every (1,241)
	plural: all
πολύς	much, many; great, large (416)
πρῶτος	first (152)
τότε	then (160)
καθώς	as, even as (182)
οὕτως	thus, so; in this manner (208)

84,041 total word occurrences out of 137,663 (61%)

CHAPTER 12

PHRASES AND CLAUSES

Thoughts are more generally expressed in groups of words and not just a single word. In Bible study and phrasing, we need to think in larger chunks of words.

ENGLISH

12.1   A **dependent** construction is one that can't grammatically stand on its own. In other words, it isn't a sentence. Do any of the following form a sentence?

> after the rain stops
>
> which I read to you

No they don't, and therefore they are *dependent* or *subordinate* clauses.

12.2   An **independent** clause is a clause that can stand on its own as a sentence.

> After the rain stops, *I will dry the car.*
>
> *Please give me the book,* which I read to you.

Normally, the author's main thought is in the independent clause, and the dependent clause modifies a main thought. This distinction will be especially important for phrasing.

12.3   A **phrase** is a group of related words that don't have a subject or a finite verb. It is a dependent construction. You've already learned one type of phrase, the prepositional phrase, but there are many other kinds of phrases.

After going home, the rain stopped.

Because of love, I will serve God.

12.4 **Clauses** are like phrases except that they have a finite verb and its subject.

After I went home, the rain stopped.

Clauses can be either dependent (as above) or independent (i.e., a sentence).

12.5 A phrase or clause is often categorized by the type of word it begins with, such as a preposition phrase. Other times a phrase is categorized by its function, such as "adverbial" or "temporal."

12.6 A **relative pronoun** is a noun substitute: who(m); whose; that; which; what(ever).

The man *who* is sitting at the table is my pastor.

The relative pronoun introduces a **relative clause**, which is comprised of the relative pronoun, a verb and its subject, and possibly other modfiers.

The disciple *whom Jesus loved* was not martyred.

12.7 **Antecedent.** The antecedent is the word replaced by the pronoun. The antecedent of "whom" in the preceding example is "disciple."

In the second sentence in 12.6, the relative pronoun "whom" is the direct object of the verb "loved." If you are unsure of the function of the relative pronoun within the clause, replace it with its antecedent.

"Whom Jesus loved" → "disciple Jesus loved" → "Jesus loved disciple"

In English, the antecedent must be the closest possible word. If you say, "I saw the student who is studying," the antecedent of "who" is "student," not "I."

12.8 **Function**. The relative clause can function as a noun ("substantival") or as an adjective ("attributive").

> *Who is not against us* is for us.

> Those *who are not for us* are against us.

GREEK NOUN PHRASES

12.9 A "noun phrase" is a phrase that has an internally consistent meaning. It's important to view them as units of thought when phrasing.

12.10 Dative noun phrases can stand somewhat on their own.

Οὐαὶ   τῷ   κόσμῳ   ἀπὸ   τῶν   σκανδάλων
woe   *to the world*   from   the   enticements
Woe *to the world* because of the things that cause people to sin! *(Matt 18:7)*

12.11 Genitive noun phrases are generally modifying something.

δείκνυσιν   αὐτῷ   πάσας   τὰς βασιλείας   τοῦ κόσμου
he showed   him   all   the kingdoms   *of the world*
He showed him all the kingdoms *of the world (Matt 4:8)*.

GREEK RELATIVE CLAUSES

12.12 The Greek **relative pronoun** is ὅς. Here is its paradigm, and the article is included for comparison. Memorization is recommended. In most cases, the pronoun is like the article but the τ is replaced by a rough breathing. At a minimum, remember that its number is GK #4005, Strong's #3739.

	relative pronoun			*article*		
nom sg	ὅς	ἥ	ὅ	ὁ	ἡ	τό
gen sg	οὗ	ἧς	οὗ	τοῦ	τῆς	τοῦ
dat sg	ᾧ	ᾗ	ᾧ	τῷ	τῇ	τῷ
acc sg	ὅν	ἥν	ὅ	τόν	τήν	τό

n/v pl	οἵ	αἵ	ἅ		οἱ	αἱ	τά
gen pl	ὧν	ὧν	ὧν		τῶν	τῶν	τῶν
dat pl	οἷς	αἷς	οἷς		τοῖς	ταῖς	τοῖς
acc pl	οὕς	ἅς	ἅ		τούς	τάς	τά

12.13 **Relative clauses** are comprised of the relative pronoun, a verb and its subject, and possibly other modifiers. The clause always starts with a relative pronoun.

καὶ ἔλεγεν, ὃς ἔχει ὦτα ἀκούειν ἀκουέτω.
and   he said   *who   has   ears   to hear*   let him hear

And he said, "*Whoever has ears to hear*, let him hear" (*Mark 4:9*).

12.14 **Gender and number**. The relative pronoun must agree with its antecedent in number and gender. So, for example, if the relative pronoun is masculine plural, look for an antecedent that is masculine plural. This is the linkage that ties a pronoun to its antecedent. In phrasing, always connect the relative pronoun to its antecedent (Eph 1:6b–7).

ἐν τῷ ἠγαπημένῳ

     ἐν ᾧ ἔχομεν τὴν ἀπολύτρωσιν διὰ τοῦ αἵματος αὐτοῦ

in the Beloved.

     in him we have received redemption through his blood

ἠγαπημένῳ is singular masculine, so the relative pronoun ᾧ must also be singular masculine.

12.15 **Case**. The case of a relative pronoun is determined by its function *inside the relative clause*. This is an important difference from the adjective. What the relative clause may (or may not) be modifying does not affect the case of the relative pronoun. Its case is determined by how it's used *inside* the relative clause.

Think of the relative clause as its own sentence. If necessary, replace the relative pronoun with its antecedent, and then ask yourself what function the relative pronoun is performing inside the relative clause. If it's the direct object of the verb, then the pronoun will be accusative. If the relative pronoun is the subject of the verb, it will be nominative.

ὁ μόνος ἔχων ἀθανασίαν... ὃν   εἶδεν οὐδεὶς ἀνθρώπων
the   only   having immortality   *whom* saw   no one   of men
who alone has immortality ... *whom* no one has ever seen
(1 Tim 6:16)

The relative pronoun ὃν is masculine singular because its antecedent ὁ ... ἔχων is masculine singular. ὃν is accusative because
it is the direct object of εἶδεν within the relative clause.

12.16 Attributive. Relative clauses can be adjectival.

κατὰ   τὸν χρόνον ὃν   ἠκρίβωσεν παρὰ τῶν μάγων
according to the time   which he had learned from the   wise men
according to the time *he had learned from the wise men* (Matt 2:16)

> κατὰ τὸν χρόνον
>
>> ὃν ἠκρίβωσεν παρὰ τῶν μάγων.
>
> according to the time
>
>> he had learned from the wise men

12.17 Substantival. Relative clauses can also act as parts of speech, like
a noun.

ὃς δ' ἂν ποιήσῃ καὶ διδάξῃ, οὗτος μέγας   κληθήσεται
who but ever he does and he teaches this   great   he will be called
But whoever does them and teaches them will be called great in the
kingdom of heaven (Matt 5:19).

The relative clause ὃς δ' ἂν ποιήσῃ καὶ διδάξῃ is the subject of
κληθήσεται. Notice that the relative clause is repeated in the pronoun οὗτος. This is not uncommon.

προσκαλεῖται οὓς ἤθελεν αὐτός
he called   whom he wished himself
He called those *whom he himself wanted* (Mark 3:13).

οὓς ἤθελεν αὐτός is the direct object of προσκαλεῖται. The relative
pronoun οὓς is the direct object of ἤθελεν inside the relative
clause.

When a relative clause functions as a noun, it is not uncommon for the antecedent to be unexpressed. Nevertheless, the number and gender of the relative pronoun are still controlled by the implied antecedent.

ὃς ... ἂν   ἀπολέσῃ   τὴν ψυχὴν   αὐτοῦ   ἕνεκεν   ἐμοῦ   εὑρήσει   αὐτήν
who ever loses   life   their   for   me   will find   it

Whoever loses their life for me will find it *(Matt 16:25).*

The relative clause ὃς ... ἂν ἀπολέσῃ τὴν ψυχὴν αὐτοῦ ἕνεκεν ἐμοῦ is the subject of εὑρήσει. Because it refers to a person, the pronoun ὅς is a (generic) masculine singular.

12.18 **Indefinite**. Relative pronouns can be changed to indefinite relative pronouns (e.g., to "whoever, whichever, whatever") when they are followed by ἄν (or an alternate form such as ἐάν).

Matthew 5:19 says, "Therefore *whoever* [ὃς ἐάν] relaxes one of the least of these commandments and teaches others to do the same will be called least in the kingdom of heaven; but *whoever* [ὃς δ' ἄν] does them and teaches others, this person will be called great in the kingdom of heaven."

TRANSLATION

12.19 **Add in words**. It's often necessary for the translator to add a word to the clause to make better sounding English. For example, in the sentence "Who will be first will be last," the relative clause "Who will be first" is the subject of the verb "will be." To make the translation smoother you could add a word such as a personal pronoun, "*He* who will be first will be last," or, "the one who ...."

μέσος   ὑμῶν   ἕστηκεν   ὃν   ὑμεῖς   οὐκ   οἴδατε
midst   of you stands   whom   you   not   know

NRSV: Among you stands *one* whom you do not know *(John 1:26).*

12.20 **Substitution**. Because Greek is an inflected language, Greek writers are comfortable separating pronouns from their antecedents by quite some distance. The linkage of the gender and number would allow the Greek reader to identify the pronoun's antecedent. However, English requires relative pronouns to be much closer to their antecedent. Because of this difference, translators sometimes substitute the antecedent for the pronoun if they think that the English reader might not be able to identify the pronoun's antecedent.

ὃ	γὰρ	ἀπέθανεν,	τῇ	ἁμαρτίᾳ	ἀπέθανεν	ἐφάπαξ
which	for	he died,	to the	sin	he died	once for all

ESV: *The death* he died he died to sin, once for all *(Rom 6:10).*

For the relative pronoun ὅ, the ESV substitutes its antecedent, "death."

12.21 **Long sentences**. Sometimes a Greek sentence is too long and must be broken into smaller units for the sake of English style. When this is done, the break often is made at the relative pronoun, and the pronoun is replaced with its antecedent. A word-for-word translation of Romans 2:5b–6 reads like this:

ἀποκαλύψεως	δικαιοκρισίας	τοῦ θεοῦ	ὃς	ἀποδώσει
revelation	of righteous verdict	of God	who	he will give judgment

ἑκάστῳ	κατὰ	τὰ ἔργα	αὐτοῦ
to each	according to	the works	of him

There is no question as to the identity of the "who" (ὅς), especially since it immediately follows "God" (θεοῦ). However, if the translators feel that the sentence is too long and they decide to start a new sentence at ὅς, the "who" becomes separated from its antecedent.

- The NASB does not start a new sentence:

    who will repay each person according to his deeds.

- The ESV starts a new paragraph at verse 6 and so it can't say "who." They substitute the personal pronoun for the relative pronoun.

    He will render to each one according to his works.

- The NIV supplies the antecedent of the relative pronoun.

    God "will repay each person according to what they have done."

12.22* Attraction. Greek, as is the case with any language, does not
always follow its own rules. All spoken languages are in a constant state of flux, so nice, neat grammatical rules often break
down.

This is the case with the relative pronoun. Its case is supposed to
be determined by its function inside the relative clause, but sometimes the relative pronoun is the same case as its antecedent, as if
it were modifying it like an adjective. This is called "attraction."

Attraction usually happens when the relative pronoun occurs in
the immediate proximity to the antecedent, when the antecedent
is dative or genitive, and when the relative pronoun normally
would be accusative.

ἤγγιζεν ὁ χρόνος τῆς ἐπαγγελίας ἧς ὡμολόγησεν ὁ θεὸς τῷ Ἀβραάμ
drew near the time   of the promise   *that* assured   God   to Abraham
The time of the promise *that* God assured to Abraham was draw-
ing near *(Acts 7:17)*.

The relative pronoun ἧς should have been the accusative ἥν
because it's the direct object of ὡμολόγησεν, but it was attracted to
the genitive case of its antecedent ἐπαγγελίας.

TYPES OF SENTENCES

12.23 There are different types of sentences, grammatically. Knowing the differences will help you in phrasing.

12.24 A **simple** sentence has one subject and one verb.

> I love Greek!

The subject and/or the verb can be compound.

> Hayden and I love Greek and Hebrew.

> Hayden
>   and   love Greek and Hebrew.
> I

12.25 A **compound** sentence has two or more independent clauses connected with a coordinating conjunction or punctuation.

> Tyler loves Greek and Hayden loves Hebrew.

> Tyler loves Greek; Hayden loves Hebrew.

> Tyler loves Greek
>   and
> Hayden loves Hebrew.

12.26 A **complex** sentence has one independent clause and one (or more) dependent clauses.

> Whenever I think back to Hebrew class, I start to sweat.

>   Whenever I think back to Hebrew class,
> I start to sweat.

12.27 A **compound-complex** sentence has two (or more) independent clauses and one (or more) dependent clauses.

> I went to class and Hayden went home because he was tired.

> I went to class
> > and
> Hayden went home
> > > because he was tired.

12.28 Greek is primarily a **hypotactic** language. This means that it tends to have a main clause with a series of dependent phrases or clauses modifying it. Paul writes with a hypotactic style.

English, and to a greater degree Hebrew, are **paratactic**. They are more linear, tending to link one independent clause to the next with coordinating conjunctions such as "and" and "but." Greek narrative in general and the Gospel of John in particular tend to be more paratactic.

The difference is important to note when phrasing.

VOCABULARY

εἰ	if (502)
ἄν	Untranslatable. Makes a word contingent. (166)
ἐάν	if (348)
ἤ	or; than (343)
τε	and (215)
μέν	on the one hand (178). Often left untranslated.
ὡς	as ("like") (503)
τίς	who? what? which? why? (554)
τις	someone/thing, anyone/thing (524)
ὅς	who (whom) (1,398)

88,771 total word occurrences out of 137,663 (65%)

CHAPTER 13

PRONOUNS

There are 16,202 pronouns in the Greek Testament, but for the most part they are easy to translate.

ENGLISH

13.1   A **pronoun** is a word that replaces a noun. In the sentence, "It is red," "It" is a pronoun referring back to something.

A personal pronoun is a pronoun that replaces a personal noun, which is a noun referring to a person. In the sentence, "My name is Bill; I will learn Greek as well as possible," "I" is a personal pronoun referring to me, Bill.

The word that a pronoun refers back to, "Bill," is the **antecedent**.

13.2   **Person**. Pronouns can be first, second, or third person. We saw this same thing with verbs and their personal endings.

- First person refers to the person speaking ("I," "we").

- Second person refers to the person being spoken to ("you").

- Third person refers to that which is spoken about ("he," "she," "it," "they"). All nouns are considered third person.

As you can see on the next page, English personal pronouns are highly inflected.

	1st person	2nd person	3rd person		
			masculine	*feminine*	*neuter*
subjective sg	I	you	he	she	it
possessive sg[1]	my	your	his	her	its
objective sg	me	you	him	her	it
subjective pl	we	you	they		
possessive pl	our	your	their		
objective pl	us	you	them		

There's no easy way to distinguish between second person singular and plural ("you"). Sometimes I'll use the southern American expression "y'all" for the plural (although technically it's not plural) especially in doing the homework.[2]

13.3 Like the relative pronoun, the number and person of a personal pronoun are determined by its antecedent.

- The **number** of the pronoun is determined by the antecedent. Because "Bill" is singular, you would use "I" and not "we."

- The **person** of the pronoun is also determined by the antecedent. If the antecedent were the person speaking (first person), you use "I," not "you."

- There is no gender in the first and second person. "I" or "you" can be either a woman or a man. The third person pronoun has gender in the singular.

13.4 The **case** of a pronoun is determined by its function in the sentence. For example, if the pronoun is the subject of the sentence, you would use "I" and not "me" since "I" is in the subjective case. You would not say, "Me would like to eat now," because "me" is objective.

---

[1] If the possessive forms are used substantivally, they are translated "mine," "yours," and "ours."

[2] In older English, "thou," "thee," and "thy, thine" were singular, and "ye," "you," and "your, yours" were plural.

GREEK FIRST AND SECOND PERSONAL PRONOUNS

13.5   The Greek personal pronouns function as they do in English. Number and gender are determined by the antecedent, and case by function.

13.6   You should memorize the first and second person personal pronouns. They are extremely common, occurring 11,139 times in the New Testament. The forms in parentheses are called the "emphatic" forms, but they have the same basic meaning as the nonemphatic.

	first person		*second person*	
nom sg	ἐγώ	I	σύ	you
gen sg	μου (ἐμοῦ)	my	σου (σοῦ)	your
dat sg	μοι (ἐμοί)	to me	σοι (σοί)	to you
acc sg	με (ἐμέ)	me	σε (σέ)	you
nom pl	ἡμεῖς	we	ὑμεῖς	you
gen pl	ἡμῶν	our	ὑμῶν	your
dat pl	ἡμῖν	to us	ὑμῖν	to you
acc pl	ἡμᾶς	us	ὑμᾶς	you

The Greek pronouns do not have gender in the first and second person, just like English.

As was the case with the article, my preference is that you memnorize the paradigm, but at a minimum remember its GK number, #1609 (first person) and #5148 (secondperson). If you use Strong's numbers, as you will see in 13.8, every form has its own number, making it extremely difficult to memorize.

13.7   **Emphatic forms.** In the first person singular, the genitive, dative, and accusative cases will sometimes include an epsilon and an accent (ἐμοῦ, ἐμοί, ἐμέ). The second person singular pronoun will not add an epsilon but can add an accent (σοῦ, σοί, σέ). These accented forms are called the emphatic forms.

The emphatic and unemphatic forms have the same basic meaning. The emphatic form can be used when the author wants to be emphatic, often in contrasting one person with another.

ἐμοὶ μαθηταί ἐστε, ἐὰν ἀγάπην ἔχητε ἐν ἀλλήλοις
to me disciples you are if love you have to one another
You are *my* disciples, if you have love for one another (*John 13:35*).

Emphatic forms also tend to be used after prepositions without any emphasis in meaning.

ἔργον γὰρ καλὸν ἠργάσατο εἰς ἐμέ
Thing for good she has done to *me*
For she has done a beautiful thing to *me* (*Matt 26:10*).

13.8 **Strong's numbers.** Strong assigned a different number for each inflected form, and separate numbers for the emphatic first person forms (in parentheses below) but not for the second person. Logos follows suit.

	first person		*Strong's*		*second person*		*Strong's*
nom sg	ἐγώ		1473		σύ		4771
gen sg	μου	(ἐμοῦ)	3450	(1700)	σου	(σοῦ)	4675
dat sg	μοι	(ἐμοί)	3427	(1698)	σοι	(σοί)	4671
acc sg	με	(ἐμέ)	3165	(1691)	σε	(σέ)	4571
nom pl	ἡμεῖς		2249		ὑμεῖς		5210
gen pl	ἡμῶν		2257		ὑμῶν		5216
dat pl	ἡμῖν		2254		ὑμῖν		5213
acc pl	ἡμᾶς		2248		ὑμᾶς		5209

Accordance connects all singular and plural forms of the first person to ἐγώ (GK #1609), and all the second person forms to σύ (GK #5148). Obviously, if you do not use Accordance or my interlinears, it is easier to memorize the Greek forms than nineteen Strong's numbers.

13.9 When the genitive of these pronouns is used to show possession, they generally follow the noun they modify.

ὁ κύριός μου καὶ ὁ θεός μου
Lord *my* and God *my*
My Lord and *my* God (*John 20:28*).

This will not be visible in my reverse interlinear.

My	Lord		and	my	God	
μου	‚ὁ	κύριός‚	καὶ	μου	‚ὁ	θεός‚
r.gs.1	d.vsm	n.vsm	cj	r.gs.1	d.vsm	n.vsm
3836	3261	2779	1609	3836	3261	2536

THIRD PERSON PRONOUN

13.10 The Greek third person pronoun has gender in both the singular and plural. You may want to memorize this paradigm as well, or at least the word's GK (#899) or Strong's (#846) number.

	masc	*fem*	*neut*	*translation*		
nom sg	αὐτός	αὐτή	αὐτό	he	she	it
gen sg	αὐτοῦ	αὐτῆς	αὐτοῦ	his	her	its
dat sg	αὐτῷ	αὐτῇ	αὐτῷ	to him	to her	to it
acc sg	αὐτόν	αὐτήν	αὐτό	him	her	it
nom pl	αὐτοί	αὐταί	αὐτά	they		
gen pl	αὐτῶν	αὐτῶν	αὐτῶν	their		
dat pl	αὐτοῖς	αὐταῖς	αὐτοῖς	to them		
acc pl	αὐτούς	αὐτάς	αὐτά	them		

13.11 There are three uses of αὐτός. The most common is as the **third person personal pronoun**, which will be translated by some form of "he, she, it; they, them, etc."

13.12 **Natural and grammatical gender.** If αὐτός is referring to a person, it will be masculine or feminine, i.e., it follows natural gender. If it's referring to something else, it will be masculine, feminine, or neuter depending on the grammatical gender of its antecedent.

This can give us the somewhat unusual situation (for the English reader) in which the grammatical gender of the pronoun does not match up with natural gender. For example, if the antecedent is πνεῦμα, which is grammatically neuter, the pronoun will be neuter (e.g., αὐτό). But if the πνεῦμα is the Holy Spirit, then we translate the neuter pronoun αὐτό as "he," not "it."

πνεῦμα κυρίου ἐπ' ἐμὲ οὗ εἵνεκεν ἔχρισέν με εὐαγγελίσασθα
spirit   lord   upon me *who* because he anointed me to preach

The Spirit of the Lord is upon me because *he* anointed me to preach (*Luke 4:18*).

οὗ is neuter because its antecedent πνεῦμα is neuter, but we refer to the Spirit of the Lord as a "he" (meaning a person).

It is the same situation with the relative pronoun.

τὸ πνεῦμα τῆς ἀληθείας, ὃ   ὁ   κόσμος οὐ δύναται λαβεῖν
the Spirit of truth   *who* the world not able   to receive

ESV: The Spirit of truth, *whom* the world cannot receive (*John 14:17*).
NIV: The Spirit of truth. The world cannot accept *him.*

Or how about ἀγάπη? The noun is feminine, so the pronoun referring back to it must be feminine (e.g., αὐτῇ), but in English we refer to "love" as "it," not "she."

καὶ αὕτη ἐστὶν ἡ   ἀγάπη ... ἵνα   ἐν αὐτῇ περιπατῆτε
and *this* is the love   in order that in *it* walk

And *this* is love ... that you should walk in *it* (*2 John 6*).

13.13 **Translation.** In translation, αὐτός is sometimes replaced by its antecedent, usually for one of two reasons.

■ There might be confusion in reading the text if the translator simply writes "he." For example, in Matthew 8:24, who was the "he" who was sleeping?

> Suddenly a furious storm came up on the lake, so that the waves swept over the boat. But *Jesus* was sleeping [αὐτὸς δὲ ἐκάθευδεν] (NIV).

The Greek only has "he (αὐτός) was sleeping," and the NIV replaces the pronoun αὐτός with its antecedent "he."

■ Sometimes at the beginning of a paragraph, the simple translation of αὐτός as "he" might also be confusing. This is especially true if the translators think the reader will be working with this one paragraph and not in the context of the preceding paragraphs. On Matthew 9:10 the ESV writes,

> And as Jesus [αὐτοῦ] reclined at table in the house, behold, many tax collectors and sinners came and were reclining with Jesus and his disciples.

The footnote on the first "Jesus" reads, "Greek *he*."

13.14* **Other uses of αὐτός.** The most common use of αὐτός is as the third person pronoun. However, it does have two other secondary uses: the intensive and the identical uses.

13.15* **Intensive.** αὐτός can function intensively when used adjectivally. In this usage, αὐτός modifies another word and is usually in the predicate position. There is no antecedent. It can be translated with the reflexive pronoun.

αὐτὸς γὰρ ὁ Ἡρῴδης ἀποστείλας ἐκράτησεν τὸν Ἰωάννην
himself For Herod sending seized John.
For Herod *himself* had sent for and arrested John *(Mark 6:17)*.

13.16* **Identical adjective.** αὐτός is sometimes used as the identical adjective meaning "same."

καὶ πάλιν ἀπελθὼν προσηύξατο τὸν αὐτὸν λόγον
And again after going away he prayed *the* *same* *word*
And again, after going away, he prayed the *same* prayer
(Mark 14:39).

If you want more details on these usages, see the handout in the online lesson for this chapter.

DEMONSTRATIVE PRONOUNS

13.17 The demonstrative pronouns in Greek are οὗτος ("this/these") and ἐκεῖνος ("that/those"). They function the same way as the demonstratives do in English, both as pronouns and as adjectives.

13.18 **Adjectival.** If a demonstrative is functioning as an adjective, it will be anarthrous. In other words, it will be in the predicate position just like πᾶς.

εἰπὲ ἵνα οἱ λίθοι οὗτοι ἄρτοι γένωνται
say that stones *these* bread become

Tell *these* stones to become bread *(Matt 4:3).*

ἐν δὲ ταῖς ἡμέραις ἐκείναις παραγίνεται Ἰωάννης ὁ βαπτιστὴς
in but days *those* appeared John the Baptist

Now in *those* days, John the Baptist appeared *(Matt 3:1).*

13.19 **Pronoun.** If a demonstrative is functioning as a pronoun, translators will sometimes add in words to make proper English.

τινες τῶν γραμματέων εἶπαν ἐν ἑαυτοῖς, οὗτος βλασφημεῖ
some of the scribes said to themselves *this* blasphemes

NRSV: Some of the scribes said to themselves, "*This man* is blaspheming" *(Matt 9:3).*

NIV: Some of the teachers of the law said to themselves, "*This fellow* is blaspheming!"

13.20 **Personal Pronoun.** Sometimes the demonstrative pronoun weakens in its force and functions as a personal pronoun.

οὗτος ἔσται μέγας καὶ υἱὸς ὑψίστου κληθήσεται
this will be great and son of Most High he will be called

He will be great and will be called "Son of the Most High" *(Luke 1:32).*

ἐκείνοις δὲ οὐ δέδοται
to those but not is given

But *to them* it's not given *(Matt 13:11).*

ANTECEDENT

13.21 The antecedent for a pronoun does not have to be in the same sentence as the pronoun. Sometimes the antecedent will be in a previous verse, and other times it will be quite a few verses back, and sometimes followed by a series of pronouns, all referring back to the same antecedent.

For example, Paul introduces both "Christ Jesus" and "God" in Rom 1:1, and in v 2 he refers to "his (αὐτοῦ) prophets" and in v 3 "his (αὐτοῦ) Son" in v 3.

In some cases, there is no expressed antecedent and you will have to determine it from context. This is especially true of relative clauses that function substantivally.

ACCENTS*

13.22* Generally, there is one accent per Greek word. However, there are times you may have seen where a word has two accents and another has no accent. What's happening?

13.23* An **enclitic** is a word that is pronounced so closely with the *preceeding* word that it moves its accent back to that word, which can result in the first word having two accents and the enclitic with none.

τὸ γὰρ ἐν αὐτῇ γεννηθὲν ἐκ πνεύματός ἐστιν ἁγίου
the for in her conceived by spirit *is* holy
For that which has been conceived in her *is* by the Holy Spirit
(*Matt 1:20*)

ἐστιν loses its accent to πνεύματός.

Common enclitics you know are μοῦ, μοί, μέ, σοῦ, σοί, σέ, τις, and most forms of εἰμί.

13.24* A **proclitic** is a word that connects itself to the *following* word, and is only accented when that word pushes its own accent back to the proclitic.

ὁ ἀγαθὸς ἄνθρωπος ἐκ τοῦ ἀγαθοῦ θησαυροῦ ἐκβάλλει ἀγαθά
the good man *out of* the good treasure brings good things
NRSV: *The* good person brings good things *out of* a good treasure
(*Matt 12:35*).

Common proclitics you know are are ὁ, ἡ, οἱ, αἱ, εἰς, ἐκ, ἐν, εἰ, and οὐ.

VOCABULARY

Pronouns you already know

ἐγώ (ἡμεῖς)	I (we)
σύ (ὑμεῖς)	you
αὐτός	he, she, it (they, them)
οὗτος	this (these)
ἐκεῖνος	that (those)

New vocabulary

οὐδείς	no one (nothing) (225)
ἑαυτοῦ	himself/herself/itself (319)
ἁμαρτία	sin (173)
νόμος	law (193)
χάρις	grace (155)
ἔργον	work, deed (169)
δόξα	glory (166)
καρδία	heart (156)
χείρ	hand (175)

90,503 word occurrences out of 137,663 (66%)

This fifth-century uncial manuscript, labeled 0301, contains John 17:1–4. It's located in Münster, Germany. The photo is provided by the Center for the Study of New Testament Manuscripts (csntm.org). Used by permission of Institut für neutestamentliche Textforschung.

See if you can figure out what this poster is advertising.

CHAPTER 14

PHRASING 101

When I started studying the Bible, I remember looking at a paragraph and having difficulty locating the main idea(s). I am a visual person, and sometimes the words blend together.

So I started working on a new way to study my Bible. I would xerox a paragraph of the Bible, cut each verse into its phrases, and lay the pieces out in a way that made sense to me visually. I would put the main thought all the way to the left, and I placed modifiers under or over the word they modified. For example (Mark 8:34):

> If anyone wishes to come after me,
>
> they must
>
>   deny himself, and
>
>   take up his cross and
>
>   follow me.

In other words, those who want to be a disciple of Jesus must do three things: "deny," "take up," "follow."

When I was done, I would xerox my reconstructed text and have something that visually helped me see the flow of the author's discussion.

As the years passed, I became more sophisticated. I used color pencils! Eventually I used a software program to get the actual text; I would copy it into my word processor and lay out the passage.

This process has helped me more than anything else to study my Bible (except knowing Greek). It forced me to identify the main point (or points) and to see the flow of the author's thought—how he moved from one main point to the next, and how he clarified the main point(s) by adding modifiers.

I eventually named this process "phrasing" because I found that it wasn't normally helpful to break a sentence into every word (which is done in grammatical diagramming). I would break the sentence into its phrases (or clauses) and found that I rarely needed to divide the phrases further. So when you see the examples of phrasing on the following pages, and if you have "baggage" from high school English classes, don't freak out. This isn't grammatical diagramming, although it uses grammar.

By the way, why am I talking about phrasing in a book designed to teach you the basics of Greek grammar? My assumption is that you want to learn to use the language tools in order to study your Bible. After trying many other methods, I discovered that the tools are best learned while you are actually doing Bible study, or what is called "exegesis."

Also, one of the goals for this textbook is to help you read good commentaries. While some good commentaries may not actually phrase the text, the essence of the commentary will be to discover the flow of the author's thought and his main points. The better you become at phrasing, the more familiar a good commentary will feel.

When I then started teaching phrasing to college and graduate students, I found that they too enjoyed the process because it helped them learn, for themselves, what the Bible was saying.

I also discovered that other people were doing the same type of procedure. They called it by different names—"sentence flow," "discourse analysis"—but they too had learned how laying a passage out visually helped them see what the author meant. Let me show you how it works.

Imagine that you have been asked to teach a Bible study on 1 Peter 1:2. I know. It's doubtful you would be assigned a salutation, but let's just pretend. How are you going to do it? How will you start?

Phrasing starts with two steps: (1) finding the beginning and the end of the passage, (2) and then breaking the passage into manageable sections. Let's walk through the process.

What is a "passage"? This is my word for the basic story that the author wants to tell us. For example, John 3:3 is part of the story of Jesus and Nicodemus, which is John 3:1–21. Romans 3:23 is part of the passage that summarizes justification by faith, which is Romans 3:21–26. In other words, a "passage" is all the verses that make up a complete idea. If your Bible has headings, a passage is probably the verses under one heading.

1:1   Peter, an apostle of Jesus Christ, To God's elect, strangers in the world, scattered throughout Pontus, Galatia, Cappadocia, Asia and Bithynia,

1:2   who have been chosen according to the foreknowledge of God the Father, through the sanctifying work of the Spirit, for obedience to Jesus Christ and sprinkling by his blood: Grace and peace be yours in abundance.

1:3   Praise be to the God and Father of our Lord Jesus Christ! In his great mercy he has given us new birth into a living hope through the resurrection of Jesus Christ from the dead,

1:4   and into an inheritance that can never perish, spoil or fade—kept in heaven for you,

1:5   who through faith are shielded by God's power until the coming of the salvation that is ready to be revealed in the last time.

1:6   In this you greatly rejoice, though now for a little while you may have had to suffer grief in all kinds of trials.

1:7   These have come so that your faith—of greater worth than gold, which perishes even though refined by fire—may be proved genuine and may result in praise, glory and honor when Jesus Christ is revealed.

1:8   Though you have not seen him, you love him; and even though you do not see him now, you believe in him and are filled with an inexpressible and glorious joy,

1:9   for you are receiving the goal of your faith, the salvation of your souls.

1:10   Concerning this salvation, the prophets, who spoke of the grace that was to come to you, searched intently and with the greatest care,

1:11   trying to find out the time and circumstances to which the Spirit of Christ in them was pointing when he predicted the sufferings of Christ and the glories that would follow.

1:12   It was revealed to them that they were not serving themselves but you, when they spoke of the things that have now been told you by those who have preached the gospel to you by the Holy Spirit sent from heaven. Even angels long to look into these things.

1:13   Therefore, prepare your minds for action; be self-controlled; set your hope fully on the grace to be given you when Jesus ... (NIV 1984)

STEP 1: FIND THE BEGINNING AND THE END OF THE PASSAGE

The biblical writers don't intend you to read a single verse in isolation from the verses around it. If you want to understand what one verse means, you have to see how it fits into its context. But which verses provide this context?

The key is to find the beginning and the end of the passage in which your verse occurs. If you are starting with the beginning of a book, the process is a little easier; you start with 1:1. But if you are studying a verse somewhere in the middle of a book, it means you must find both the beginning and the end of the passage.

You find the limits of the passage by reading and rereading the surrounding verses until the limits become apparent. You are looking for the natural breaks in the passage, where the author changes topics, even slightly. To put it another way, you are looking for a unifying theme that ties the verses together. Let the Bible tell you when the author shifts topics. Here are a few of the indicators that the topic has changed.

- Major shifts in the topic of discussion (e.g., Paul has stopped making one point and has gone on to another).

- Shifts in audience (e.g., Jesus stops talking to the Pharisees and starts talking to the disciples).

- Shifts of other types, such as moving from describing what Jesus did to what he is teaching.

- Changes in key words and repeated themes.

- Transitional phrases (e.g., "the next day," "after this").

This can be trickier than you think, and the temptation is to trust the chapter, paragraph, and verse divisions of your Bible. But none of these were part of the original Bible, and while usually helpful they can often get in the way. They can also rob you of the joy of exploring and deciding for yourself, and sometimes they are wrong. There were times when I was teaching at university where I would give the students the Gospel of Mark without any paragraphs, verses, or headings, and they would use that to learn where the natural divisions were. It was a good discipline. Read the first part of 1 Peter to the left over and over. Where is the end of the first passage? Go ahead and discover it for yourself. Don't turn the page until you have done so.

SALUTATION

1:1   Peter, an apostle of Jesus Christ, To God's elect, strangers in the world, scattered throughout Pontus, Galatia, Cappadocia, Asia and Bithynia,

1:2   who have been chosen according to the foreknowledge of God the Father, through the sanctifying work of the Spirit, for obedience to Jesus Christ and sprinkling by his blood: Grace and peace be yours in abundance.

This is a different approach than many Bible study methods that recommend getting into the details right away. But I think the big picture is more important; and if you run out of time and can't do all your preparation for your Bible study or Sunday School class, it's much better to know the big picture than lots of details.

You probably saw rather quickly that verses 1–2 form the letter's salutation. Once you have found the beginning and the end, write out your heading for 1:1–2. If you are not sure what to call it, make a guess; you can always change it later.

Writing out the headings is crucial: your goal is to get the main point out of each section and then to state that main point in the heading. I call this the "passage heading" as opposed to another type of heading we'll meet in a few pages.

STEP 2: IDENTIFY THE SECTIONS

The next step is to break the passage into sections. You do this by reading and rereading the passage you identified in Step 1 until the natural sections of the passage suggest themselves to you. In my terminology, a "passage" divides into "sections," and sections divide into "phrases." You then label each section with the main point being made in that section. Writing out the section heading is crucial, just like writing out the passage heading, since the initial goal of phrasing (and exegesis) is to identify the main point. If you are not sure what to write, write it in pencil or phrase using a computer so you can change it later if necessary.

Don't be in a hurry to get into the details of the passage but take the time to get the *big* picture. So many times when studying the Bible we want to jump right in and see what this word or that phrase "means to me." That's where we are headed, but don't be in a rush. Take your time. God's Word is worth it. Be content to sit back and let the overall picture develop.

During this part of the process you may notice words and phrases that seem important, but you don't know what they mean. Don't stop now to look them up; we're concentrating on the big picture, and the day's own trouble is sufficient. Let's concentrate on getting the big picture.

Don't be so concerned with the *meaning* of the verses. Concentrate on seeing the *structure* of the passage, the flow of the author's thought. Ask yourself how the different parts are related to each other. As you read and reread the passage, thinking primarily about structure, you will be surprised at how the passage starts to show you its structure.

Try this now with 1 Peter 1:1–2 before turning the page and seeing what I have done with it.

SALUTATION

WRITER

1:1   Peter, an apostle of Jesus Christ,

RECIPIENTS

To God's elect, strangers in the world, scattered throughout Pontus, Galatia, Cappadocia, Asia and Bithynia,

1:2   who have been chosen according to the foreknowledge of God the Father, through the sanctifying work of the Spirit, for obedience to Jesus Christ and sprinkling by his blood:

GREETING

Grace and peace be yours in abundance.

What did you find? You can see my suggestions to the left. I decided that there are three main sections that identify the writer ("Peter"), the recipients ("To God's elect"), and the greeting ("Grace and peace be yours in abundance").

Let me say it again: what you are doing is learning to study your Bible by breaking up the passage into manageable sections. Of course, you can always cheat yourself out of the joy of discovering the Bible's meaning for yourself and look at a study Bible, or check out a commentary, or ask a friend. But along with losing the joy of discovery, what makes you think that the next time you need help there will be a friend nearby or a study Bible within reach?

One of the nice aspects of phrasing is that if you run out of time after Step 2, you at least have learned something that will help you teach the passage. You know the verses that make up the passage, the main point of the passage, the passage's sections, and the main thought of each section.

STEP 3: IDENTIFY THE PHRASES

Now that you have identified the passage (Step 1) and its sections (Step 2), it's time to look at each individual section and divide it into its phrases.

What's a phrase? A phrase is an assertion, a proposition, something that means something. I am using the word "phrase" in a broader way than its grammatical usage. However, many phrases are grammatical phrases such as prepositional phrases, or adverbial phrases, or dependent and independent clauses. As you will see on the next page, many of the phrases I have identified are in fact grammatical phrases and clauses.

For example, if I said, "My mom, Jean, likes to eat chocolate ice cream and drink iced tea," how many assertions did I make? How many phrases are there? In one sense, I only made one assertion. But can you break it down into smaller assertions that have meaning?

Is "Jean" by itself a phrase? Not really. While it may name my mother, it says nothing more. How about "to eat chocolate ice cream" and "drink iced tea"? Sure, these are two phrases that have meaning. They may not make complete sense all by themselves (they are dependent constructions), but they do mean something. What does my mother like? She likes (at least) two things: ice cream; iced tea.

Here is where phrasing and grammatical diagramming are different. In grammatical diagramming, every word is shown in its grammatical relationship to other words, and you get something like what you see below. This is not what phrasing is, and if you subdivide your phrases too far, the process loses its effectiveness.

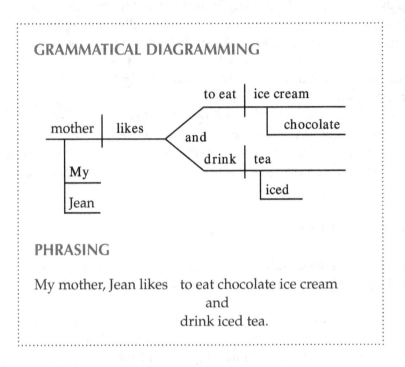

GRAMMATICAL DIAGRAMMING

PHRASING

My mother, Jean likes   to eat chocolate ice cream
                              and
                        drink iced tea.

Let me explain it another way. In the sentence, "I want to go to the park but I must study first," how many words does it take until you have a phrase that has real meaning?

1. I
2. I want
3. I want to
4. I want to go
5. I want to go to
6. I want to go to the
7. I want to go to the park
8   I want to go to the park but
9. I want to go to the park but I
10. I want to go to the park but I must
11. I want to go to the park but I must study
12. I want to go to the park but I must study first.

While individual words have meaning, you don't really have a phrase that makes any sense until line 7. When you get to line 12, you realize that you have two phrases joined with the conjunction "but": "I want … but I must …."

Okay, back to 1 Peter. You have identified 1 Peter 1:1–2 as a passage and have seen that it has three sections. Now, break the two verses into its phrases. When done, check my work on the next page.

In "Section 1" ("writer"), Peter identifies himself by name and by office. In "Section 2" ("recipients") Peter addresses them as "God's elect" and follows with a series of descriptions. "Section 3" ("greeting") contains the letter's greeting.

Many signs in modern Greece are written in both Greek and English. See if you can pronounce the Greek words on this sign in Corinth.

SALUTATION

1:1   Peter,

       an apostle of Jesus Christ,

RECIPIENTS

       To God's elect,

       strangers in the world,

       scattered throughout Pontus, Galatia, Cappadocia, Asia and Bithynia,

1:2   who have been chosen

       according to the foreknowledge of God the Father,

       through the sanctifying work of the Spirit,

       for obedience to Jesus Christ and

       sprinkling by his blood:

GREETING

       Grace and peace be yours in abundance.

STEP 4: IDENTIFY THE MAIN PHRASE(S) AND MODIFYING PHRASES

Now comes the real fun. You have established the limits of the passage and its sections, and have broken it down into its phrases. As you have been reading and rereading the passage, you have started to identify the main points and the secondary points, and have seen how those secondary points relate to the main one. Now it's time to make a commitment as to what is the main point (or points).

Identify the main point(s) in each section and place its phrase furthest to the left. These "main" phrases will be stating the main points the author is making. Most likely a main phrase will have a subject and a verb, and in many cases the verb will be in the indicative mood (and not the subjunctive or a participle).

Indent the other phrases under or over the word they modify. Use extra spacing to separate subsections of thought. If you find it helpful, underline or highlight words or themes that run throughout the discussion. When done, recheck your passage and section headings to be sure they are right. You can see my work on the next page.

PHRASING #1

SALUTATION

WRITER

1:1   <u>Peter</u>,
        an apostle of Jesus Christ,

RECIPIENTS

      <u>To God's elect</u>,
             strangers in the world,

                        scattered throughout Pontus,
                        Galatia, Cappadocia, Asia and
                        Bithynia,

1:2   who have been chosen

                according to the foreknowledge of God the
                Father,
                  through the sanctifying work of the Spirit,
                for   obedience to Jesus Christ and
                    sprinkling by his blood:

GREETING

      <u>Grace and peace</u> be yours in abundance.

PHRASING #2

RECIPIENTS

      <u>To God's elect</u>,
             strangers in the world,
                scattered throughout Pontus, Galatia,
                Cappadocia, Asia and Bithynia,

1:2   who have been chosen

                according to the foreknowledge of God the Father,
                through the sanctifying work of the Spirit,
                for
                  obedience to Jesus Christ and
                  sprinkling by his blood:

Phrasing #1 is how I phrase 1 Peter 1:1–2. Are there other ways this passage could have been laid out? Sure. Since "elect" and "chosen" are the same thing, it would have been nice to align the phrase "strangers ...," "according ...," "through ...," and "for ..." in a straight column so you could see that Peter is giving us four descriptions of who the elect are, as in Phrasing #2. (Actually, there is no Greek behind the phrase "who have been chosen." The NIV [1984] inserted it because they wanted the reader to understand that the following prepositional phrases modify the idea of "elect.")

The two phrases "obedience to Jesus Christ" and "sprinkling by his blood" could have been placed under the preposition "for" (Phrasing #2), but when a word has multiple objects, I like to add the extra space to the right of the word (e.g., "for") so you can see that the following phrases are parallel (Phrasing #1).

I also could have listed the five place names ("Pontus, Galatia ...") in a column, and often I will do this for a series. It didn't seem to make that much difference here.

WALK THROUGH 1 PETER 1:1–2

Now that we have 1 Peter 1:1–2 laid out, let's walk through the passage to see what Peter has to tell us. Here is your Bible study lesson.

Peter begins his letter with a three-part salutation. He first identifies himself by name and adds the qualifier that he is Jesus' apostle.

Peter then identifies to whom he is writing. His primary description is that they are the elect, Christians. He continues by explaining that this means they are strangers, scattered throughout five different areas in modern-day Turkey. Although they still live on the earth, they are strangers to this land because they are elect. But what is perhaps more significant is the following theological description of the elect. Their election was "according to the foreknowledge of God," an election accomplished "through the sanctifying work of the Spirit," and an election that has as its goal "obedience to Jesus Christ" and made possible by the "sprinkling by his blood," Christ's death on the cross.

Peter then concludes with the actual greeting.

Can you see how much help phrasing can be? It helps you get started, rewards you with some understanding of the passage if you are short of time (after Steps 1 and 2), and helps you dig deeper into the passage and discover its primary and secondary points.

1:3	Praise be to the God and Father of our Lord Jesus Christ! In his great mercy he has given us new birth into a living hope through the resurrection of Jesus Christ from the dead,
1:4	and into an inheritance that can never perish, spoil or fade—kept in heaven for you,
1:5	who through faith are shielded by God's power until the coming of the salvation that is ready to be revealed in the last time.
1:6	In this you greatly rejoice, though now for a little while you may have had to suffer grief in all kinds of trials.
1:7	These have come so that your faith—of greater worth than gold, which perishes even though refined by fire—may be proved genuine and may result in praise, glory and honor when Jesus Christ is revealed.
1:8	Though you have not seen him, you love him; and even though you do not see him now, you believe in him and are filled with an inexpressible and glorious joy,
1:9	for you are receiving the goal of your faith, the salvation of your souls.
1:10	Concerning this salvation, the prophets, who spoke of the grace that was to come to you, searched intently and with the greatest care,
1:11	trying to find out the time and circumstances to which the Spirit of Christ in them was pointing when he predicted the sufferings of Christ and the glories that would follow.
1:12	It was revealed to them that they were not serving themselves but you, when they spoke of the things that have now been told you by those who have preached the gospel to you by the Holy Spirit sent from heaven. Even angels long to look into these things.
1:13	Therefore, prepare your minds for action; be self-controlled; set your hope fully on the grace to be given you when Jesus Christ is revealed.
1:14	As obedient children, do not conform to the evil desires you had when you lived in ignorance.
1:15	But just as he who called you is holy, so be holy in all you do;
1:16	for it's written: "Be holy, because I am holy."
1:17	Since you call on a Father who judges each man's work impartially, live your lives as strangers here in reverent fear.
1:18	For you know that it was not with perishable things such as silver or gold that you were redeemed from the empty way of life handed down to you from your forefathers,
1:19	but with the precious blood of Christ, a lamb without blemish or defect.
1:20	He was chosen before the creation of the world, but was revealed in these last times for your sake.
1:21	Through him you believe in God, who raised him from the dead …

Let's try the process again with another passage. Try to do the work on your own before seeing how I do it. We might as well check out the verses following Peter's salutation.

STEP 1: FIND THE BEGINNING AND THE END OF THE PASSAGE

Read through the verses until you decide where Peter stops his discussion.

———————————————————————

It's a little difficult isn't it? Peter changes his topic several times, and yet each time the new subject is explicitly connected to the previous. Peter starts by describing our salvation, our new birth (vv. 3–5). Then he moves from rejoicing in that salvation to suffering because of that salvation (vv. 6–9), to how the prophets wanted to see the salvation (vv. 10–12), and into how we should live in light of all this (vv. 13–17).

The "therefore" that starts verse 13 shows Peter is not starting a totally new topic, and yet Peter changes from discussing salvation (vv. 3–12) to specifics on how that salvation is to show itself, so perhaps verse 13 is a good place to mark the end of the passage.

STEP 2: IDENTIFY THE SECTIONS

While you were working on Step 1, you were also getting ready for Step 2. How many basic sections do you find in verses 3–12? Break the passage into its sections and put a heading with each.

———————————————————————

SALVATION

1:3   Praise be to the God and Father of our Lord Jesus Christ! In his great mercy he has given us new birth into a living hope through the resurrection of Jesus Christ from the dead,

1:4   and into an inheritance that can never perish, spoil or fade—kept in heaven for you,

1:5   who through faith are shielded by God's power until the coming of the salvation that is ready to be revealed in the last time.

SALVATION AND SUFFERING

1:6   In this you greatly rejoice, though now for a little while you may have had to suffer grief in all kinds of trials.

1:7   These have come so that your faith—of greater worth than gold, which perishes even though refined by fire—may be proved genuine and may result in praise, glory and honor when Jesus Christ is revealed.

1:8   Though you have not seen him, you love him; and even though you do not see him now, you believe in him and are filled with an inexpressible and glorious joy,

1:9   for you are receiving the goal of your faith, the salvation of your souls.

SALVATION AND THE PROPHETS

1:10   Concerning this salvation, the prophets, who spoke of the grace that was to come to you, searched intently and with the greatest care,

1:11   trying to find out the time and circumstances to which the Spirit of Christ in them was pointing when he predicted the sufferings of Christ and the glories that would follow.

1:12   It was revealed to them that they were not serving themselves but you, when they spoke of the things that have now been told you by those who have preached the gospel to you by the Holy Spirit sent from heaven. Even angels long to look into these things.

STEP 3: IDENTIFY THE PHRASES

There is still too much in verses 3–12 for one Bible study (but just the right amount for a three-part series). Let's work with just the first section, verses 3–5. Go through the passage and break it down into its phrases.

_____

It looks as if verse 3 begins with the theme statement, and then Peter follows with a series of prepositional phrases and a few relative clauses. As you are dividing these three verses into phrases, you will be starting to get a feel for the main assertions of the section. Here's how I did it.

> 1:3   Praise be to the God and Father of our Lord Jesus Christ!
> In his great mercy he has given us new birth
> into a living hope
> through the resurrection of Jesus Christ from the dead,
> 1:4   and into an inheritance
> that can never perish, spoil or fade—
> kept in heaven for you,
> 1:5   who through faith are shielded by God's power
> until the coming of the salvation
> that is ready to be revealed in the last time.

STEP 4: IDENTIFY THE MAIN PHRASE(S) AND MODIFYING PHRASES

Now it's time to identify the main point (or points). Move those phrases to the left, and the modifying phrases under the word they modify. Keep parallel phrases equally indented from the left margin. Go ahead and do it now, and then turn the page.

_____

1:3   <u>Praise</u> be to the God and Father of our Lord Jesus Christ!

> In his great mercy
>
> <u>he has given us new birth</u>
>
> > {1} into a living hope
>
> > through the resurrection of Jesus Christ from the dead,

1:4   {2} and into an inheritance

> > that can never perish, spoil or fade—
>
> > kept in heaven for you,

1:5   who through faith are shielded by God's power

> > until the coming of the salvation
>
> > that is ready to be revealed in the last time.

By the way, this is great biblical theology. Saying "Praise God" is not praising him. That is not the biblical pattern. To praise God is to give him glory, to describe his character and proclaim his deeds.

The main affirmation of the passage is that we are to praise God. The reason for praising God is that he has given us new birth, and he did this because he is merciful.

Peter then specifies that this new birth has two results. The first is that we now have a living hope. But how was that hope made available? The answer is Jesus' resurrection. Notice from my placement that the prepositional phrase ("through ...") modifies the verb "given," telling us how it was given. But I wanted to show that "into a living hope" and "and into an inheritance" are parallel, both telling us something about our new birth. But they are separated by the prepositional phrase "through...." This illustrates one of the problems with phrasing—words can get in the way. One solution is to number them as I have. I always use curly brackets when I insert something into the phrasing that is not in the text. I don't want to confuse my words with God's!

The second result of our new birth is that we have an inheritance. But it's not just any inheritance. It's an inheritance that can never perish. Why? Because it's kept in heaven for you. This illustrates another problem of phrasing, but one easily remedied. Due to the nature of how we construct discussions, the visual representation of the flow of thought keeps moving to the right. But eventually you will run out of paper, so I use a line to pull the discussion back to the left. The line should connect a word with what it's modifying. It's especially good to connect pronouns to their antecedents.

"Kept in heaven for you" isn't parallel with "that can never perish, spoil, or fade." It's telling you why our inheritance can never "perish, spoil, or fade." If I wanted to indicate this, I could have placed "kept ..." under "never," or I could have drawn a line under the phrase "perish, spoil, or fade" and drawn a second line from it to "kept." In other words, you can make your phrasing more or less specific, depending upon what you need to do in order to understand the passage.

Peter adds one last note to his description of "you." While we look forward to our inheritance in heaven, we live out our lives here and now shielded by God's power. How long will this shielding last? Until our salvation comes in its fullness. When will that be? "In the last time." It's ready right now and waits for the end of time.

Can you see how this simple process of working through the text, seeing its sections, and identifying the main affirmations can make such a significant difference in your Bible study? I hope so.

CHAPTER 15

NOMINATIVE, VOCATIVE, AND ACCUSATIVE

It's time to see how the Greek case system is more flexible than perhaps you have realized. The term in bold at the beginning of each category below is its technical name. These are the terms commentators will use.

NOMINATIVE

15.1 **Subject**. We learned that the nominative can be used to indicate the subject of a verb.

φωνὴ ἐγένετο ἐκ τῶν οὐρανῶν, σὺ εἶ ὁ υἱός μου ὁ ἀγαπητός
voice came   out of heaven   *you* are son   my the beloved
A *voice* came from heaven, "*You* are my Son, the Beloved" *(Mark 1:11)*.

φωνή does the action of the verb ἐγένετο. σύ is the subject of the verb εἶ.

15.2 **Unexpressed subject**. We learned that a Greek sentence does not require an expressed subject. A verb by itself can be a complete sentence. The verb ἀκούω means, "I hear," which is a sentence. The subject is supplied by the personal ending on the verb.

οἴδαμεν δὲ ὅτι, καλὸς ὁ νόμος
we know but that good   the law
But *we know* that the law is good *(1 Tim 1:8)*.

There is no expressed subject "we," so it's derived from the personal ending on the verb οἴδαμεν.

15.3   If a simple pronoun derived from the verb's personal ending might be confusing, translators will sometimes supply the actual subject. Take, for example, Hebrews 4:7–9.

> He again sets a certain day, "Today," saying through David after so long a time just as has been said before, "Today if you hear His voice, Do not harden your hearts." For if Joshua had given them rest, He would not have spoken of another day after that. Consequently, there remains a Sabbath rest for the people of God. (NASB)

Who is the "He" who "would not have spoken"? It may appear, initially, to be Joshua; that is what the normal rules of English grammar would require. However, the subject of the verb is "God," who is alluded to in the context. That is why the NASB capitalizes "He," and why the NIV replaces "He" with "God." The ESV also supplies the antecedent "God" and adds a footnote, "Greek *he*," as is its custom in this situation.

οὐκ ἂν περὶ   ἄλλης ἐλάλει   μετὰ ταῦτα ἡμέρας
not would concerning another *he was speaking* after   these   days
ESV: *God* would not have spoken of another day later on (Heb 4:8).

Another example is Romans 3:9, where the ESV adds "Jews" and marks it with a footnote, "Greek *Are we*."

τί   οὖν;   προεχόμεθα; οὐ πάντως;
what therefore *we are better off* not at all
ESV: What then? Are we *Jews* any better off? No, not at all.
CSB: What then? Are we any better off? Not at all!

15.4   **Predicate nominative**. We also learned that the nominative is used for a predicate nominative, primarily with εἰμί and γίνομαι.

ἐγώ εἰμι ὁ   χριστός
I   am *the Christ*
I am *the Christ* (Matt 24:5).

χριστός is predicating something about ἐγώ.

15.5   **Simple apposition**. A word in the nominative can be in apposition to another substantive in the nominative. "Apposition" means that the second word refers to the same entity as the first and is telling us something more about that entity. The two substantives will be next to each other and in the same case. Simple apposition occurs in all four cases.

παραγίνεται Ἰωάννης ὁ βαπτιστὴς κηρύσσων ἐν τῇ ἐρήμῳ
came John the Baptist preaching in the desert

NIV: John *the Baptist* came, preaching in the wilderness *(Matt 3:1)*.

ὁ βαπτιστής is referring to the same person as Ἰωάννης, and identifies this John as opposed to other Johns.

Παῦλος ἀπόστολος Χριστοῦ Ἰησοῦ διὰ θελήματος θεοῦ
Paul apostle of Christ Jesus through will of God

Paul, an apostle of Christ Jesus through the will of God *(Eph 1:1)*

Paul is the apostle writing the letter.

VOCATIVE

15.6 **Simple address**. We learned that the vocative case is used for *direct address*. When speaking directly to a person, the word used is in the vocative.

ἔρχου κύριε Ἰησοῦ
come Lord Jesus

Come, *Lord Jesus!* *(Rev 22:20)*

15.7 **Emphatic address**. We also learned that ὦ may be included if there is deep emotion or emphasis.

ὁ Ἰησοῦς εἶπεν αὐτῇ, ὦ γύναι, μεγάλη σου ἡ πίστις
Jesus said to her O woman great your the faith

ESV: Then Jesus answered her, "*O woman*, great is your faith!" *(Matt 15:28)*

NET: Then Jesus answered her, "Woman, your faith is great!"

15.8 **Nominative for vocative**. In many instances, the nominative is used in place of the vocative, so don't be surprised when you mouse over the word, thinking it should be a vocative, but it parses as a nominative.

ἡ παῖς, ἔγειρε
Child   arise
Child, get up! *(Luke 8:54)*

παῖς is nominative, and the child is being directly addressed.

ACCUSATIVE

15.9 **Direct object**. We have seen how the accusative is used for the direct object (5.13).

καὶ εἶχον   ἰχθύδια ὀλίγα
also they had *fish*   few
They also had a few small *fish* *(Mark 8:7)*.

15.10 **Object of a preposition**. We have also seen the accusative used for the object of certain prepositions (6.8).

ἰδοὺ   μάγοι ἀπὸ   ἀνατολῶν παρεγένοντο εἰς Ἰεροσόλυμα
behold Magi from East   came   to *Jerusalem*
Magi from the east came to *Jerusalem (Matt 2:1)*.

Ἰεροσόλυμα is the object of the preposition εἰς, which takes its object in the accusative.

15.11 **Simple apposition**. The accusative can be in an appositional relationship to another substantive in the accusative.

εἶδεν   Σίμωνα καὶ   Ἀνδρέαν τὸν ἀδελφὸν   Σίμωνος
he saw Simon   and Andrew   *the brother*   of Simon
He saw Simon and Andrew, Simon's *brother (Mark 1:16)*.

This Andrew was in fact Simon's brother.

15.12 **Unexpressed direct object.** It's common for Greek to drop a verb's direct object, and English translators must add them back in (since English doesn't allow this, for the most part). This often happens when there is a parallelism in the sentence, and words from the first half are assumed in the second.

ἔλαβεν ὁ Πιλᾶτος τὸν Ἰησοῦν καὶ ἐμαστίγωσεν
took Pilate Jesus and flogged
Pilate took Jesus and flogged *him* (John 19:1).

Ἰησοῦν is the direct object of ἔλαβεν, and also the implied direct object of ἐμαστίγωσεν.

15.13* **Double accusative.** Some verbs require two objects to complete their meaning. This construction falls into two categories.

Person-thing. Sometimes the two objects will be a personal (e.g., "you") and a nonpersonal (e.g., "things") word.

ἐκεῖνος ὑμᾶς διδάξει πάντα
he you he will teach *all things*
He will teach *you all things* (John 14:26).

The coming Holy Spirit will teach the disciples ("you"), and he will teach everything ("all things") Jesus taught them.

Object-complement. The other category is the object-complement. This means that one word will be the direct object and the second will predicate something about the direct object.

δεῦτε ὀπίσω μου, καὶ ποιήσω ὑμᾶς ἁλιεῖς ἀνθρώπων
follow after me and I will make *you* *fishermen* of men
ESV: Follow me, and I will make *you* [to be] *fishers* of men
(Matt 4:19).

Jesus is going to make the disciples (ὑμᾶς) into fishermen (ἁλιεῖς ἀνθρώπων).

Sometimes a translation will add a word like "as" or "to be" before the second accusative to help you understand its meaning.

ἀπέστειλεν τὸν υἱὸν αὐτοῦ ἱλασμὸν
He sent the son of him propitiation

NIV: he ... sent his Son *as an atoning sacrifice (1 John 4:10).*

NASB: He ... sent His Son *to be the propitiation.*

15.14* **Subject of an infinitive**. A word in the accusative can function as if it were the subject of an infinitive. Infinitives are "in-finite" in that they are not limited by a subject, but a word in the accusative can act as if it were a subject.

ὁ θεός ... οὐκ ἐάσει ὑμᾶς πειρασθῆναι ὑπὲρ ὃ δύνασθε
God not will allow *you* *to be tempted* beyond what you are able

NIV: God... will not let *you* be tempted beyond what you can bear *(1 Cor 10:13).*

ὑμᾶς is accusative and is functioning as the subject of the infinitive πειρασθῆναι.

15.15* **Measure**. The word in the accusative can behave as an adverb, modifying the verb.

ζητεῖτε πρῶτον τὴν βασιλείαν τοῦ θεοῦ
seek *first* the kingdom of God

Seek *first* the kingdom of God *(Matt 6:33).*

πρῶτον is technically an adjective, but here it's functioning as an adverb.

15.16* **Time how long**. When used with time designations, the accusative is used to indicate length of time. This can be called the "accusative of time how long."

ἦν ἐν τῇ ἐρήμῳ τεσσεράκοντα ἡμέρας πειραζόμενος ὑπὸ τοῦ σατανᾶ
he was in the desert *forty* *days* being tempted by Satan

He was in the wilderness *forty days*, tempted by Satan *(Mark 1:13).*

VOCABULARY

ὄχλος	crowd (175)
πόλις	city; town (163)
ἔθνος	nation (162) plural: Gentiles
ἡμέρα	day (389)
ὄνομα	name (229)
Ἰουδαῖος	Jewish (195) noun: a Jew
Παῦλος	Paul (158)
Πέτρος	Peter (156)

92,130 word occurrences out of 137,663 (67%). Congratulations. You now know two-thirds of all word occurrences in the Greek Testament.

CHAPTER 16

DATIVE AND GENITIVE

DATIVE

16.1 In general terms, the dative expresses the ideas of "to," "in," "by," and "with," and a word in the dative will often be the object of a preposition. "Locative," "instrumental," and "association" are subcategories of the dative we use to describe those three basic meanings.

Dative	"to"
Locative	"in"
Instrumental	"by"
Association	"with"
Object of preposition	

16.2 **Without prepositions**. Many of the times when English uses prepositions, Greek uses the dative case (often without prepositions).

ὕπαγε πρῶτον διαλλάγηθι τῷ ἀδελφῷ σου
go   first   be reconciled   *to*   *brother*   your
First, go be reconciled *to* your *brother (Matt 5:24).*

Since English does not have a dative case, the translator will often use an extra word in the translation of the dative such as "to." They are normally prepositions. In *IRU*, you will see these words with arrows under them. The arrow is pointing to the word in the dative case (or one of the other cases) that requires this helping word, such as "by" in Ephesians 2:8.

For	it	is	by	grace		you	have	been	saved
γὰρ	→	ἐστε	→	τῇ	χάριτί	→	→	→	σεσωσμένοι
cj		v.pai.2p		d.dsf	n.dsf				pt.rp.npm
1142		1639		3836	5921				5392

In my Greek-English interlinear, this phrase looks like this:

	τῇ	γὰρ	χάριτί	ἐστε	σεσωσμένοι
For	by	*For*	grace	∟you have been┘	saved
1142	3836	1142	5921	1639	5392
	d.dsf	cj	n.dsf	v.pai.2p	pt.rp.npm

Because there is an article (τῇ) with χάριτι, I put the key word "by" under the article.

BASIC USES OF THE DATIVE

16.3 **Object of a preposition**. We have seen the dative used as the object of a preposition (6.8).

ἐβαπτίζοντο		ἐν	τῷ	Ἰορδάνῃ	ποταμῷ	ὑπ᾽	αὐτοῦ
they were being baptized		in	the	Jordan	river	by	him

They were being baptized by him in the *Jordan* River *(Matt 3:6)*.

Ἰορδάνῃ is the object of the preposition ἐν, which takes the dative.

16.4 **"To."** We have seen that the dative can express the idea of "to," especially as an indirect object (5.14).

λέγει	αὐτοῖς,	Δεῦτε	ὀπίσω	μου
He says	*to them*	Follow	After	me

He says *to them*, "Follow me" *(Matt 4:19)*.

ἀποδώσεις	δὲ	τῷ	κυρίῳ	τοὺς	ὅρκους	σου
Carry out	but	*to the Lord*	the	oaths	you	

But carry out your oaths made *to the Lord (Matt 5:33)*.

16.5 **"In."** The dative can express the idea of the sphere or realm in which something occurs. Its technical term is "locative of sphere."

μακάριοι	οἱ	καθαροὶ	τῇ	καρδίᾳ
Blessed	the	pure	*in*	the heart

NIV: Blessed are the pure *in heart (Matt 5:8)*.

NLT: God blesses those whose hearts are pure.

What type of purity is Jesus talking about? Cultic purity? No, but purity within the sphere of a person's heart.

16.6 **"By."** The dative can also show the means (or the instrument) by which an action is accomplished. Its technical term is "instrumental dative." The word in the dative will be an impersonal object like "hair." Greek tends to use the preposition ὑπό with an object in the genitive when the object is personal.

Μαριὰμ ...	ἐκμάξασα	τοὺς πόδας	αὐτοῦ	ταῖς θριξὶν	αὐτῆς
Mary	wiped	feet	his	*with hair*	her

Mary wiped his feet *with* her *hair (John 11:2)*.

The instrument with which Mary wiped Jesus' feet was her hair.

τῇ	γὰρ	χάριτί	ἐστε	σεσῳσμένοι
the	for	*by grace*	you are	being saved

For it is *by grace* you have been saved *(Eph 2:8)*.

The means by which we are saved is grace.

16.7 **"With."** The dative can indicate the idea of "with." Its technical term is "dative of association."

μὴ	γίνεσθε	ἑτεροζυγοῦντες	ἀπίστοις
Not	you become	unequally yoked	*with unbelievers*

ESV: Do not be unequally yoked *with* unbelievers *(2 Cor 6:14)*.

Believers are not to be yoked in association with nonbelievers.

16.8 **Simple apposition**. A word in the dative can be used in simple apposition.

ἠγαλλίασεν	τὸ πνεῦμά	μου	ἐπὶ	τῷ θεῷ	τῷ σωτῆρί	μου
rejoices	spirit	my	in	God	*savior*	my

My spirit rejoices in God my *Savior (Luke 1:47)*.

"God" is also our "Savior," and so σωτῆρι is in the dative as is θεῷ.

16.9 **Direct object**. Some verbs take a direct object in the dative. If you think through the meaning of the verb, you will often see why this makes sense.

ἔπεσεν ἐπὶ πρόσωπον παρὰ τοὺς πόδας αὐτοῦ εὐχαριστῶν αὐτῷ
falling   on face   at   feet   his   thanking   to him

NIV: He threw himself at Jesus' feet and thanked *him* (Luke 17:16).

You can see that εὐχαριστῶν (εὐχαριστέω) means "give thanks to," and hence is followed by the dative αὐτῷ.

ADVANCED USES OF THE DATIVE*

16.10* **Reference**. The dative can indicate what in English is awkwardly expressed by the phrase "with respect to," also called the "dative of respect."

λογίζεσθε ἑαυτοὺς εἶναι νεκροὺς τῇ ἁμαρτίᾳ
consider   yourselves to be   dead   to the sin

ESV: Consider yourselves dead *to sin* (Rom 6:11).
TEV: You are to think of yourselves as dead, *so far as sin is concerned*.

They were dead, but in what sense? Physical? No. Their death was with respect to sin.

16.11* **Interest**. The dative can express the idea of "for."

ἡ γυνή σου Ἐλισάβετ γεννήσει υἱόν σοι
wife   your Elizabeth   she will bear son   to you

Your wife Elizabeth will bear a son *for you* (Luke 1:13).
NET: Your wife Elizabeth will bear you a son.

Elizabeth did not bear a son "to" Zechariah; it was "for" him. When the word in the dative expresses an idea that is to the person's advantage, as here, we call it a "dative of advantage." When context tells us that it's not for the person's advantage, we call it a "dative of disadvantage" and often use a different preposition based on the meaning of the phrase.

μαρτυρεῖτε ἑαυτοῖς
you testify   *to yourselves*
NRSV: You testify *against yourselves* (Matt 23:31).

Here the testifying is not "for" the Pharisees in a positive sense but is rather hostile; in English we say this with the preposition "against."

16.12* **Time**. A time designation in the dative specifies when something occurs.

τῇ   τρίτῃ   ἡμέρᾳ   ἐγερθήσεται
to the *third*   *day*   he will be raised.
NET: *On the third day* he will be raised (*Matt 17:23*).

This can also be called the "dative of time when" to keep it distinct from the "accusative of time how long."

GENITIVE

16.13 **Descriptive**. We have seen that the most generic use of the genitive is to establish a simple modifier relationship (5.17).

μακάριοι οἱ εἰρηνοποιοί, ὅτι αὐτοὶ υἱοὶ θεοῦ κληθήσονται
blessed   the peacemakers for they sons *of God* will be called
Blessed are the peacemakers, for they will be called the sons *of God* (*Matt 5:9*).

They will not be called just anyone's sons, but God's sons.

This is, as it were, the catchall category. If context doesn't allow a more specific meaning, we tend to classify it as a "descriptive genitive."

16.14 **Possessive**. We have seen that the head noun can be possessed by the word in the genitive (5.18). The word can be a personal pronoun or a noun.

ὕπαγε πώλησόν σου   τὰ ὑπάρχοντα
Go   sell   *of you* the things belonging
Go, sell *your* possessions (*Matt 19:21*).

He was to sell his own possessions.

Παῦλος ἀπόστολος Χριστοῦ Ἰησοῦ κατ'   ἐπιταγὴν θεοῦ
Paul   apostle   *of Christ Jesus* because of command *of God*
Paul, an apostle *of Christ Jesus* because of the command *of God*
(1 Tim 1:1).

Paul was Christ's apostle, and his apostolic ministry was not due
to a general command but a specifc command from God.

16.15 **Object of a preposition.** We have also seen that the word in the
genitive can be the object of a preposition (6.8).

πατέρα   μὴ καλέσητε ὑμῶν ἐπὶ τῆς γῆς
father   not call   your   on   *earth*
Do not call anyone on *earth* your "father" (*Matt 23:9*).

γῆς is in the genitive because it's the object of the preposition ἐπί,
which can take the genitive.

16.16 **Simple apposition.** The word in the genitive can indicate an
appositional relationship.

χάρις ὑμῖν καὶ εἰρήνη ἀπὸ θεοῦ πατρὸς ἡμῶν
grace to you and peace from God *father* our
Grace to you and peace from God our *father* (*Col 1:2*).

Paul's blessing comes from God, who is also our Father.

16.17 **Direct object.** Some verbs take a direct object in the genitive.
If you think through the meaning of the verb, you will often see
why this makes sense.

εἴ τις   ἐπισκοπῆς ὀρέγεται, καλοῦ ἔργου ἐπιθυμεῖ
if anyone office of overseer aspires   *good* *work* he desires
If anyone aspires to the office of overseer, he desires *a good thing*
(1 Tim 3:1).
NLT: If someone aspires to be an elder, he desires *an honorable
position.*

You can see that ἐπιθυμεῖ (ἐπιθυμέω) means "to be desirous of,"
and hence is followed by the genitive.

ADVANCED USES OF THE GENITIVE*

16.18* This category and the next are quite important. They occur with a head noun that expresses a verbal idea (i.e., the root of the noun can also occur as a verb). They often present the translator with significantly different interpretations.

16.19* **Subjective**. Sometimes the word in the genitive functions as if it were the subject of the verbal idea implicit in the head noun. In other words, if you can turn the head noun into a verb, the word in the genitive would become its subject. You can use the helping word "produced" to help identify this usage. The ambiguous "the love of Christ" becomes "the love produced by Christ," which means Christ's love for us.

τίς   ἡμᾶς χωρίσει   ἀπὸ   τῆς ἀγάπης   τοῦ Χριστοῦ;
who   us   will separate   from   the love   *of Christ*
NIV: Who shall separate us from the love *of Christ*? *(Rom 8:35)*
NLT: Can anything ever separate us from Christ's love?

The NLT is making it clear that Χριστοῦ is a subjective genitive, that Paul is talking about Christ's love for us and not our love for Christ.

16.20* **Objective**. The word in the genitive can function as the direct object of the verbal idea implicit in the head noun. This is the opposite of the subjective genitive. In other words, if the head noun were a verb, the word in the genitive would be its direct object. You can use the key word "receives." "The blasphemy received by the Spirit" would mean our blasphemy of the Spirit.

ἡ   τοῦ πνεύματος βλασφημία οὐκ ἀφεθήσεται
The   *of the Spirit*   blasphemy   not   will be forgiven
The blasphemy *of the Spirit* will not be forgiven *(Matt 12:31)*.
NIV: Blasphemy against the Spirit will not be forgiven.

16.21* **Genitive of apposition**. A word in the genitive can be part of another type of appositional relationship. It is also called the "epexegetical genitive."

- In the case of the simple apposition (16.16), the head noun and the word in the genitive are roughly equivalent, and both words must be in the genitive.

- With the genitive of apposition, the head noun represents a larger group (often ambiguous), and the genitive is a smaller, perhaps more specific part of the larger group. The head noun does not have to be in the genitive.

In this case, the two words refer to the same thing, but they are not exactly the same.

σημεῖον ἔλαβεν   περιτομῆς σφραγῖδα τῆς δικαιοσύνης τῆς πίστεως
sign   he received of circumcision seal   of righteousness   by faith

NIV: He received *circumcision* as a sign, a seal of the righteousness that he had by faith *(Rom 4:11)*.

ESV: He received the sign *of circumcision* as a seal of the righteousness that he had by faith.

"Seal" is the head noun for "circumcision" and is the larger category; "circumcision" is the smaller, more specific concept. Paul is not talking about seals in general but of a specific seal, the seal of circumcision.

ἐκεῖνος δὲ ἔλεγεν   περὶ   τοῦ ναοῦ τοῦ σώματος αὐτοῦ
he   but was speaking concerning the temple   of body   his

NRSV: But he was speaking of the temple *of* his *body (John 2:21)*.

NIV: But the temple he had spoken of was his *body*.

NLT: But when Jesus said "this temple," he meant his own *body*.

Jesus was speaking of the temple, and the specific temple was his body.

λήμψεσθε   τὴν δωρεὰν τοῦ ἁγίου   πνεύματος
You will receive   the gift   of the Holy   Spirit

You will receive the gift, *which is the Holy Spirit (Acts 2:38)*.

NIV: You will receive the gift *of the Holy Spirit*.

TEV: You will receive God's gift, the Holy Spirit.

Of all the gifts we can receive, the gift here is the Holy Spirit himself.

16.22* **Attributive**. The substantive in the genitive gives an attribute of the head noun. As such, it's similar to a simple adjective; however, it uses a substantive to in effect modify another substantive, and it's more emphatic in its force than an adjective. This is a common contruction and is sometimes called an "Hebraic genitive" as it reflects a Hebraic idiom.

καταργηθῇ   τὸ σῶμα   τῆς ἁμαρτίας
abolished   the body   of sin

ESV: the body *of sin* might be brought to nothing *(Rom 6:6)*
NIV: the body *ruled by sin* might be done away with

"Body of sin" becomes "sinful body."

Some of these constructions can be tricky, since the translator must make up his or her mind whether to use the "of" construction ("gospel of the glory") or to translate the genitive as an attributive ("glorious gospel").

κατὰ   τὸ εὐαγγέλιον τῆς δόξης τοῦ   μακαρίου θεοῦ
according to the gospel   of the glory of the blessed   God

ESV: in accordance with the gospel *of the glory* of the blessed God *(1 Tim 1:11)*
NASB: according to the *glorious* gospel of the blessed God
NRSV: that conforms to the *glorious* gospel of the blessed God

Is Paul saying that the gospel is glorious, or that the gospel is about the glory of God? The first printings of the ESV read, "in accordance with the glorious gospel of the blessed God," but the committee later changed it.

16.23* **Time**. The genitive can describe the kind of time, or the time within which, the head noun takes place.

οὗτος ἦλθεν πρὸς αὐτὸν νυκτός
he   came   to   him   of night

He came to him *at night (John 3:2)*.

Nicodemus came to Jesus as one who comes in the night, either because Pharisees studied at night or else Nicodemus did not want to be seen with Jesus (hence, secretly). John is not simply telling us when Nicodemus came. In that case, νυκτός would have been in the dative.

νηστεύω δὶς   τοῦ σαββάτου
I fast   twice   of the week
I fast *twice a week* (Luke 18:12).

The Pharisee fasts two times within the week.

VOCABULARY

ἰδού	Look! Behold! (200)
γράφω	I write (190)
εὑρίσκω	I find (176)
ἵστημι	intransitive: I stand (153)
	transitive: I cause to stand

92,849 total word occurrences out of 137,663 (67%)

You are done learning all 109 words occurring 150 times or more in the Greek Testament (and two more). Congratulations. All the vocabulary words are listed at the end of this book organized by part of speech.

CHAPTER 17

CONJUNCTIONS

Conjunctions are important words since they show us the flow of the author's thought. They are generally little words and often quite difficult to translate, and some can be translated with punctuation.

17.1   Conjunctions are (normally) the little words that connect words, phrases, clauses, and sentences (e.g., and, but, for, or, so, yet). They are broken down into three categories.

- **Coordinating** conjunctions connect equal elements (*paratactic*).

  The Word was with God *and* the Word was God.

- **Subordinate** conjunctions begin a dependent clause and often link it to an independent clause (*hypotactic*).

  I studied *because* I want to pass this class.

- **Correlative** conjunctions work in pairs.

  Kiersten has *both* strength *and* speed.

SIGNIFICANCE

17.2   In exegesis (and phrasing), conjunctions are important because they tell us the specific relationship between different units of thought. By seeing this, we can better understand the author's flow of thought and therefore his meaning.

17.3   However, Greek can use conjunctions differently than we do in English. One-third of all the sentences in John begin with καί, which generally means "and." It's poor English style to start so many sentences with conjunctions, so they are often dropped in translation. But they are there, and sometimes might give us a clue as to the relationship between ideas.

17.4 **Conjunctions, punctuation, and flow of thought**. As you recall, when the Greek Testament was originally written, there was no punctuation, not even spaces between words. To clarify the nature of the connection between a sentence and the preceding, most sentences begin with a conjunction.

However, today we use punctuation, including paragraphs, to group our throughts. In other words, punctuation can sometimes do for us what conjunctions did for Greek.

In addition, English allows the flow of thought to clarify the relationship between ideas. In the sentence, "A and B," what is the relationship between A and B? Contextually, it could be clear that we mean "A *and then* B." However, contextually, it could also mean "A *but* B." In other words, "and" can contextually mean either "and" or "but."

This explains some of the variations among translations. Do we say "and" and allow the context to clarify that we mean "and" or "but," or do we translate "but"?

17.5 It's especially important to highlight the main conjunctions when phrasing.

- Coordinating conjunctions should be set off on their own line, indented the same distance from the left to highlight the flow of thought.

> *And*
> > upon entering the house
> they saw the child with Mary his mother,
> > *and*
> > > falling to their knees
> they worshiped him.
> > *And*
> > > opening their treasure chests,
> they presented him with gifts,   gold and
> > > > frankincense and
> > > > myrrh.

- Subordinate conjunctions are indented under the word they modify, on the same line as their following phrase or clause.

> Blessed are the poor in spirit,
>> *for* theirs is the kingdom of heaven *(Matt 5:3)*.

- If the conjunction simply ties a series of words together, the conjunction does not need to be highlighted. See the first example above: "gold and frankincense and myrrh."

Conjunctions are so important that you should memorize all the ones listed in this chapter.

17.6   In what follows, I usually list two translations. The first illustrates the point I am making, and the second shows another translation that treats the conjunction differently.

COORDINATING CONJUNCTIONS

17.7   Coordinate conjunctions connect grammatically equal units. They can connect two independent clauses (i.e., two sentences), two direct objects, two subjects, etc. They can even link paragraphs. Following are the main coordinate conjunctions in Greek.

καί

17.8   **Copulative.** καί is the most common of all Greek conjunctions. It can mean "and."

NASB: The things you have learned *and* [καί] received *and* [καί] heard *and* [καί] seen in me, practice these things, *and* [καί] the God of peace will be with you *(Phil 4:9)*.

NIV: Whatever you have learned *or* [καί] received *or* [καί] heard from me, *or* [καί] seen in me—put it into practice. *And* [καί] the God of peace will be with you.

17.9   **Ascensive.** καί can add emphasis to a word, as in the English "even" or "also."

NRSV: For if you love those who love you, what reward do you have? Do not *even* [καί] the tax collectors do the same? *(Matt 5:46)*

NIV: For those God foreknew he *also* [καί] predestined to be conformed to the image of his Son, that he might be the firstborn among many brothers and sisters *(Rom 8:29)*.

17.10 **Adversative.** καί can also be used in a context in which the two clauses contrast each other, and καί is translated "but" by some translations while others use "and."

NLT: When an evil spirit leaves a person, it goes into the desert, seeking rest *but* [καί] finding none *(Matt 12:43)*.

NIV: When an impure spirit comes out of a person, it goes through arid places seeking rest *and* [καί] does not find it.

17.11 **Continuation.** When καί occurs at the beginning of a sentence, it's often marking the simple fact that the sentence is a continuation of the previous discussion. This use of καί is often left untranslated because we group sentences by paragraphs, which conveys the same idea.

CSB: [καί] Therefore [διὰ τοῦτο], he is the mediator of a new covenant, so that those who are called might receive the promise of the eternal inheritance *(Heb 9:15)*.

KJV: And [καί] for this cause [διὰ τοῦτο] he is the mediator of the new testament, that by means of death, for the redemption of the transgressions that were under the first testament, they which are called might receive the promise of eternal inheritance.

δέ

17.12 **Coordinating.** δέ is a weaker connective, which means all it necessarily says is that there is a connection between the preceding and following. Often, when a sentence starts with δέ, it's not translated. The NET Bible has literally hundreds of footnotes that indicate every place they did not translate δέ.

NIV: Abraham was the father of Isaac, [δέ] Isaac the father of Jacob, [δέ] Jacob the father of Judah and his brothers *(Matt 1:2)*.

ESV: Abraham was the father of Isaac, *and* [δέ] Isaac the father of Jacob, *and* [δέ] Jacob the father of Judah and his brothers.

17.13 **Continuation**. Sometimes the force of the δέ is a little stronger and is translated as "and."

RSV: And [δέ] this is the judgment, that the light has come into the world, and [καί] men loved darkness rather than light, because their deeds were evil *(John 3:19)*.

NIV: [δέ] This is the verdict: Light has come into the world, but [καί] people loved darkness instead of light because their deeds were evil.

17.14 **Adversative**. δέ can also introduce a contrasting idea and is translated "but." However, δέ is a weak adversative, which means it indicates only a slight adversative relationship, so slight that at times δέ can't be translated.

NASB: [καί] They tried to give Him wine mixed with myrrh; *but* [δέ] He did not take it *(Mark 15:23)*.

NIV: Then [καί] they offered him wine mixed with myrrh, *but* [δέ] he did not take it.

ESV: But [δέ] it's easier for heaven and [καί] earth to pass away than for one dot of the Law to become void *(Luke 16:17)*.

NIV: [δέ] It's easier for heaven and [καί] earth to disappear than for the least stroke of a pen to drop out of the Law.

NIV: Some, *however*, [δέ] made fun of them and said, "They have had too much wine" *(Acts 2:13)*.

NLT: But [δέ] others in the crowd ridiculed them, saying, "They're just drunk, that's all!"

NIV: Yet [δέ] to all who did receive him, to those who believed in his name, he gave the right to become children of God *(John 1:12)*.

ESV: But [δέ] to all who did receive him, who believed in his name, he gave the right to become children of God.

17.15 However, at times context shows that the adversative nature of δέ is quite pronounced. Usually, when a strong adversative is needed, Greek will use ἀλλά (see 17.20).

NKJV: [δέ] I thank God—through Jesus Christ our Lord! So then, with the mind I myself serve the law of God, *but* [δέ] with the flesh the law of sin *(Rom 7:25).*

17.16 **Continuation.** Sometimes the δέ is helping the story to continue, and "now" or "then" among other words is used.

NIV: Now [δέ] there were staying in Jerusalem God-fearing Jews from every nation under heaven *(Acts 2:5).*

NLT: At that time [δέ] there were devout Jews from every nation living in Jerusalem.

NIV: Then [δέ] their eyes were opened and [καί] they recognized him, and [καί] he disappeared from their sight *(Luke 24:31).*

ESV: And [δέ] their eyes were opened, and [καί] they recognized him. And [καί] he vanished from their sight.

NLT: Suddenly [δέ], their eyes were opened, and [καί] they recognized him. And [καί] at that moment he disappeared!

17.17 If you want to get even more sophisticated, you can see that the paragraph marker can perform the same function as δέ, since it indicates a change of some sort. Luke 24:36–43 contains one of Jesus' post-resurrection appearances. Verse 44 starts a new paragraph introduced with δέ.

NIV: [δέ] He said to them, "This is what I told you while I was still with you: Everything must be fulfilled that is written about me in the Law of Moses, the Prophets and the Psalms" *(Luke 24:44).*

NASB: Now [δέ] He said to them, "These are My words which I spoke to you while I was still with you, that all things which are written about Me in the Law of Moses and the Prophets and the Psalms must be fulfilled."

ESV: Then [δέ] he said to them, "These are my words that I spoke to you while I was still with you, that everything written about me in the Law of Moses and the Prophets and the Psalms must be fulfilled."

In Matthew 28:11–15 we read about the Jewish leaders formulating the lie to explain away the empty tomb. Verse 16, in essence, starts a new paragraph by telling us what the disciples did.

NASB: But [δέ] the eleven disciples proceeded to Galilee, to the mountain which Jesus had designated *(Matt 28:16).*

RSV: Now [δέ] the eleven disciples went to Galilee, to the mountain to which Jesus had directed them.

NIV: Then [δέ] the eleven disciples went to Galilee, to the mountain where Jesus had told them to go.

How does the translator know when to translate δέ and when to drop it? Context! Are you seeing why translations can be so different? The translators' sense of English style and how they want to express the relationships between phrases will vary.

γάρ

17.18 **Explanatory.** γάρ gives the reason or explanation for something. It's usually translated "for."

NASB: A woman of Samaria came to draw water. Jesus said to her, "Give Me a drink." *For* [γάρ] His disciples had gone away into the city to buy food *(John 4:7–8).*

NLT: Soon a Samaritan woman came to draw water, and Jesus said to her, "Please give me a drink." He was alone at the time *because* [γάρ] his disciples had gone into the village to buy some food."

ESV: For [γάρ] as in one body we have many members, and the members do not all have the same function ... *(Rom 12:4]*

CSB: Now [γάρ] as we have many parts in one body, and all the parts do not have the same function, ...

17.19 **Continuation.** γάρ can also indicate that the author is simply continuing his discussion, and these occurrences are usually not translated, as illustrated by the second occurrence of γάρ in Romans 1:19–20 in the RSV.

RSV: For [διότι] what can be known about God is plain to them, *because* [γάρ] God has shown it to them. [γάρ] Ever since the creation of the world his invisible nature, namely, his eternal power and [καί] deity, has been clearly perceived in the things that have been made. So they are without excuse.

NIV: since [διότι] what may be known about God is plain to them, *because* [γάρ] God has made it plain to them. *For* [γάρ] since the creation of the world God's invisible qualities—his eternal power and [καί] divine nature—have been clearly seen, being understood from what has been made, so that people are without excuse.

People who don't know Greek often criticize translators for not translating every occurrence of γάρ. But when γάρ simply indicates continuation, translating γάρ as "for" mistranslates since the English "for" always indicates a reason and never continuation.

ἀλλά, οὖν, ἤ

17.20 **Adversative.** ἀλλά is a strong adversative conjunction, indicating that the following clause stands in contrast to the preceding. It's usually translated "but," but it can be translated many other ways that indicate a contrast.

NIV: Do not think that I have come to abolish the Law or the Prophets; I have not come to abolish them *but* [ἀλλά] to fulfill them *(Matt 5:17).*

NLT: Don't misunderstand why I have come. I did not come to abolish the law of Moses or the writings of the prophets. No [ἀλλά], I came to accomplish their purpose.

NIV: Neither do people light a lamp and [καί] put it under a bowl. *Instead* [ἀλλά] they put it on its stand, and [καί] it gives light to everyone in the house *(Matt 5:15).*

ESV: Nor do people light a lamp and [καί] put it under a basket, *but* [ἀλλά] on a stand, and [καί] it gives light to all in the house.

NASB: Nor do people put new wine into old wineskins; otherwise [δέ] the wineskins burst, and [καί] the wine pours out and [καί] the wineskins are ruined; *but* [ἀλλά] they put new wine into fresh wineskins, and [καί] both are preserved *(Matt 9:17)*.

NIV: Neither do people pour new wine into old wineskins. [δέ] If they do, the skins will burst; [καί] the wine will run out and [καί] the wineskins will be ruined. *No* [ἀλλά], they pour new wine into new wineskins, and [καί] both are preserved.

NIV: If not [ἀλλά], what did you go out to see? A man dressed in fine clothes? No, those who wear fine clothes are in kings' palaces *(Matt 11:8)*.

ESV: What *then* [ἀλλά] did you go out to see? A man dressed in soft clothing? Behold, those who wear soft clothing are in kings' houses.

RSV: For [γάρ] there is nothing hid, except to be made manifest; nor is anything secret, *except* [ἀλλά] to come to light *(Mark 4:22)*.

NIV: For [γάρ] whatever is hidden is meant to be disclosed, and whatever is concealed is meant [ἀλλά] to be brought out into the open.

NIV: For if we have been united with him in a death like his, we will *certainly* [ἀλλά] also [καί] be united with him in a resurrection like his *(Rom 6:5)*.

NLT: Since we have been united with him in his death, we will [ἀλλά] also [καί] be raised to life as he was.

17.21 **Inferential**. οὖν is the main inferential conjunction and is often translated "therefore."

NASB: Therefore [οὖν] I urge you, brothers *and sisters*, by the mercies of God, to present your bodies a living and [*no Greek conjunction*] holy sacrifice, acceptable to God, *which is* your spiritual service of worship *(Rom 12:1)*.

NLT: And so [οὖν], dear brothers and sisters, I plead with you to give your bodies to God because of all he has done for you. Let them be a living and [no Greek conjunction] holy sacrifice—the kind he will find acceptable. This is truly the way to worship him.

17.22 **Continuation**. οὖν can weaken to indicate a transition or continuation of the narrative without any sense of inference.

ESV: The Jews [οὖν] did not believe that he had been blind and [καί] had received his sight *(John 9:18)*.

NASB: The Jews *then* [οὖν] did not believe it of him, that he had been blind and [καί] had received sight.

17.23 ἤ is the main conjunction for saying "or."

NIV (1984): For [γάρ] truly I say to you, until heaven and [καί] earth pass away, not the smallest letter *or* [ἤ] stroke shall pass from the Law until all is accomplished *(Matt 5:18)*.

ESV: For [γάρ] truly, I say to you, until heaven and [καί] earth pass away, not an iota, [ἤ] not a dot, will pass from the Law until all is accomplished.

Did you notice how the comma performs the function of ἤ in the ESV example above?

SUBORDINATE CONJUNCTIONS

17.24 Subordinate conjunctions introduce dependent clauses, which will modify a word often in the main clause. This is significant for phrasing as you attempt to differentiate primary and secondary thoughts.

17.25 ὅτι can indicate the basis for an action and is usually translated "because."

RSV: And [δέ] hope does not disappoint us, *because* [ὅτι] God's love has been poured into our hearts through the Holy Spirit which has been given to us *(Rom 5:5)*.

17.26 ὅτι can be the equivalent of "that" after certain types of verbs, such as verbs expressing the idea of "to say" or "to perceive."

RSV: If the world hates you, know *that* [ὅτι] it has hated me before it hated you *(John 15:18).*

17.27 ὅτι can introduce either direct and indirect speech. If the translator thinks it's direct speech, ὅτι is translated with quotation marks. If it is indirect speech, ὅτι is translated as "that."

CSB: How can he now say [λέγει], "[ὅτι] I have come down from heaven"? *(John 6:42)*

The Spirit clearly says [λέγει] *that* [ὅτι] in the last times some of the faith will apostasize *(1 Tim 4:1).*

17.28 ἵνα generally indicates *purpose* and can be translated "in order that," or "so that."

NASB: Do not judge *so that* [ἵνα] you will not be judged *(Matt 7:1).*

ESV: Judge not, *that* [ἵνα] you be not judged.

NIV: Do not judge, *or* [ἵνα] you too will be judged.

NLT: Do not judge others, *and* [ἵνα] you will not be judged.

NLT: For [γάρ] this is how God loved the world: He gave his one and only Son, *so that* [ἵνα] everyone who believes in him will not perish but [ἀλλ'] have eternal life *(John 3:16).*

NIV: For [γάρ] God so loved the world that he gave his one and only Son, *that* [ἵνα] whoever believes in him shall not perish but [ἀλλ'] have eternal life.

17.29 ἵνα can also indicate *result,* translated with "that."

NIV: But [δέ] this has all taken place *that* [ἵνα] the writings of the prophets might be fulfilled *(Matt 26:56).*

The difference between purpose and result is subtle. If there was intention, it's purpose. If the action simply occurred, it's result.

17.30 ἵνα can also lose all of its purpose/result nuance and simply introduce the content of what is expressed by the verb.

ESV: And as you wish *that* [ἵνα] others would do to you, do so to them *(Luke 6:31).*

CSB: Just as you want [ἵνα] others to do for you, do the same for them.

The NASB (and others] reverses the order of the phrases and so the conjujnction is not actually translated.

NASB: Treat people the same way you want them to treat you.

17.31 εἰ (and an alternate form ἐάν] is the main *conditional* conjunction meaning "if."

If [εἰ] you are the Christ, tell us *(Luke 22:67).*

NASB: You are the salt of the earth; but [δέ] if [ἐάν] the salt has become tasteless, how can it be made salty *again? (Matt 5:13).*

CORRELATIVE CONJUNCTIONS

17.32 Correlative conjunctions are pairs of conjunctions that work together. The most common are:

μέν ... δέ	on the one hand ... but on the other
καί ... καί	both ... and
ἤ ...ἤ	either ... or
μήτε ... μήτε	neither ... nor
οὔτε ... οὔτε	neither ... nor
οὐκ ... ἀλλά (or δέ)	not ... but
τε ... καί	both ... and

RSV: I know your works: you are *neither* [οὔτε] cold *nor* [οὔτε] hot. Would that you were cold or [ἤ] hot! *(Rev 3:15)*

17.33 Sometimes the first of the pair is not translated because of English style. This is especially true of μέν ... δέ.

CSB: Then he said to his disciples, "[μέν] The harvest is abundant, *but* [δέ] the workers are few." *(Matt 9:37)*

17.34 The translation of conjunctions can become quite nuanced. For example, in the NASB of 1 Corinthians 7:7 the μέν ... δέ is represented by the change from "one" to "another."

one [μέν] in this way, and *another* [δέ] in that.

17.35 The correlatives can often be tricky to spot because of intervening words.

ὑπο ἀνθρώπων μὲν ἀποδεδοκιμασμένον παρὰ δὲ θεῷ ἐκλεκτόν
by men rejected before *but* God chosen

rejected by men *but* chosen by God *(1 Peter 2:4)*

Notice how μέν comes after ὑπὸ ἀνθρώπων and δέ after παρά since they are postpositives. In my reverse interlinear, I listed μέν and δέ as the first word in each phrase.

rejected		by	men	but	chosen	by	God
μὲν	ἀποδεδοκιμασμένον	ὑπὸ	ἀνθρώπων	δὲ	ἐκλεκτὸν	παρὰ	θεῷ
pl	pt.rp.asm	p.g	n.gpm	cj	a.asm	p.d	n.dsm
525	627	5679	476	1254	1723	4123	2536

VOCABULARY

You have already learned these words, but I have grouped all of them here for your review. All of them are especially important in phrasing.

CONJUNCTIONS

ἀλλά	but
γάρ	for
δέ (δ᾿)	and; but
ἐάν	if
εἰ	if
ἵνα	in order that; so that; that
καθώς	as, even as
καί	and; even, also
οὖν	therefore
ὅτι	that; because
τε	and
ὡς	as ("like")

PARTICLES

ἄν	makes contingent
ἤ	or; than
μέν	on the one hand
μή	not, lest
οὐ	not

ADVERB

οὕτως	thus, so; in this manner
τότε	then

INTERJECTION

ἰδού	Look! Behold!

CHART OF CONJUNCTIONS

	καί	δέ	γάρ	ἀλλά	οὖν	ἤ	ὅτι	ἵνα	εἰ/ἐάν
copulative	and	and							
ascensive	also even								
contrast (weak)	but	but							
contrast (strong)		but		but					
continuation		now, then	now						
change transition		now, then			now, then				
explanatory			for						
inferential					there-fore				
alternative		or				or			
cause							be-cause		
content							that	that	
purpose								that	
result								in order that, so that	
condition									if

CHAPTER 18

PHRASING 102

In chapter 14 we learned the basics of phrasing. Let's review! The purpose of phrasing is to identify the beginning and end of the passage, divide it into manageable sections if necessary, find the main point(s) of each section, and then see how the remaining phrases relate to those main points.

We are going to do some more phrasing, this time with the letter of Jude. This is a harder book to phrase, but if you can get through Jude, you can deal with most of the New Testament.

JUDE

I have listed the NIV (1984) text of Jude on the next two pages without paragraphs and headings. Work from it, not your Bible, or copy the text from your Bible software and paste it into your word processor.

STEP 1: FIND THE BEGINNING AND THE END

Because we want to phrase all of Jude, this step is done for us. We are going to work with all twenty-five verses.

STEP 2: IDENTIFY THE SECTIONS

Work through Jude on the next two pages and discover how many basic sections it has. Place headings with each.

JUDE

1:1   Jude, a servant of Jesus Christ and a brother of James,

To those who have been called, who are loved by God the Father and kept by Jesus Christ:

1:2   Mercy, peace and love be yours in abundance.

1:3   Dear friends, although I was very eager to write to you about the salvation we share, I felt I had to write and urge you to contend for the faith that was once for all entrusted to the saints.

1:4   For certain men whose condemnation was written about long ago have secretly slipped in among you. They are godless men, who change the grace of our God into a license for immorality and deny Jesus Christ our only Sovereign and Lord.

1:5   Though you already know all this, I want to remind you that the Lord delivered his people out of Egypt, but later destroyed those who did not believe.

1:6   And the angels who did not keep their positions of authority but abandoned their own home—these he has kept in darkness, bound with everlasting chains for judgment on the great Day.

1:7   In a similar way, Sodom and Gomorrah and the surrounding towns gave themselves up to sexual immorality and perversion. They serve as an example of those who suffer the punishment of eternal fire.

1:8   In the very same way, these dreamers pollute their own bodies, reject authority and slander celestial beings.

1:9   But even the archangel Michael, when he was disputing with the devil about the body of Moses, did not dare to bring a slanderous accusation against him, but said, "The Lord rebuke you!"

1:10   Yet these men speak abusively against whatever they do not understand; and what things they do understand by instinct, like unreasoning animals—these are the very things that destroy them.

1:11   Woe to them! They have taken the way of Cain; they have rushed for profit into Balaam's error; they have been destroyed in Korah's rebellion.

1:12   These men are blemishes at your love feasts, eating with you without the slightest qualm—shepherds who feed only themselves. They are clouds without rain, blown along by the wind; autumn trees, without fruit and uprooted—twice dead.

1:13   They are wild waves of the sea, foaming up their shame; wandering stars, for whom blackest darkness has been reserved forever.

1:14   Enoch, the seventh from Adam, prophesied about these men: "See, the Lord is coming with thousands upon thousands of his holy ones

1:15   to judge everyone, and to convict all the ungodly of all the ungodly acts they have done in the ungodly way, and of all the harsh words ungodly sinners have spoken against him."

1:16   These men are grumblers and faultfinders; they follow their own evil desires; they boast about themselves and flatter others for their own advantage.

1:17   But, dear friends, remember what the apostles of our Lord Jesus Christ foretold.

1:18   They said to you, "In the last times there will be scoffers who will follow their own ungodly desires."

1:19   These are the men who divide you, who follow mere natural instincts and do not have the Spirit.

1:20   But you, dear friends, build yourselves up in your most holy faith and pray in the Holy Spirit.

1:21   Keep yourselves in God's love as you wait for the mercy of our Lord Jesus Christ to bring you to eternal life.

1:22   Be merciful to those who doubt;

1:23   snatch others from the fire and save them; to others show mercy, mixed with fear—hating even the clothing stained by corrupted flesh.

1:24   To him who is able to keep you from falling and to present you before his glorious presence without fault and with great joy—

1:25   to the only God our Savior be glory, majesty, power and authority, through Jesus Christ our Lord, before all ages, now and forevermore! Amen.

Salutation

1:1   Jude, a servant of Jesus Christ and a brother of James,

To those who have been called, who are loved by God the Father and kept by Jesus Christ:

1:2   Mercy, peace and love be yours in abundance.

Occasion for Writing

1:3   Dear friends, although I was very eager to write to you about the salvation we share, I felt I had to write and urge you to contend for the faith that was once for all entrusted to the saints.

1:4   For certain men whose condemnation was written about long ago have secretly slipped in among you. They are godless men, who change the grace of our God into a license for immorality and deny Jesus Christ our only Sovereign and Lord.

Description and Condemnation of the Troublemakers

1:5   Though you already know all this, I want to remind you that the Lord delivered his people out of Egypt, but later destroyed those who did not believe.

. . . . .

Call to Perseverance

1:20   But you, dear friends, build yourselves up in your most holy faith and pray in the Holy Spirit.

1:21   Keep yourselves in God's love as you wait for the mercy of our Lord Jesus Christ to bring you to eternal life.

1:22   Be merciful to those who doubt;

1:23   snatch others from the fire and save them; to others show mercy, mixed with fear—hating even the clothing stained by corrupted flesh.

Doxology

1:24   To him who is able to keep you from falling and to present you before his glorious presence without fault and with great joy—

1:25   to the only God our Savior be glory, majesty, power and authority, through Jesus Christ our Lord, before all ages, now and forever-more! Amen.

So how did you do? I see five basic sections. The salutation (vv. 1–2) and doxology (vv. 24–25) are pretty evident. Verses 3–4 then tell us why Jude wrote and introduces us to the troublemakers.

The heart of the letter is verses 5–23, but there is a shift between verse 19 and verse 20 as Jude moves from describing the troublemakers to encouraging the church to persevere. In other words, there is a shift from the troublemakers to the church, and a shift in his basic message.

Some people don't split it this way. Some see a shift at 1:17, especially because of the beginning "Dear friends." That's okay. I may not be right. But when I break a passage into its sections, what I am looking for is a unifying theme, something that holds the verses together. In verses 5–23 I see Jude doing the same thing: whether he is describing people or explicitly judging them, all of it functions as a condemnation of sin, asserting that God always punishes evil.

STEPS 3–4

Go ahead and phrase the salutation. It has similarities to 1 Peter 1:1–2 and shouldn't give you a problem. Also phrase verses 3–4. Pay special attention to why Jude says they are godless.

When you are done, check my work on the next page.

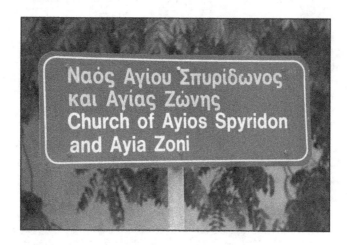

A sign of a church. Can you spot any variances from the transliteration scheme you were instructed in this book?

Salutation

1:1   Jude,

> a servant of Jesus Christ and
>
> a brother of James,

To those

> who have been called,
>
> who are   loved by God the Father and
>
> > kept by Jesus Christ:

1:2   Mercy, peace and love be yours in abundance.

Occasion for Writing

1:3   Dear friends,

> although I was very eager to write to you about the salvation we share,

I felt I had to write and urge you to contend for the faith

> that was once for all entrusted to the saints.

1:4   For

certain men ... have secretly slipped in among you.

> whose condemnation was written about long ago
>
> They are godless men,
>
> > who change the grace of our God
> > into a license for immorality and
> >
> > deny Jesus Christ our only
> > Sovereign and Lord.

We have the usual three-part salutation, with Jude emphasizing that those who have been called are also loved and kept both by God the Father and Jesus Christ. This is an important affirmation in light of the overall negative emphasis of the letter.

Jude then moves into the occasion for writing. He had wanted to write a different type of letter, one about the salvation he shares with the church; but instead, because of the troublemakers, he felt the need to encourage the church to fight for the faith. Why? Because certain godless men had snuck into the church, and their heresy was twofold. They taught that holiness didn't matter, that God's grace gave them license to live immoral lives. Second, they denied that Jesus was the believer's only Sovereign and Lord.

I connected the "For" in verse 4 with the line back to "felt," precisely identifying verse 4 as the *reason* for why Jude felt this way. Without the line, it may not have been visually clear that "For" explains why he felt this way. If there had been more room on the page to the right, I would have indented all of verse 4.

Notice the use of ellipsis in verse 4: "certain men … have secretly slipped in." While I prefer to keep the word order of the translation, sometimes it's not possible. In biblical order, the phrase, "whose condemnation was written about long ago," separates the subject "men" from its verb "slipped in" and is parallel with the following phrase, "they are godless men." So I pulled the phrase out, marked its place with an ellipsis, and placed it under "men."

Notice also what I did with the last two statements ("who …" and "deny …"). They were too long to fit on one line, and it might look like "who …"and "into …" were parallel phrases. This is why I put a little extra space between paragraphs, so wrapped lines still appear to be the same phrase. This is how you do it in a word processor.

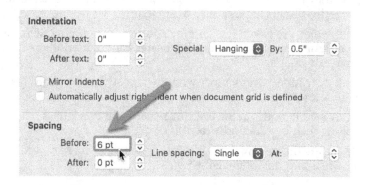

Description and Condemnation of the Troublemakers

1:5 Though you already know all this, I want to remind you that the Lord delivered his people out of Egypt, but later destroyed those who did not believe.

1:6 And the angels who did not keep their positions of authority but abandoned their own home—these he has kept in darkness, bound with everlasting chains for judgment on the great Day.

1:7 In a similar way, Sodom and Gomorrah and the surrounding towns gave themselves up to sexual immorality and perversion. They serve as an example of those who suffer the punishment of eternal fire.

1:8 In the very same way, these dreamers pollute their own bodies, reject authority and slander celestial beings.

1:9 But even the archangel Michael, when he was disputing with the devil about the body of Moses, did not dare to bring a slanderous accusation against him, but said, "The Lord rebuke you!"

1:10 Yet these men speak abusively against whatever they do not understand; and what things they do understand by instinct, like unreasoning animals—these are the very things that destroy them.

1:11 Woe to them! They have taken the way of Cain; they have rushed for profit into Balaam's error; they have been destroyed in Korah's rebellion.

1:12 These men are blemishes at your love feasts, eating with you without the slightest qualm—shepherds who feed only themselves. They are clouds without rain, blown along by the wind; autumn trees, without fruit and uprooted—twice dead.

1:13 They are wild waves of the sea, foaming up their shame; wandering stars, for whom blackest darkness has been reserved forever.

1:14 Enoch, the seventh from Adam, prophesied about these men: "See, the Lord is coming with thousands upon thousands of his holy ones

1:15 to judge everyone, and to convict all the ungodly of all the ungodly acts they have done in the ungodly way, and of all the harsh words ungodly sinners have spoken against him."

1:16 These men are grumblers and faultfinders; they follow their own evil desires; they boast about themselves and flatter others for their own advantage.

1:17 But, dear friends, remember what the apostles of our Lord Jesus Christ foretold.

1:18 They said to you, "In the last times there will be scoffers who will follow their own ungodly desires."

1:19 These are the men who divide you, who follow mere natural instincts and do not have the Spirit.

REPEAT OF STEPS 1 AND 2

What are we going to go with verses 5–19? Jude is describing the troublemakers and condemning them, and he is talking about other people who got in trouble. But verses 5–19 are probably too many verses to handle at one time, so what is a "phraser" to do?

Basically, we treat the section (vv. 5–19) as a new passage, and repeat Step 2 by dividing the section into its subsections. Read and reread verses 5–19 until the Bible tells you where the natural breaks are. Go ahead and do it now, and be sure to write a heading for each subsection. (Write the subsection headings in some form that differentiates them from the main section headings.) Then do Steps 3 and 4 for each subsection. My work is on the next few pages.

This is a lectionary from the thirteenth to fourteenth century, containing parts of Matthew and John. Photo provided by the Center for the Study of New Testament manuscripts (www.csntm.org) and used by permission of Institut für neutestamentliche Textforschung.

1:5   Though you already know all this,
       I want to remind you that

       {1} the Lord delivered <u>his people</u> out of Egypt,
       but later destroyed those who did not believe.

1:6   And
       {2} the <u>angels</u> who did not keep their positions of authority but
       abandoned their own home
            —these he has kept in darkness, bound with everlasting
            chains for judgment on the great Day.

1:7   In a similar way,
       {3} <u>Sodom and Gomorrah</u> and the surrounding towns gave them-
       selves up to sexual immorality and perversion.
            They serve as an example of those who suffer the punishment
            of eternal fire.

DESCRIPTION OF THE TROUBLEMAKERS

1:8   In the very same way,

       <u>these dreamers</u>

                {1} pollute their own bodies,
                {2} reject authority and
                {3} slander celestial beings.

1:9   But even the archangel <u>Michael</u>, →

                     when he was disputing with the devil about
                     the body of Moses,
            →   did not dare to bring a slanderous accusation against
                him,
            but said, "The Lord rebuke you!"

1:10   Yet

       <u>these men</u>

                {4} speak abusively against whatever they do not under-
                stand; and
                {5} what things they do understand by instinct, like unrea-
                soning animals—these are the very things that destroy them.

I see six subsections.

(1) Verses 5–7 spell out *three situations* that parallel the situation Jude is addressing: people delivered from Egypt; angels; Sodom and Gomorrah. The parallelism is that these three groups represent the fact that God always punishes sin. The first two groups are especially privileged people, and even they were punished. The implication is that these "certain men" in Jude's time will likewise be punished for their sins. I underlined the main words to make the three groups obvious.

Notice that I numbered the three points. As I said earlier, whenever I want to add something in my phrasing to the biblical text, I use curly brackets so I never confuse my scribblings with God's Word.

I could have broken verse 6b into two parts, showing that the angels {1} have been kept in darkness and {2} are bound with everlasting chains. But I divided it up the way I did because I like to see the symmetry of three groups of beings who each experienced punishment: the Israelites were destroyed; the angels are bound in darkness; the people of Sodom and Gomorrah were punished with fire. You may also have noticed that Jude likes triplets — a series of three items.

(2) In verses 8–10 I see Jude doing two things. First, he is describing the troublemakers, the "dreamers," and emphasizing how bad they are. In verse 8 he gives three characteristics, and two more in verse 10. But what is verse 9 about?

As you worked on your phrasing, hopefully you saw that verse 9 goes with the third description of the dreamers. They "slander celestial beings" (v. 8), but even the archangel Michael wouldn't slander Satan but simply said, "The Lord rebuke you!" (Don't go looking for this story in your Bible.)

Notice my use of space between verses 8–9 and between verses 9–10 to group different ideas. Notice also how underlining the most essential elements of the discussion helps you focus on the basics of the passage and not become lost in the details.

In verse 9 the subject ("Michael") and the main verb ("did not dare") are separated by the temporal clause ("when …"). The arrows are my way of hooking "Michael did not dare" together.

STATEMENT OF JUDGMENT

1:11   Woe to them!

      {1} They have taken the way of Cain;

      {2} they have rushed for profit into Balaam's error;

      {3} they have been destroyed in Korah's rebellion.

1:12   {4} These men are blemishes at your love feasts,

             eating with you without the slightest qualm

             —shepherds who feed only themselves.

      {5} They are clouds without rain, blown along by the wind;

      {6} autumn trees, without fruit and uprooted—twice dead.

1:13   {7} They are wild waves of the sea, foaming up their shame;

      {8} wandering stars, for whom blackest darkness has been reserved forever.

PROPHECIES

1:14   Enoch, the seventh from Adam, prophesied about these men:

      "See, the Lord is coming with thousands upon thousands of his holy ones

1:15   to judge everyone, and

          to convict all the ungodly

             of all the ungodly acts they have done in the ungodly way, and

             of all the harsh words ungodly sinners have spoken against him."

CONTINUED DESCRIPTIONS

1:16   {1} These men are grumblers and faultfinders;

      {2} they follow their own evil desires;

      {3} they boast about themselves and flatter others for their own advantage.

(3) The third subsection moves into Jude's statements of woe, his statement of judgment on these dreamers (vv. 11–13). Again, notice the numbering of the series.

(4) Jude continues by pointing out that Enoch prophesied about these men (vv. 14–15). Enoch didn't prophesy specifically that these specific men would come, but that the Lord would judge all the ungodly for what they said and did.

(5) In verse 16 Jude resumes his description of the dreamers. If you wanted to connect them back to verses 11–13, you could continue the numbering with {9}, {10}, and {11}. However, to emphasize Jude's uses of triplets, I numbered them {1}, {2}, and {3}.

The entrance to an archaeological site of ancient Corinth.

1:17   But, dear friends,

remember what the apostles of our Lord Jesus Christ foretold.

1:18   They said to you,

"In the last times there will be scoffers

who will follow their
own ungodly desires."

1:19   These are the men   who divide you,

who follow mere natural instincts and

do not have the Spirit.

Call to Perseverance

1:20   But you, dear friends, build yourselves up in your most holy faith and pray in the Holy Spirit.

1:21   Keep yourselves in God's love as you wait for the mercy of our Lord Jesus Christ to bring you to eternal life.

1:22   Be merciful to those who doubt;

1:23   snatch others from the fire and save them; to others show mercy, mixed with fear—hating even the clothing stained by corrupted flesh.

Doxology

1:24   To him who is able to keep you from falling and to present you before his glorious presence without fault and with great joy—

1:25   to the only God our Savior be glory, majesty, power and authority, through Jesus Christ our Lord, before all ages, now and forevermore!

(6) In the sixth subsection, Jude refers to the prophecies of the apostles, that evil people will come in the last days; the dreamers are the fulfillment of those prophecies (vv. 17–19). What is important to note, in all these descriptions, is that Jude is also condemning them, and that note of judgment is what ties verses 5–19 together.

Some people see a major break at verse 17, which starts with what appears to be a transitional phrase ("But, dear friends") and which addresses the church directly. It's good to have a sensitivity to this type of change. However, because the overall thrust of this subsection is to describe the dreamers as evil people and so continue the judgment theme, I prefer to keep verses 17–19 with the preceeding and not start a new subsection.

How do my subsections compare to yours? How about my headings? If you found a different structure, you may want to go back and reread the passage. But again let me stress that the point here is for *you* to study *your* own Bible and to let the Bible and the Holy Spirit talk to *you* about what it's saying.

Okay, we are almost done. Phrase verses 20–25 and then turn the page.

It's probably a good thing both Greek and English are written here. The Greek phrase literally reads, "Do not come near."

CALL TO PERSEVERANCE

1:20   But you, dear friends,

       {1} build yourselves up in your most holy faith and

       {2} pray in the Holy Spirit.

1:21   {3} Keep yourselves in God's love

          as you wait for the mercy of our Lord Jesus Christ to bring you to eternal life.

1:22   {4} Be merciful to those who doubt;

1:23   {5} snatch others from the fire and save them;

       {6} to others show mercy, mixed with fear

       {7}—hating even the clothing stained by corrupted flesh.

DOXOLOGY

1:24   To him

         who is able   to keep you from falling and

               to present you before his glorious presence

                   without fault and with great joy—

1:25   to the only God our Savior

    be glory, majesty, power and authority,

       through Jesus Christ our Lord,

       before all ages, now and forevermore!

    Amen.

Verses 20–23 are a call to perseverance in face of the opposition from the dreamers. This is the point to which Jude has been heading. He is not describing them just to condemn them; he wants his "dear friends" to see that the dreamers are evil people and to stand firm in the face of their opposition.

Verses 24–25 end with a glorious doxology. Did you notice the themes in the doxology that were introduced in verses 1–2? These themes of God's protection and the person of Jesus Christ serve as theological bookends to Jude's call for perseverance.

Let me again stress that while phrasing is not grammatical diagramming, recognizing conjunctions and dependent clauses goes a long way in helping us see the author's flow of thought.

Do you see what just happened? You took twenty-five verses that perhaps were not the easiest to understand, you discovered their main points, you identified several modifying assertions, and you can now see how they all relate to the main points. Welcome to the heart of Bible study!

You figure out what works for you. That's the point. There isn't always a right and wrong way to phrase. You can take this basic process and mold and shape it until it works for you, until you find a way that helps you see most clearly what the Bible is saying. And what works for me may not work for you. But take the time, experiment, and let the Bible teach you what it says and means.

One last point. One of the purposes of this book is to help you be able to read better commentaries. The kind of work we have been doing here is what you will find in them. Perhaps the commentary authors will not be as deliberate and obvious as I have been with phrasing, but this is precisely the type of work that underlies a good commentary. You will see an example of this in Phrasing 104 (chapter 24).

When I was pastoring, we had three people "sneak" into our church and try to deceive the people, especially the youth group. I preached a three-part sermon on Jude and laid down the groundwork by which we would either agree to disagree or else to ask people to leave. The links to the sermons are on the lesson page of the online class. If you listen to the sermons, you'll see how I put phrasing into practice.

CHAPTER 19

GREEK VERBS (ASPECT)

The genius of the Greek verbal system is not to define time, when something happens, but aspect, the kind of action.

VERBAL ASPECT

19.1   **Primacy of aspect**. In the Greek indicative, aspect is as significant as time, and sometimes is more important than time. This is why I have previously made statements like, "The aorist indicates an undefined action *normally occurring in the past.*" While a tense in the indicative may convey something about the time of the action, the aspect of the action is as important.

I introduced aspect in chapter 8, but I need to delve deeper into them. There are three aspects: undefined; continuous; perfective.

19.2   **Undefined ("perfective")**. The verb with an undefined aspect tells you nothing about the nature of the action of the verb. It doesn't say whether it was instantaneous, occurred over a period of time, or was repeated a number of times. It views the action from the outside as it were, as a whole, without interest in the precise nature of the action. This is the default aspect, used when the writer does not want to say anything special about the kind of action described by the verb. The meaning of this aspect will soon become clearer when we look at the other aspects.

Linguists are starting to use the term "perfective" for this aspect, which unfortunately is easily confused with the perfect tense. When I use this term with regard to aspect, I will always say "perfective aspect" as opposed to the "perfect tense."

The aorist and future tenses express undefined actions.

ἠλεήθην, ὅτι ἀγνοῶν ἐποίησα ἐν ἀπιστίᾳ

I was shown mercy because being ignorant I acted in unbelief

I was shown mercy since, being ignorant, I *had acted* in unbelief
(1 Tim 1:13).

Paul's acts of unbelief were many, but that is not what he wants to emphasize here. He uses the aorist ἐποίησα to simply state what was.

19.3 **Continuous ("imperfective").** The verb with a continuous aspect is describing an ongoing action. It looks at the action from the inside as it were, focusing on the progress of the action, not concerned about the beginning or the end.

Linguists are starting to use the term "imperfective" for this aspect in that it is incomplete, which unfortunately is easily confused with the imperfect tense. When I use this term with regard to aspect, I will always say "imperfective aspect" as opposed to the "imperfect tense."

The present.tense usually describes a continuous action; the imperfect tense always describes a continuous action.

οἱ ἀκολουθοῦντες ἔκραζον λέγοντες, ὡσαννὰ τῷ υἱῷ Δαυίδ

Those following were crying out saying Hosanna to the Son of David

Those that followed *were shouting*, "Hosanna to the Son of David!" *(Matt 21:9)*

As you would suspect from the meaning of the verb ἔκραζον, the aspectual significance of the verbal form (imperfect) is that they were shouting over and over.

ὁ ἀγαπῶν τὸν ἀδελφὸν αὐτοῦ ἐν τῷ φωτὶ μένει

the one who loves brother his in the light remains

The one who loves his brother *is living* in the light *(1 John 2:10)*.

μένει is present tense, and as you would suspect, "remaining" ("is living in") is a continuous action.

19.4 **Perfective ("combinative").** The verb with a perfective aspect describes a completed action whose ongoing effects are felt in the present (of the speaker). In a sense, it's the combination of the two prior aspects. The action is completed (undefined) and the state resulting from the action is ongoing (continuous).

The perfect tense describes perfective actions.

ἠλπίκαμεν ἐπὶ θεῷ ζῶντι, ὅς ἐστιν σωτὴρ πάντων ἀνθρώπων
we have hoped in God living who is savior of all people
We have placed our hope in the living God, who is the Savior of all people *(1 Tim 4:10).*

Paul and Timothy had already placed their hope in God, and as a result they were able daily to toil and strive.

Linguists are starting to use the term "combinative," suggesting a combination of the previous two aspects. Don't confuse "perfective" meaning "combinative" with the same term used for the perfect tense. I still prefer the old terminology. If you are in a class, be sure to ask your teacher whether you should use the old ("undefined, continuous, perfective") or new ("perfective, imperfective, combinative") terminology.

19.5   **Portrayal of Reality**. Remember that language does not describe what necessarily is but how the speaker choses to portray it (cf. 7.26). We define the indicative mood as the mood of fact, of what *is*, but that is a simplification. The indicative mood is used when the speaker wants to express something as reality, as fact; but we still lie in the indicative. It's an issue of what the speaker wants to express. There is not a necessary link between reality and my description of that reality.

NARROWBAND

19.6   Let's look at how these different aspects play out in describing real life events. "Narrowband" means that the action of the verb occurs over a relatively short period of time, relative, that is, to the context and the point the speaker is making.

19.7 **Instantaneous.** The action occurs relatively instantly.

Αἰνέα, ἰᾶταί σε Ἰησοῦς Χριστός.... καὶ εὐθέως ἀνέστη
Aeneas *heals* you Jesus Christ and immediately he got up
Aeneas, Jesus Christ *heals* you.... And immediately he got up
(*Acts 9:34*).

Peter uses the present tense of ἰᾶται to describe something that happened immediately.

19.8 **Progressive.** The action occurs over a period of time. The length of the time is determined by context.

εἰς τοῦτο γὰρ κοπιῶμεν καὶ ἀγωνιζόμεθα
into this for *we are toiling* and *we are struggling*
for with respect to this reason *we are toiling* and *struggling*
(*1 Tim 4:10*)

Paul and his team continually toiled and struggled day after day for the gospel.

19.9 **Ingressive** means that the emphasis is on the beginning of an action. Sometimes the meaning of the verb or the context is enough to show that the action has begun; other times the translators will add in a word like "began" to make it clear.

ἐξαλλόμενος ἔστη καὶ περιεπάτει καὶ εἰσῆλθεν σὺν αὐτοῖς
jumping up he stood and *walk around* and entered with them

εἰς τὸ ἱερὸν
into the temple
NRSV: Jumping up, he stood and *began to walk*, and he entered the temple with them (*Acts 3:8*).

The point is not that he jumped, stood, walked, and entered. It's that he jumped up to a standing position, and began to walk (showing his full recovery), and then entered the temple.

BROADBAND

19.10 "Broadband" is used of actions occurring over a longer period of time, including actions that have nothing to do with time. As with "narrowband," "longer" is relative to the point the speaker is making.

19.11 Iterative. This type of action is continual in that it happens over a period of time; however, it does not happen continually but rather repeatedly.

ἐγὼ μὲν ὑμᾶς βαπτίζω ἐν ὕδατι εἰς μετάνοιαν
I — you *baptize* in water for repentance
I *baptize* you in water for repentance *(Matt 3:11)*.

John was not constantly baptizing, but he baptized (βαπτίζω is present tense) people one at a time, over and over.

19.12 Customary. These actions occur on a regular basis.

τοιαύταις παραβολαῖς πολλαῖς ἐλάλει   αὐτοῖς τὸν λόγον
such   parables   many   *he was speaking* to them the word
NIV: With many similar parables *Jesus spoke* the word to them
(Mark 4:33).

It was Jesus' custom to speak in parables. Mark is not thinking of any one particular speaking event, but rather of what Jesus did on a regular basis.

19.13 Gnomic. This action is timeless ("gnomic" denotes a general aphorism). The speaker is not thinking of any specific event, but of an action that is always true.

πᾶς ὁ ἀρνούμενος τὸν υἱὸν οὐδὲ τὸν πατέρα ἔχει
Each one who denies the Son   not   the Father   *has*
No one who denies the Son *has* the Father *(1 John 2:23)*.

It's always true that anyone who denies allegiance to Jesus does not have (ἔχει is present tense) the Father. John is not thinking of any one particular act of denial; he is stating an axiomatic truth.

19.14 In the following chapters, you will see how this issue of aspect plays itself out in the different tenses and moods.

AKTIONSART

19.15 Meaning is not conveyed only by aspect. There are many different parts that make up the whole, so to speak. Aktionsart (yes, it's a German word) is a way of discussing all these different parts.

19.16 Aktionsart is the full meaning of a word in context, made up of these and perhaps other considerations:

- Lexical meaning of the word
- Tense (present, future, imperfect, aorist, perfect)
- Aspect (undefined, continuous, perfective)
- Grammar
- Context (e.g., narrative, poetry)

19.17 When you are exegeting a verse and studying a particular verb, that verb will always have a context that affects its meaning. For example, if you saw the verb "weep," does the fact that the author might use a continuous verbal form surprise you? No. The author could have used a continuous or an undefined form since the meaning of the word is inherently continuous. However, the continuous aspect fits the actual meaning of the verb, assuming of course that the speaker wants to emphasize the ongoing nature of this particular act of weeping.

So as you are studying a verb, don't look just for aspect. Language uses a plethora of tools to convey meaning, and aspect is just one part, albeit an important part.

19.18 How do you know if a particular verb indicates an action that is undefined, continuous, or perfective? How do you know if a verb is instantaneous or gnomic? That is a function of the tense of the verb, the meaning of the verb, and its context. I will delve into these mysteries in the next chapter.

CHAPTER 20

GREEK VERBS (TENSE)

Now that you have a feel for aspect, we can delve into the tenses and see how they combine time and aspect. While a tense may have a general meaning, you'll discover that it may have many nuances and variations.

20.1   This chart is the key to this chapter, showing the relationship between the tenses and aspects. You should memorize it (but not the Greek example), and I will explain it throughout this chapter.

tense	time (normally)	aspect	example
Present	present	continuous	λύω
Future	future	undefined	λύσω
Aorist	past	undefined	ἔλυσα
Imperfect	past	continuous	ἔλυον
Perfect	past and present	perfective	λέλυκα

20.2   What follows are some of the more common ways in which tenses and aspects work together. The primary function of these examples is to give you a feel for the variety of usages and to see why so much of translation is interpretive and therefore why translations are often different.

Remember the different ways that aspects function that we saw in the last chapter:

■ Instantaneous	happens immediately
■ Progressive	happens over a period of time
■ Ingressive	emphasis is on the beginning of the action
■ Iterative	happens repeatedly
■ Customary	happens on a regular basis, not thinking of any one instance
■ Gnomic	happens without any time constraints

20.3   I will not show you all the usages; there are too many. But I have picked the common usages to give you a feel for the tense. This means you will come across passages in the Bible that illustrate one of those omitted uses. There are Greek grammars that discuss all the uses (such as Daniel Wallace's *The Basics of New Testament Syntax*, and his larger *Greek Grammar Beyond the Basics*).

20.4   How do translators decide which of these usages is correct in any one instance? It's easier than you may think, but it does involve some "linguistic sensitivity," otherwise known as "interpretation." We look at the context and especially the meaning of the word, and make a decision. But learning a language is both a science (i.e., there are rules to follow) and an art. It's the art side that takes years to develop, and it's the art side that ultimately enables the translator to make these types of decisions.

20.5   Let's take a break and talk about humility. I have heard too many people who know too little Greek abuse the information in the rest of the chapter. So here are three principles.

■ You don't know enough Greek to say a verbal form has a certain nuance if you can't find the same thing being said in a commentary. What you will know is enough Greek to be able understand the nuances of the different translations.

■ You don't know enough Greek to say that a standard commentary is wrong if you can't find your opinion voiced in another commentary. What you will know is enough Greek to be able to follow a commentary's discussion.

- You don't know enough Greek to say that a translation is wrong. I have never seen a random translation in a Bible that was not a possible interpretation. It doesn't mean you have to agree with a certain translation. You can certainly prefer one translation's interpretive position over another, but you don't know enough to say that one translation is necessarily wrong.

It's not a little knowledge that is dangerous. It is a lack of humility that is dangerous.

PRESENT

20.6   In 8.17 we saw that the present tense describes an action normally occuring in the present time; its aspect covers the gamut from instantaneous to gnomic.

NARROWBAND

20.7   **Instantaneous**. Sometimes a Greek present describes an action that happens immediately. In other words, it has no discernable continuous nature.

τέκνον, ἀφίενταί   σου αἱ ἁμαρτίαι
child   *they are forgiven* your   the sins
My son, your sins *are forgiven* (Mark 2:5).

Once Jesus made the pronouncement, the sins were instantly forgiven.

20.8   **Progressive**. The Greek present can describe an ongoing action, even though in real time the action does not last very long. This is the default category for the present tense.

ἐὰν γὰρ προσεύχωμαι γλώσσῃ, τὸ πνεῦμά μου προσεύχεται
if   for   I am praying   tongue,   the spirit   my   *is praying*
ESV: For if I pray in a tongue, my spirit *prays* (1 Cor 14:14).

The prayer is an ongoing action, but probably for a short time.

20.9 **Iterative**. Some actions occur repeatedly.

πολλάκις   γὰρ   πίπτει   εἰς   τὸ πῦρ
often   for   *he falls*   into   the fire

For often *he falls* into the fire (*Matt 17:15*).

The boy is not constantly falling into the fire (an impossible notion), but he falls in time and time again.

20.10 **Customary**. Actions can occur regularly but not necessarily constantly.

νηστεύω   δὶς   τοῦ σαββάτου
I fast   twice   the week

I *customarily fast* twice a week (*Luke 18:12*).
NIV: I fast twice a week.

It's not that he fasts constantly, but that this is his regular habit.

20.11 **Gnomic**. The Greek present tense can express a timeless fact.

ἱλαρὸν   δότην   ἀγαπᾷ   ὁ θεός
cheerful   giver   *he loves*   the God

God loves a cheerful giver (*2 Cor 9:7*).

Paul is not thinking of any one specific response of love, but rather of God's constant response to cheerful giving.

20.12* **Historical**. Because the Greek verb system views time as secondary to aspect, it's possible for the Greek present tense to refer to an action that occurs in the past. The idea is to make the telling of the past event more vivid by using the present tense. We have the same construction in English, but the Greeks used it much more than we do, so this usage is often translated with the past tense.

βλέπει   τὸν Ἰησοῦν   ἐρχόμενον   πρὸς   αὐτόν
he sees   the Jesus   coming   to   him

ESV: The next day he *saw* Jesus coming toward him (*John 1:29*)

As John is recounting the event, the time frame was past, but using the present βλέπει makes the story more vivid.

20.13* **Futuristic.** The present tense can also refer to a future event, and the fact that it is present tense emphasizes the immediacy or certainty of the event.

Χριστὸς ἐγερθεὶς   ἐκ νεκρῶν οὐκέτι ἀποθνῄσκει
Christ   having been raised from dead   never   *dies*
NASB: Christ, having been raised from the dead, *is* never *to die* again *(Rom 6:9)*.
NRSV: We know that Christ, being raised from the dead, *will* never *die* again.

Paul is convinced that Christ will never die, not now nor in the future.

FUTURE

20.14 Of all the Greek tenses, the future has the strongest emphasis on time, describing an action that will occur in the future. As a general rule, the future is translated with the undefined aspect ("I will eat") rather than the continuous ("I will be eating").

20.15 **Predictive.** In 8.18 we saw that the basic use of the future is to describe something that will happen in the future.

ὁ ἐναρξάμενος ἐν ὑμῖν ἔργον ἀγαθὸν ἐπιτελέσει
the one beginning in you   work   good   *will complete*
He who began a good work in you *will bring it to completion* *(Phil 1:6)*.

20.16 **Imperatival.** As in English, the Greek future can express a command.

ἀγαπήσεις   κύριον τὸν θεόν σου
you will love Lord   the God   your
ESV: You shall love the Lord your God *(Matt 22:37)*.
NET: Love the Lord your God.

Because we use the future in English the same way, this usage is easy to understand.

20.17 Gnomic. The future can state that a generic event will occur. It does not say that a particular occurrence is in mind, but that such events do occur.

οὐκ ἐπ᾽ ἄρτῳ μόνῳ ζήσεται ὁ ἄνθρωπος
not on bread alone *will live* man

NASB: Man *shall* not *live* on bread alone *(Matt 4:4)*.
NRSV: One *does* not *live* by bread alone.

Jesus is not thinking of one particular meal, but of how life should be lived.

AORIST

20.18 The aorist tense describes an action normally occuring in the past time; its aspect is always undefined (8.20). Remember that the aorist is the default past-time tense; there may be no real significance to the fact that a particular verb is aorist other than time.[1]

20.19 Constative. The aorist looks at an action as a whole and does not necessarily tell us anything about the precise nature of the action. This is the default category for the aorist tense.

ἐνέβη εἰς τὸ πλοῖον καὶ ἦλθεν εἰς τὰ ὅρια Μαγαδάν
he got into the boat and *he went* into the region of Magadan

He got into the boat and *went* to the region of Magadan *(Matt 15:39)*.

Even though getting into the boat and traveling across the Sea certainly was a continuous action (lots of rowing or working with the sails), it was not important for Matthew to convey this emphasis, so he uses the aorist.

---

[1] There is meaning in the fact that a verb is aorist, but it's often so subtle a nuance that for now you should view it as the default past tense and let it go at that.

20.20 **Ingressive.** The aorist can place emphasis on the beginning of an action.

ὁ   δὲ βασιλεὺς ὠργίσθη
the but king   *he was angry*
NLT: Then the king *became furious (Matt 22:7).*
RSV: The king *was angry.*

This is a matter of interpretation, but the NLT thinks that the emphasis was on the fact that he started to get angry ("became"), not the simple fact that he was angry.

20.21 **Gnomic.** The aorist can be used to describe a timeless truth. These are often translated with the English present tense. This use of the aorist is rare; Greek tends to use the present tense to express the gnomic idea.

ἐξηράνθη ὁ χόρτος καὶ τὸ ἄνθος ἐξέπεσεν
withered   the grass   and the flower   *fell off*
NET: The grass *withers* and the flower *falls off (1 Pet 1:24).*

Peter is not thinking of any one event in which the grass and flowers die, but rather of the timeless truth that this is what happens.

20.22 **Punctiliar.** One of the primary areas of confusion in Greek exegesis comes when people confuse the Greek aorist with the English punctiliar aspect. The English punctiliar describes an action that occurs in a single point of time. "The tidal wave *hit* the boat." However, the Greek aorist is not necessarily punctiliar. It tells you nothing about the action of the verb other than it happened.

It is interesting that Luke's version of Jesus' statement on discipleship is a little different from Mark's. He says,

> If anyone wishes to come after me, let him deny himself and *take up* his cross *daily*, and follow me *(Luke 9:23).*

Luke includes the adverb "daily" to emphasize that the action of "taking up" occurs every day, even though the verb is aorist.

Does this contradict the Markan account (Mark 8:34) that simply says "take up" using the aorist? No. Both Mark and Luke use the same undefined aspect—the aorist—when saying "take up." The verb does not specify the nature of the action; it merely says it should occur. But Luke includes the adverb "daily" to clarify that this action is a daily action. He could have just as easily used the continuous aspect for "take up" and arrived at the same meaning.

Part of the misconception surrounding the aorist and its aspect is because it *can* be used to describe a punctiliar action. However, such a verb is punctiliar not because it is an aorist but because of the context and the meaning of the word. You will find this mistake in many commentaries, so be careful.

IMPERFECT

20.23 In 8.21 we saw that the imperfect tense describes an action normally occuring in the past time; its aspect is always continuous.

NARROWBAND

20.24 **Progressive**. The imperfect tense describes an ongoing action that generally happened in the past. This is the default category for the imperfect.

ἐδίδασκεν   τοὺς μαθητὰς αὐτοῦ
He was teaching   the disciples   his
NIV: *He was teaching* his disciples *(Mark 9:31)*.
KJV: *He taught* his disciples.

"Teaching" is by definition an ongoing activity.

20.25 **Ingressive**. The imperfect tense can also place emphasis on the beginning of the action.

ἄγγελοι προσῆλθον καὶ διηκόνουν   αὐτῷ
angels   *they came*   *and*   *they were ministering*   *to him*
NASB: Angels came and *began to minister* to Him *(Matt 4:11)*.
NIV: Angels came and *attended* him.

It's an exegetical decision as to whether Matthew's emphasis is on the angels ministering to Jesus over a period of time, or whether Matthew emphasizes the beginning of the action, that they began to minister.

20.26 Iterative. Some continuous actions do not occur constantly but rather repetitively.

ἤρχοντο   πρὸς αὐτὸν καὶ ἔλεγον,   χαῖρε
They were coming to   him   and *they were saying* Hail!
NRSV: They kept coming up to him, saying, "Hail" (John 19:3).
NIV: (They) *went up* to him *again and again, saying, "Hail."*
NASB: They repeatedly came up to Him and *said,* "Hail."

The imperfect makes it explicit that they taunted our Lord over and over.

20.27 Customary. Other actions occur regularly, such as expressed by the English "used to."

Κατὰ δὲ ἑορτὴν ἀπέλυεν   αὐτοῖς ἕνα   δέσμιον
at   now feast   *he was releasing* for them one   prisoner
NASB: Now at *the Passover* feast *he used to release* for them *any* one prisoner *(Mark 15:6).*
NET: During the feast *it was customary to release* one prisoner to the people.
NIV: Now *it was the custom* at the festival *to release* a prisoner.
KJV: Now at that feast he *released* unto them one prisoner.

20.28* The imperfect can describe what a person wishes to do (**voluntative**), tries to do (**conative**), or almost does (**tendential**). Often it is difficult to tell the difference between these three, and, as always, context is the guide.

ηὐχόμην   γὰρ ἀνάθεμα εἶναι αὐτὸς ἐγώ
I was wishing for curse   to be   myself I
NASB: For *I could wish* that I myself were accursed *(Rom 9:3).*
NLT: I would be willing to be forever cursed.

ἐδίωκον   τὴν ἐκκλησίαν τοῦ θεοῦ καὶ ἐπόρθουν   αὐτήν
I was persecuting the church   of God   and *I was destroying* it
NASB: I *used to persecute* the church of God ... and *tried to destroy* it *(Gal 1:13).*

ESV: I *persecuted* the church of God … and *tried to destroy* it.

NRSV: I *was violently persecuting* the church of God and *was trying to destroy* it

ὁ   δὲ Ἰωάννης διεκώλυεν   αὐτόν
the but John   *he was preventing* him

NIV: But John *tried to deter* him (*Matt 3:14*).

ESV: John *would have prevented* him.

PERFECT

20.29 In 8.23 we saw that the perfect tense describes a completed action, with the results of that action felt in the present (of the speaker).

20.30 **Consummative**. Sometimes the emphasis is on the fact that the action was completed.

ἡ ἀγάπη τοῦ θεοῦ ἐκκέχυται   ἐν ταῖς καρδίαις ἡμῶν
the love of the God *has been poured* in the hearts   of us

ESV: God's love *has been poured* into our hearts (*Rom 5:5*).

KJV: The love of God *is shed abroad* in our hearts.

While the effects of that love are still felt by Paul, the context requires that the emphasis is on the accomplished fact that the love has in fact been poured out. The KJV disagrees.

20.31 **Intensive**. Other times the emphasis is on the continuing effect of the past action and is generally translated with the English present.

ἄνθρωπε, ἀφέωνταί   σοι αἱ ἁμαρτίαι σου
man   *have been forgiven* to you the sins   your

ESV: Man, your sins *are forgiven* you (*Luke 5:20*).

The forgiveness is an accomplished fact, but contextually the emphasis is on the man's current state of being forgiven, as evidenced by his getting up and walking out of the house.

SUMMARY

20.32 Summary chart

	Present	Future	Aorist	Imperfect	Perfect
Narrowband					
Instantaneous	✓		(punctiliar)		
Constative			✓		
Progressive	✓			✓	
Ingressive	✓		✓	✓	
Broadband					
Iterative	✓			✓	
Customary	✓			✓	
Gnomic	✓	✓	✓		
Consummative					✓
Intensive					✓
Predictive		✓			
Imperatival		✓			
Advanced uses					
Historical*	✓				
Futuristic*	✓				
Voluntative*				✓	
Conative*				✓	
Tendential*				✓	

CHAPTER 21

PHRASING 103

By now you are experienced in English phrasing, and in doing so you are learning how to understand the better commentaries. But Greek answers many mysteries in the phrasing world, and it's time to jump into Greek phrasing.

21.1   Be sure to work through the exercises for this chapter in the online class. It's crucial to develop the right habits in using Greek-English interlinears, and so I have made a number of screencasts where you can watch me walk through the verses.

21.2   Also, be patient with yourself. Now that we are moving into the Greek text, you are going to see things that will not make sense to you. Some of them will be explained in the remaining chapters of this book, but you will have to skip others since no approach to first and second year Greek is able to teach you everything.

21.3   There are two ways to include Greek into phrasing. The first method, which I have cleverly named "Method 1," is what you will learn in this chapter, Phrasing 103. "Method 2" is in chapter 24, Phrasing 104. Method 1 is for students who are still a little uncomfortable with Greek and have not been learning the vocabulary in this book. Method 2 is for those of you who are more adventurous and have been learning the vocabulary. I suspect that eventually most of you will graduate to Method 2.

21.4   In this chapter we are going to work with Titus. You have already phrased three passages in Phrasing 102, and so we are going to start with those phrasings and take the next step into Greek. I will walk through 1:1–4 in the text, and 2:11–14 and 3:1–7 are your homework.

21.5   There are two things we are looking for as we study the Greek.

1. Did I do my English phrasing right? My guess is that most of the time you will have phrased properly, and the Greek will not add much to your understanding apart from identifying significant Greek vocabulary. And yet at times the Greek will correct your phrasing.

2. The Greek should also help with uncertainty. There will be times when you are phrasing in English and you are not sure how to line up the phrases. Hopefully, the Greek will help in the vast majority of these situations.

21.6   The first step is to set up your computer. You, of course, are welcome to do it any way that you find helpful, but here is what I do.

■ I have my word processor to the left (I am using Microsoft Word) and Accordance on the right. You can download the English (and Greek) text for this chapter from the online lesson.

■ One pane of Accordance is my translation and the other is a Greek interlinear (not reverse interlinear). I show the key number, lexical form, and an English translation. As you will see, this allows for several levels of double checking.

■ I also make sure the Instant Details windows is showing along the bottom so I can see parsing information.

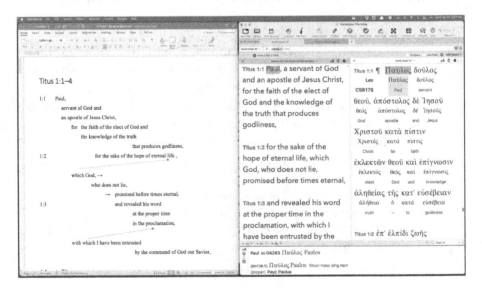

21.7 Here is the English phrasing of the salutation in Titus 1:1–2a that we did in Phrasing 102 in the video lesson.

1:1   Paul,

           a servant of God and

           an apostle of Jesus Christ,

                for   the faith of the elect of God and

                     the knowledge of the truth

                                that produces godliness,

1:2   for   the sake of the hope of eternal life,

21.8 Let's start our double checking. As you move the mouse over the English, you will see that "Paul" translates Παῦλος, and "servant" (δοῦλος) and "apostle" (ἀπόστολος) translate two nouns in the same case, number, and gender as Παῦλος. The Greek words δοῦλος and ἀπόστολος are therefore in apposition to to Παῦλος. This confirms lines 2 and 3 of the phrasing.

This is why I show the English in the interlinear. It confirms that I am mousing over the right Greek word.

At this point you need to decide if remembering any of these Greek words is important for your Bible study. Whereas major connectors are always important, other words are a matter of personal choice. If they are important, then put them into the phrasing with curly brackets rather than parentheses or square brackets, since both of these appear in some English and Greek texts.

1:1   Paul {Παῦλος},

           a servant {δοῦλος} of God and

           an apostle {ἀπόστολος} of Jesus Christ,

When using Greek, I indent under the Greek word (Παῦλος) and not the English (Paul). However, sometimes the page isn't wide enough, so I will put the line under the English from time to time.

21.9 "For" translates the preposition κατά, and from the English it looks like there are two objects of κατά. The nouns πίστιν and ἐπίγνωσιν are both accusatives, confirming this assumption.

for {κατά}   the faith {πίστιν} of the elect of God and

the knowledge {ἐπίγνωσιν} of the truth

When the text is simply listing a series like "one, two, and three," I tend to not make a big deal about the conjunction and leave it at the end of the line after the preceeding word. But when the conjunction joins two significant ideas, I might put the conjunction on its own line and indent it a little.

for {κατά}   the faith {πίστιν} of the elect of God

and

the knowledge {ἐπίγνωσιν} of the truth

This is totally a matter of choice depending on whether it helps you see the structure of the passage or not.

21.10 This introduces a challenge, and how you deal with it is a matter of personal preference. When I copy and paste the Greek, I am copying the inflected form (πίστιν). If you are okay with that, then fine. But if you want the lexical form (πίστις), which would be helpful for word studies, the easiest way is to simply type it. I showed you in lesson 2 in the online course how to switch to a Greek keyboard on your computer.

In Accordance, if you don't want to type the lexical form, you could always triple click on the inflected form and bring up a Greek dictionary. It will start with the lexical form, which you can then copy.

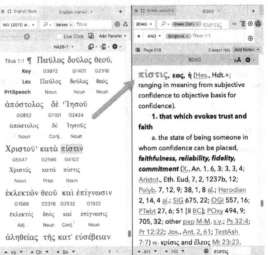

In Logos, you can copy the interlinear entry and paste it into your word processor. Then you would copy the lexical form and paste that into your phrasing.

πίστιν

πίστις

or faith

In The Bible Study App (OliveTree), you can click on the inflected word and copy the lexical form from the popup window.

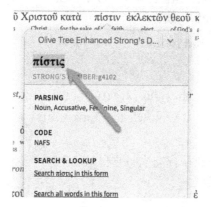

I think "faith" refers to coming to faith in Jesus (conversion), and "knowledge" refers more to growing in our relationship with Jesus (sanctification). The two halves create a nice description of the Christian life. Paul wasn't concerned only with evangelism but also with spiritual growth.

21.11 So what is the relationship between "that" and the preceding? At first glance you might think "that" represents a relative pronoun, but actually it is the article ὁ (τῆς). You should also have noticed that what follows it is a prepositional phrase, κατ᾽ εὐσέβειαν. In this situation, the article is telling you that the prepositional phrase is acting as an attributive (second attributive position). What does it modify? The article is genitive singular feminine, so start moving to the left and see the first eligible word.

It is ἀληθείας, so it is the truth that should lead to godliness.

> for {κατά}   the faith {πίστιν} of the elect of God and
>   the knowledge {ἐπίγνωσιν} of the truth {ἀληθείας}
>
>   ————————————————————————————▶
>
> that {τῆς} leads to godliness,

21.12 The first phrase in verse 2 is a bit troublesome: "in the hope of eternal life." It is a prepositional phrase {ἐπί} and can therefore be adverbial or attributive. In other words, the Greek doesn't really help except that it allows you some flexibility of interpretation.

One option is that it modifies εὐσέβειαν, giving the result of true godliness.

> for {κατά}   the faith {πίστιν} of the elect of God and
>   the knowledge {ἐπίγνωσιν} of the truth {ἀληθείας}
>
>   ————————————————————————————▶
>
> that {τῆς} leads to godliness {εὐσέβειαν},

1:2   in {ἐπ'} the hope of eternal life.

Another option is that it is the result of our πίστιν and ἐπίγνωσιν.

21.13 As you look at the Greek of the "which" clause in verse 2b, you see that the order of the Greek is quite a bit different from English, but it is good Greek nonetheless.

> which (τῆς) God, →
>   who does not lie,
>   → promised before times eternal,

You remember that I use arrows when the verb is separated from its subject. The Greek construction ἐπηγγείλατο ὁ ἀψευδὴς θεὸς is verb, article, modifier, noun—the standard order of Greek words with the modifier ἀψευδής being in the first attributive position.

21.14 We now come to the end of the first third of the salutation. The Greek verb ἐπηγγείλατο is parallel with ἐφανέρωσεν, and πρὸ χρόνων αἰωνίων is parallel with καιροῖς ἰδίοις. We also learn that the "truth" that was revealed is τὸν λόγον αὐτοῦ.

which (τῆς) God, →

who does not lie,

→ promised {ἐπηγγείλατο} before times eternal,

1:3 and revealed {ἐφανέρωσεν} his word {λόγον}

21.15 When was it revealed? καιροῖς ἰδίοις. How was it revealed? ἐν κηρύγματι

1:3 and revealed his word {λόγον}

at the proper time {καιροῖς ἰδίοις}

in the proclamation {ἐν κηρύγματι},

While Paul does not explicitly specify what was proclaimed, you understand contextually that it was τὸν λόγον αὐτοῦ, and Paul will add that this was the content of his apostolic ministry.

21.16 We now find our first relative pronoun. How do you find a pronoun's antecedent? Same gender and number. Always put the Greek pronoun and its antecedent into your phrasing. If you need to pull your phrasing to the left, then connect the two with an arrow.

in the proclamation {ἐν κηρύγματι},

with which {ὃ} I have been entrusted

by {κατ'} the command of God our Savior,

21.17 Moving to the second part of the salutation, we find that our English phrasing is accurate.

1:4 to Titus,

a true son in a common faith:

21.18 Now we arrive at the greeting. Did you see that there is one preposition (ἀπὸ) with two objects?

> Grace {χάρις} and peace {εἰρήνη} from {ἀπὸ}
>> God the Father and
>> Christ Jesus our Savior.

This point is advanced Greek, but it is significant that there is one preposition controlling the two objects. It is one of the interesting indicators of how Paul thinks of God the Father and God the Son. The single preposition does not mean the two members of the Godhead are identical, but it does show that Paul thought of them as working so closely in unison that he only needs to use one preposition. If they were totally different, we would have expected the preposition to be repeated.

21.19 So that's it. We have used Greek to confirm and correct our English phrasing, and we have also used Greek where we weren't quite sure about some of the relationships between clauses.

21.20 If you want to use a paper resource like one of my interlinears, they work well. You will have to type the Greek in yourself, or do your phrasing on paper.

21.21 Let me repeat. You should not be able to do everything I did in this chapter on your own. Some of these issues are well beyond even second year Greek. But you should have been able to follow what I did and it should have made sense. This is what will happen in the commentaries. What they discuss may sound foreign, but you should be able to follow their discussion and make sense of the exegesis.

21.22 So much for Method 1, Phrasing 103. In Phrasing 104, we will include all of the Greek words in the phrasing and also learn about semantic tags.

1:1   Paul {Παῦλος},

        a servant {δοῦλος} of God and
        an apostle {ἀπόστολος} of Jesus Christ,

    for {κατά} the faith {πίστιν} of the elect of God and
        the knowledge {ἐπίγνωσιν} of the truth {ἀληθείας}

1:2   in {ἐπ'} the hope of eternal life {ζωῆς}.

  which (τῆς) God, →
      who does not lie,
       → promised {ἐπηγγείλατο} before times eternal,
1:3   and revealed {ἐφανέρωσεν} his word {λόγον}
          at the proper time {καιροῖς ἰδίοις}
          in the proclamation {ἐν κηρύγματι},

  with which {ὃ} I have been entrusted

        by the command of God our Savior,

1:4 to Titus,
    a true son in a common faith:

  Grace {χάρις} and peace {εἰρήνη} from {ἀπὸ} God the Father and
                   Christ Jesus our Savior.

CHAPTER 22

GREEK VERBS (MOODS)

Now it's time to look at the nonindicative moods. I'll cover participles in chapter 23.

TIME AND ASPECT

22.1 **Aspect**. A Greek verb has time significance only in the indicative. The only significance that a verb has in the other moods is one of aspect.

22.2 I have made this point several times, but it is so important that I want to repeat it one more time.

- Forms built on the *aorist* tense stem indicate an *undefined* action.

- Forms built on the *present* tense stem indicate a *continuous* action.

- Forms built on the *perfect* tense stem indicate a *perfective* action: a completed action with its effects felt in the present (of the speaker).

22.3 It's difficult to bring the sense of the continuous into the translation of a nonindicative mood. Sometimes translators add in words like "continue" but only rarely. As a result, the nonindicative moods are often under-translated.

MOOD

22.4 You remember that the mood of a verb defines its relationship to reality. We have been looking primarily at the indicative mood. There are two other moods, the subjunctive and imperative, but we will start by reviewing the indicative.

INDICATIVE

22.5   We saw in 9.2 that the indicative mood is the mood of reality. When you want to state what is—or at least what you want to portray as being real—you use the indicative mood.

22.6   **Declarative.** In 8.37, we saw that the simplest use of the indicative is to make a statement, a declaration.

> ὑπερεπλεόνασεν   δὲ   ἡ χάρις   τοῦ κυρίου   ἡμῶν
> *completely overflowed*   and   the grace   of Lord   our
>
> And the grace of our Lord *completely overflowed* (1 Tim 1:14).

22.7   **Interrogative.** The indicative is also used to ask a question. There is no difference in the form of the verb when asking a question; it's a matter of context, the editorial help of punctuation, and sometimes the presence of an interrogative word, such as "where," "why," who," etc.

> ποῦ   ἐστιν   ὁ τεχθεὶς   βασιλεὺς   τῶν Ἰουδαίων;
> where   *is*   the one born   king   of the Jews
>
> Where *is* the one who is born king of the Jews? *(Matt 2:2)*

SUBJUNCTIVE

22.8   **Purpose.** In 9.3 we saw that the subjunctive is frequently used in statements of purpose. The purpose clause is often introduced with ἵνα.

> ἐπηρώτησαν αὐτὸν ...   ἵνα   κατηγορήσωσιν   αὐτοῦ
> they questioned   him   in order that   *they might accuse*   him
>
> NET: They asked Jesus ... so that *they could accuse* him *(Matt 12:10)*.
> NIV: Looking for a reason to bring charges against Jesus, they asked him.

His enemies asked Jesus the question for the purpose of accusing him. It wasn't an honest question.

22.9 Conditional. In 9.4 we saw that the subjunctive can be used to express a condition. Sometimes the author is thinking of a specific event in the future, and the suggestion is that it probably will happen. This is called a "**future more probable**" condition.

ταῦτά   σοι   πάντα δώσω, ἐὰν πεσὼν   προσκυνήσῃς μοι
these things to you all   I will give if   falling down *you worship*   me

I will give you all these things, if you will fall down and *worship* me *(Matt 4:9)*.

It is interesting that Satan used this form of the conditional sentence. Surely he knew Jesus would not accept the offer.

Other times the speaker is not thinking of any specific event but of an action in general. This is a "**present general**" condition.

ἐάν τις   περιπατῇ ἐν τῇ ἡμέρᾳ, οὐ   προσκόπτει
if   anyone *walks*   in the day   not   he stumbles

Anyone who *walks* in the daytime *does* not *stumble* (John 11:9).

22.10 Indefinite. When the word ἄν (by itself or in combination with another word such as ἐάν) makes a statement more general, the verb will be in the subjunctive.

ὃς δ' ἂν φονεύσῃ, ἔνοχος ἔσται τῇ κρίσει
who and *ever* *murders*   liable   will be to judgment.

Whoever murders will be liable to judgment *(Matt 5:21)*.

Jesus is not thinking of any one event in particular, but rather is making a general statement that applies to anyone who murders.

22.11 Hortatory. A subjunctive in the first person (singular or plural) can be used as an exhortation. The translator will usually have added words such as "let us."

τὸ δὲ καλὸν ποιοῦντες μὴ ἐγκακῶμεν
the and good   doing   not *let us get tired*

Let us not *get tired* of doing good *(Gal 6:9)*.

22.12 Deliberative. The subjunctive can also be used to express a question in which the answer is in doubt, or the question is rhetorical.

θέλεις οὖν ἀπελθόντες συλλέξωμεν αὐτά;
do you wish so going *pull up* them
CSB: So, do you want us to go and *pull* them *up*? *(Matt 13:28)*.

The servants were not sure what their master wanted them to do.

IMPERATIVE

22.13 Command. As we saw in 9.5, the imperative mood is used when a verb expresses a command. It can be either second or third person.

ἀκολούθει μοι
you follow me
Follow me! *(Mark 2:14)*

μὴ οὖν βασιλευέτω ἡ ἁμαρτία ἐν τῷ θνητῷ ὑμῶν σώματι
not therefore *let reign* sin in mortal your body
Therefore, *do* not *let* sin reign in your mortal body *(Rom 6:12)*.

22.14 Entreaty. The imperative may also express a request, as is appropriate when addressing a superior, such as God.

κύριε, δίδαξον ἡμᾶς προσεύχεσθαι
Lord *you teach* us to pray
Lord, *teach* us to pray *(Luke 11:1)*.

Obviously, the disciples were not able to command Jesus to do anything, but when you make a request of a superior, you still use the imperative form of the verb.

ἐλθέτω ἡ βασιλεία σου· γενηθήτω τὸ θέλημά σου
let come the kingdom your *let be* the will your
NASB and most translations: Your kingdom *come*, your will *be done* *(Matt 6:10)*.
NET: May your kingdom *come*, *may* your will *be done*.
NLT: May your Kingdom *come* soon. *May* your will *be done*.

This gives what I think is an example of an unfortunate translation. I would guess that virually no one who prays the Lord's Prayer with the traditional "Your kingdom come" knows that they are using an imperative to call on God to send his kingdom. The NET and NLT bravely make an attempt to convey the clear meaning of the Greek, placing clarity of translation above tradition.

22.15 The **aorist imperative** commands an undefined action.

μετανοήσατε, καὶ βαπτισθήτω ἕκαστος ὑμῶν
repent and *be baptized* each of you
Repent and *be baptized*, each of you *(Acts 2:38).*

22.16 The **present imperative** commands a continuous action.

μετανοεῖτε· ἤγγικεν γὰρ ἡ βασιλεία τῶν οὐρανῶν
repent has come near for the kingdom of heaven
Repent, for the kingdom of heaven is at hand *(Matt 3:2).*

22.17 The **perfect imperative** only occurs four times in the Greek Testament, so it is not worth learning (Mark 4:39, Acts 15:29, Eph 5:5, Jas 1:19).

22.18 **Future indicative**. The future indicative can also express a command, as it does in English (20.16).

ἅγιοι ἔσεσθε, ὅτι ἐγὼ ἅγιος
holy *you will be* because I holy
NRSV: You shall be holy, for I am holy *(1 Pet 1:16).*
NIV: Be holy, because I am holy.

NEGATION

22.19 οὐ is used to negate the indicative, and μή is used in all other moods, including participles and infinitives.

22.20 **Emphatic negation**. If the speaker uses μή or οὐ μή with the aorist subjunctive, the negation is exceptionally strong. οὐ μή is more emphatic than μή, and the double negatives do not cancel each other out as in English. Often the translator will add a word like "never" to make the prohibition more emphatic.

μὴ   φοβηθῇς   παραλαβεῖν Μαρίαμ τὴν γυναῖκά σου
not   you be afraid   to take   Mary   wife   your
Do not be afraid to take Mary home as your wife *(Matt 1:20).*

οἱ λόγοι   μου οὐ μὴ   παρέλθωσιν
the words   my   not   not   they will pass away
NIV: My words *will never pass away (Matt 24:35).*
NRSV: My words *will not pass away.*

"Never" is really over-translation because the construction is only an emphatic negation; it is not a statement about "forever." But English does not have a construction equal to the strength of this strong negation, so sometimes this is as close as we can get to the Greek when it fits the context, as in Matthew 24:35 above.

22.21 **μὴ γένοιτο.** Another strong way to say "No" is with the expression, μὴ γένοιτο.

ἁμαρτήσωμεν, ὅτι οὐκ ἐσμὲν ὑπὸ νόμον ἀλλὰ ὑπὸ χάριν; μὴ γένοιτο.
should we sin   since not   we are   under law   but   under grace   not be
NIV: Shall we sin because we are not under law but under grace? *By no means! (Rom 6:15)*

You can watch the translations struggle with how to say "No" in the strongest possible terms.

- "Absolutely not!" (CSB, NET)

- "May it never be!" (NASB 1995)

- "God forbid" (KJV)

- "Of course not!" (NLT)

- "Out of the question!" (NJB)

I actually think the KJV has it right, even though the Greek words for "God" and "forbid" don't occur. Is there any stronger negation in English than "God forbid"?

PROHIBITION

22.22 **μή + imperative**. In Greek there are different ways to state a prohibition, to tell someone not to do something. The aorist prohibits an undefined action, and the present negates a continuous action.

μὴ γνώτω ἡ ἀριστερά σου τί   ποιεῖ ἡ δεξιά σου
not allow left   *your what does* right   *your*
Do not let your left hand know what your right hand is doing
(*Matt 6:3*).

μὴ φοβοῦ, μόνον πίστευε
not fear   *only*   *believe*
Do not fear; just believe (*Mark 5:36*).

γνώτω is aorist and φοβοῦ is present.

22.23 **οὐ + future indicative**. You can also use οὐ and the future indicative to indicate prohibition.

οὐκ ἐκπειράσεις κύριον τὸν θεόν σου
not *put to the test* Lord   God   *your*
NRSV: *Do not put* the Lord your God to the test (*Matt 4:7*).
ESV: *You shall not put* the Lord your God to the test.

22.24 **Past mistake**. For many years it was believed that μή with a persent tense imperative was a prohibition to stop something currently in progress. μή with an aorist tense imperative was a prohibition to not even start an action. Although you will find this distinction throughout the commentaries, grammarians today are agreed that this distinction is invalid.

I comment in *BBG* (p. 317): "This has tremendously important ramifications for exegesis. For example, Paul tells Timothy to have nothing to do with silly myths, using a present imperative (παραιτοῦ; 1 Tim 4:7). If the present imperative commands cessation from an action currently under way, this means Timothy was participating in the myths. This creates a picture of Timothy that is irreconcilable with his mission at Ephesus and what we know of him elsewhere. But if a present imperative does not carry this meaning, then Paul is stating a command regarding a 'general precept' that is continuous in nature—continually stay away from the myths—and is saying nothing about Timothy's current involvement, or noninvolvement, in the Ephesian myths."[1]

INFINITIVE

22.25 **Verbal noun.** We've seen that the infinitive is a verbal noun (7.13). It's formed with a verb but it functions as a noun, and yet with tense and voice. It can have a direct object and adverbial modifiers, but no person or number. It will usually be preceded by a neuter singular definite article, which will be declined according to its usage in the sentence. This construction can be translated with "to" and the verb, although normally the translators find another way to say it.

ἐμοὶ τὸ ζῆν Χριστὸς καὶ τὸ ἀποθανεῖν κέρδος
to me   the to live Christ   and   the to die   gain
For to me, *to live* is Christ and *to die* is gain (*Phil 1:21*).

Both infinitives, ζῆν and ἀποθανεῖν, are the subject of the unexpressed verb "is," and each infinitive has a predicate nominative: Χριστός and κέρδος.

ἤδη   ποτὲ ἀνεθάλετε   τὸ ὑπὲρ ἐμοῦ φρονεῖν
already at last you have revived the for   me   concern
NRSV: Now at last you have revived your *concern* for me (*Phil 4:10*).

The articular infinitive τὸ … φρονεῖν is the direct object of the verb ἀνεθάλετε with the prepositional phrase ὑπὲρ ἐμοῦ in the first attributive position: article–modifier–noun.

μετέβη   ἐκεῖθεν τοῦ διδάσκειν καὶ κηρύσσειν ἐν ταῖς πόλεσιν αὐτῶν
he went on from there to teach   and to preach   in the   cities   their
He went on from there *to teach* and *preach* in their cities (*Matt 11:1*).

---

[1]   If someone wants the technical discussion, they can read it in *Verbal Aspect in New Testament Greek* by Buist Fanning (Oxford), pp. 325–88.

22.26 **Complementary**. We saw that an infinitive is often used to complete the meaning of a finite verb (9.8).

ἤρξαντο λαλεῖν ἑτέραις γλώσσαις
they began *to speak* other tongues
They began *to speak* in other tongues *(Acts 2:4)*.

"Began" by itself does not make any sense; it needs "to speak" to complete its meaning.

22.27 **Purpose**. We also saw that the infinitive can express purpose, "in order that" (9.9). There are different ways the infinitive can do this, but one is the infinitive by itself.

ἐδόθη αὐτῷ ποιῆσαι πόλεμον μετὰ τῶν ἁγίων καὶ νικῆσαι αὐτούς
it was given to him *to make* war against the saints and *to conquer* them
He was given power *to make* war against the saints and *to conquer* them *(Rev 13:7)*.

The dragon gave his authority to the beast for the purpose of making war against the saints and conquering them.

22.28 **Result**. A common way of indicating the result of some action is to use a clause introduced by ὥστε. In this case ὥστε will usually not be followed by a finite verb but by an infinitive. Because we do not have a similar use of the infinitive in English, we must translate this infinitive with a finite verb.

ἔπλησαν ἀμφότερα τὰ πλοῖα ὥστε βυθίζεσθαι αὐτά
they filled both the boats *so that to sink* them
NIV: They ... filled both boats so full *that* they *began to sink* (Luke 5:7).
NASB: They ... filled both of the boats, *to the point that they were sinking.*

The disciples filled the boat with fish, and the result was that the boats began to sink. The difference between purpose and result is intention. The dragon gave his power to the beast for the *purpose* of making war; the *result* of the catch of fish was the near sinking of the disciples' boat.

22.29 Subject. We saw that because an infinitive is not a finite verbal form (which has subjects), it technically cannot have a subject (15.14). However, there is often a word in the accusative —often a pronoun—that acts as if it were the subject of the infinitive.

μεταβαλόμενοι ἔλεγον αὐτὸν εἶναι θεόν
changing minds they said *he* *to be* god
They changed their minds and said that *he was* a god (*Acts 28:6*).

αὐτόν is accusative, acting as the subject of the infinitive εἶναι.

22.30* Appositional. An infinitive can stand in apposition to a substantive. The infinitive usually gives a specific example of the broader category expressed by the noun. Often you can add "namely" in front of the infinitive.

θρησκεία... αὕτη ἐστίν, ἐπισκέπτεσθαι ὀρφανοὺς καὶ χήρας
religion... this is *to visit* orphans and widows
This is ... religion, *to visit* orphans and widows (*Jas 1:27*).

True religion shows itself in many ways. One way is to visit those rejected by society.

CHAPTER 23

GREEK VERBS (PARTICIPLES)

In chapter 9 we learned the basic grammar of the participle. Now it is time to fill out our understanding of this flexible verbal form.

REVIEW

23.1 We have seen that a participle is a *verbal adjective* (7.14).

- It is formed from a verb but with case endings.

- The participle therefore has tense and voice as well as case, number, and gender.

- It can function adverbially or adjectivally. If it is adjectival, it can function either as an attributive or substantive.

- The form of the participle is identical whether it is adverbial or adjectival. The presence or absence of the article is the main clue as to the meaning of the participle.

- There is no absolute time outside of the indicative, so the different tense forms of the participle indicate different aspects.

ASPECT

23.2 **Aorist**. The participle formed on the aorist tense stem is undefined in its aspect.

ἐνεδυναμώθη   τῇ πίστει, δοὺς δόξαν τῷ θεῷ
he was strengthened   in faith   *giving* glory   to God
[He] was strengthened in faith, *giving* glory to God *(Rom 4:20)*.

23.3 **Present**. The participle formed on the present tense stem is continuous in its aspect.

φάσκοντες εἶναι σοφοὶ ἐμωράνθησαν
professing *to be* *wise* *they became fools*
Professing to be wise, they became fools *(Rom 1:22)*.

23.4 The participle formed on the perfect tense stem is perfective in its aspect.

ἐδέξαντο αὐτὸν οἱ Γαλιλαῖοι πάντα ἑωρακότες ὅσα ἐποίησεν
they welcomed him *the Galileans* *all* *having seen* *whatever* *he did*
The Galileans welcomed him, *having seen* all that he had done
(John 4:45).
NIV: The Galileans welcomed him. They had seen all that he had done.
CSB: The Galileans welcomed him because they had seen everything he did.
NRSV: the Galileans welcomed him, since they had seen all that he had done.

ADJECTIVAL PARTICIPLE

23.5 **Attributive**. A participle can function as an adjective, agreeing with the word it modifies in case, number, and gender. It is *usually* articular.

Ἡρῴδης... ἠκρίβωσεν παρ᾽ αὐτῶν τὸν χρόνον τοῦ φαινομένου ἀστέρος
Herod *learned* *from them* *the time* *of the appearing* *of the star*
Herod learned from them the time *of the appearing* of the star
(Matt 2:7).
ESV: Herod summoned the wise men secretly and ascertained from them *what time* the star *had appeared*.

φαινομένου is preceded by the article τοῦ and hence is articular and therefore adjectival, modifying ἀστέρος.

When the participial phrase is functioning as an attributive, it will normally be in the second attributive position: article–noun–article–modifier.

ὁ λαὸς ὁ καθήμενος ἐν σκότει φῶς εἶδεν μέγα
the people *the sitting* in darkness light saw great
The people *living in darkness* have seen a great light *(Matt 4:16).*

23.6 **Substantival.** Like any adjective, a participle can also function as a noun. Its case is determined by its function in the sentence, and its gender and number by what it stands for. It will often not have an expressed antecedent, but there is at least theoretically a word it is modifying and which determines gender and number.

τὸ εἰ δύνῃ, πάντα δυνατὰ τῷ πιστεύοντι
the if you are able all are possible *to the one who believes*
"If you can"! All things are possible *for the one who believes* *(Mark 9:23).*

ADVERBIAL PARTICIPLES

23.7 An adverbial participle is *always* anarthrous and will modify a verb, agreeing with the subject of the verb in case, number, and gender.

ἐταράχθη Ζαχαρίας ἰδὼν καὶ φόβος ἐπέπεσεν ἐπ᾽ αὐτόν
he was troubled Zechariah *seeing* and fear fell on him
Zechariah was troubled *when he saw* him and fear fell on him *(Luke 1:12).*

ἰδὼν modifies the verb ἐταράχθη and therefore agrees with its subject, Ζαχαρίας, in case, number, and gender.

The translator may add the appropriate pronoun to this construction to make better English sense. Which pronoun is used is determined by the word the participle is modifying.

Καὶ παράγων ὁ Ἰησοῦς ἐκεῖθεν εἶδεν ἄνθρωπον
And *going along* Jesus from there he saw man
And Jesus, as *he was passing on* from there, saw a man *(Matt 9:9).*

To show that it was Jesus who was passing on, I added "he."

23.8 **Temporal**. We saw that adverbial participles can indicate a temporal action relative to the verb, sometimes preceded by the words "after" or "when/while" (9.13).

ἐκτείνας τὴν χεῖρα ἥψατο αὐτοῦ λέγων, θέλω, καθαρίσθητι
reaching out hand touched his saying I am willing be cleansed
After reaching out his hand, he touched him saying, "I am willing; be cleansed" *(Matt 8:3)*.
CSB: Reaching out his hand, Jesus touched him, saying, "I am willing; be made clean."

σοῦ δὲ ποιοῦντος ἐλεημοσύνην μὴ γνώτω ἡ ἀριστερά σου
your but doing acts of mercy not let it know the left your
NET: But *when* you *do* your giving, do not let your left hand know .... *(Matt 6:3)*.

ταῦτα εἰπὼν βλεπόντων αὐτῶν ἐπήρθη
these saying *watching* they he was lifted up
When he had said these words, *while* they *were watching*, he was lifted up *(Acts 1:9)*.

23.9 **Purpose**. The adverbial participle can indicate the purpose of the finite verb. These are often translated as infinitives.

ἴδωμεν εἰ ἔρχεται Ἡλίας σώσων αὐτόν
let's see if he comes Elijah *saving* him
NIV: Let's see if Elijah comes *to save* him *(Matt 27:49)*.
NLT: Let's see whether Elijah comes *to save* him.

They waited for the purpose of seeing if Elijah would come.

23.10 **Result**. The adverbial participle can indicate the result of the finite verb. This is close to the participle of purpose; the difference is whether the force of the particple is on the intention or the result.

τοὺς δύο κτίσῃ ἐν αὐτῷ εἰς ἕνα καινὸν ἄνθρωπον ποιῶν εἰρήνην
the two he create in him into one new man *making* peace
NIV: His purpose was to create in himself one new humanity out of the two, *thus making* peace *(Eph 2:15)*.

Peace was the result of creating the one new man. It could also be purpose.

23.11 Means. The participle can indicate the means by which the action of the finite verb occurs.

κοπιῶμεν ἐργαζόμενοι ταῖς ἰδίαις χερσίν
we toil *working* with the own hands

We toil *by working* with our own hands *(1 Cor 4:12)*.
ESV: We labor, *working* with our own hands.
NIV: We *work* hard with our own hands.

The means by which Paul toils is by working with his hands. I used "by" in my translation to make this clear; the NIV uses "with." The ESV leaves it up to context.

23.12 Cause. The participle can indicate the cause or reason or ground of the action of the finite verb.

ἠγαλλιάσατο πανοικεὶ πεπιστευκὼς τῷ θεῷ
he rejoiced with his whole house *having believed* in God

NIV: He was filled with joy *because he had come to believe* in God *(Acts 16:34)*.
NASB: He ... was overjoyed, *since he had become* a believer in God.

The Philippian jailer rejoiced because he had believed. The NIV clarifies the relationship between verb and participle by using "because." The NASB leaves it up to context.

23.13 Conditional. The participle can indicate a condition that must be fulfilled if the action of the finite verb is to be accomplished.

πάντα ὅσα ἂν αἰτήσητε ... πιστεύοντες λήμψεσθε
all whatever you might ask *believing* you will receive

RSV: And whatever you ask in prayer, you will receive, *if you have faith* (Matt 21:22).
NASB: And whatever you ask in prayer, *believing*, you will receive it all.

If the condition of faith is met, then you will have what you pray for. The RSV clarifies the relationship by using "if." The NASB leaves it up to context.

23.14 **Concessive**. The participle can indicate that the action of the finite verb is true despite the action of the participle.

Καὶ ὑμᾶς ὄντας νεκροὺς τοῖς παραπτώμασιν
and you *being* dead the tresspasses
NET: And *although you were* dead in your transgressions *(Eph 2:1)*
NIV: You *were* dead in your transgressions.
RSV: And you he made alive, *when you were* dead through the trespasses.

The concessive idea is that *even though* we were dead in our sins, God made us alive. The NET clarifies the relationship by using "although." The NIV leaves it up to context. The RSV sees ὄντας as temporal.

23.15 **Attendant circumstances**. An adverbial participle can describe an action that is coordinate with the regular verb. In most cases, the participle is translated as a regular verb and the conjunction "and" is inserted.

εὐθὺς ἀφέντες τὰ δίκτυα ἠκολούθησαν αὐτῷ
immediately *leaving* the nets they followed him
NASB: Immediately they *left* their nets *and* followed Him *(Mark 1:18)*.

ἀφέντες is a participle, and ἠκολούθησαν is the main verb.

καὶ περιβλεψάμενος ὁ Ἰησοῦς λέγει τοῖς μαθηταῖς αὐτοῦ
and *looking around* Jesus says to the disciples his
ESV: And Jesus *looked around* and said to his disciples *(Mark 10:23)*

περιβλεψάμενος is a participle, and λέγει is the main verb.

23.16 **Dividing a sentence**. When Greek sentences get too long for English translations, it is often easiest to treat a long participial phrase as an independent sentence. Ephesians 1:3–14 is one such sentence. Verse 5 begins with a participial phrase, and many translations start a new English sentence by turning the participle into a finite verb, supply a subject, and hence turn a participial phrase into an independent sentence. The NET adds, "He did this," keeping the participial construction. The NRSV adds "He," changing the participle into an indicative verb.

προορίσας ἡμᾶς εἰς υἱοθεσίαν διὰ   Ἰησοῦ Χριστοῦ
predestining us   to   adoption   through Jesus   Christ

KJV: Having predestinated us unto the adoption of children by Jesus Christ to himself *(Eph 1:5).*

NET: He did this by predestining us to adoption as his legal heirs through Jesus Christ.

NRSV: He destined us for adoption as his children through Jesus Christ.

This is not necessarily bad translation practice. After all, the point of translation is to make something understandable. However, because it blurs the grammatical distinction between independent and dependent constructions, and because the author's main thought tends to be in the independent clauses, this practice can make exegesis more difficult when based on the English text.

23.17 The opposite can also happen; an independent clause can be translated as dependent.

μὴ ἀσθενήσας τῇ πίστει κατενόησεν τὸ ἑαυτοῦ σῶμα
not *weakening* in faith   *he considered* the his own   body

NRSV: He did not *weaken* in faith when he *considered* his own body *(Rom 4:19)*

"Did not weaken" is a participle in a subordinate clause. "When he considered" is the main verb in Greek, but in the NRSV it is a temporal subordinate clause. Paul's point is how Abraham looked at his aging body ("considered"), and adds that in doing so he "did not weaken" in his faith, a fact obscured by the NRSV. The NIV does a better job in this regard.

> *Without weakening* in his faith, he *faced the fact* that his body was as good as dead—since he was about a hundred years old.

Another good example is the "Great Commission" (Matt 28:19–20). The NIV reads,

> Therefore *go* and *make disciples* of all nations, *baptizing* them in the name of the Father and of the Son and of the Holy Spirit, and *teaching* them to obey everything I have commanded you.

What is the main point? It appears that the apostles are told to do two things: "Go!" and "Make disciples!" However, if you look at the Greek, you will find that there is only one imperative: "Make disciples!" "Go" is a participle, like "baptizing" and "teaching." Jesus is telling his disciples (and us): "Therefore, as you go, make disciples by baptizing and by teaching." Wherever you are, wherever you go (whether, I would add, you are in full-time ministry as a missionary or as a stay-at-home Christian), you are to make disciples. Nevertheless, you still have to "go" if you are going to make disciples.[2]

ADVANCED: ADVERBIAL PARTICIPLES AND RELATIVE TIME

23.18* In the indicative, verbs indicate what we call "**absolute time.**" This means that if an aorist has temporal significance, it's in past time regardless of the other verbal forms around it. If the verb is present tense and it has temporal significance, then it indicates an action occurring in the present time.

23.19* Adverbial participles (not so much adjectival) indicate what is called "**relative time.**"

- The participle built on the *aorist* tense stem indicates an action occurring *prior to* the time of the main verb.

- The participle built on the *present* tense stem indicates an action occurring at the *same time* as the time of the main verb.

---

[2] It is not quite this simple. The participle does pick up some of the imperatival force of the imperative. But the basic point I am making is valid.

main verb	participle	time and aspect
present	present	present continuous
present	aorist	past undefined
past	present	past continuous
past	aorist	past undefined

As you will see from the examples below, the relative time is not always expressed in translation, but the sequence of events should make the relative time clear.

23.20* For example, let's assume the main verb is *aorist*.

■ The present participle is translated as *past continuous*.

Περιπατῶν δὲ παρὰ τὴν θάλασσαν τῆς Γαλιλαίας
walking and alongside the sea of Galilee,

εἶδεν δύο ἀδελφούς.
he saw two brothers

And *as he was walking* alongside the Sea of Galilee, he *saw* two brothers *(Matt 4:18).*

■ The aorist participle is translated as *past undefined*.

Ἡρῴδης λάθρα καλέσας τοὺς μάγους ἠκρίβωσεν
Herod secretly *calling* the magi *found out*

παρ' αὐτῶν τὸν χρόνον
from them the time

NASB: Herod secretly *called* the magi and *determined* from them the exact time *(Matt 2:7).*

23.21* But what if the main verb is *present*?

■ The present participle is translated as *present continuous*.

πᾶν   δένδρον μὴ   ποιοῦν καρπὸν καλὸν ἐκκόπτεται καὶ
Every   tree   not   *bearing* fruit   good   *is cut down*   and

εἰς   πῦρ βάλλεται
into   fire   *is thrown*

Every tree *not bearing* good fruit *is cut down* and *thrown* into
the fire *(Matt 7:19)*.

■ The aorist participle is translated as *present undefined*.

ἐλθόντες   εἰς τὴν οἰκίαν εἶδον   τὸ παιδίον μετὰ Μαρίας
after entering into the house   *they saw* the child   with   Mary

τῆς μητρὸς αὐτοῦ
mother   his

After entering into the house, *they saw* the child with Mary, his
mother *(Matt 2:11)*.

This is the outside of a Greek scroll made of papyrus about eight inches long. Writing on a scroll's exterior may indicate an important text. Its text is by a practiced scribe and it came originally from Alexandria, Egypt through a chain of custody to Dr. Randall Price (World of the Bible Collection). It is dated tentatively to the early 3rd century AD. It is scheduled for digital unwrapping which will fully reveal its inner text. Used with permission.

CHAPTER 24

PHRASING 104

In Phrasing 103 you were introduced to Method 1 of Greek Phrasing. In Phrasing 104 we're going to plunge into Method 2. We will also look at using semantic tags. This is the last (and most difficult) chapter on phrasing, and doing the homework is incredibly important.

24.1 We will start with the phrasing of Titus 1:1–4 you did in Phrasing 103, but without the key Greek words inserted. You can download a fresh copy from lesson 24 in the online class. Instead of just inserting the key Greek words to our English phrasing, we're going to use the full Greek text. The challenge will be that you will now be exposed to all the intricacies of Greek grammar. If you have not been learning your vocabulary or grammar, Phrasing 104 is too difficult for you. As we work through the passage, I will explain anything you will meet in the text that I haven't yet taught.

24.2 **Greek and English order.** Some students prefer to list the Greek below the English, others above. This is merely a matter of personal preference. I am going to put the Greek above the English.

24.3 **Screen setup.** Begin by setting up your computer to show your word processor and Accordance (see next page). My personal preference is to keep the phrasing to the left and two panels open in Accordance on the right. The left panel is the Greek text, and the right panel is my translation in interlinear format. I am showing the English, the Greek lexical form, and the ESV translation. In the left pane I can see the inflected form and Greek word order, and in Instant Details I can see the word's GK number and parsing.

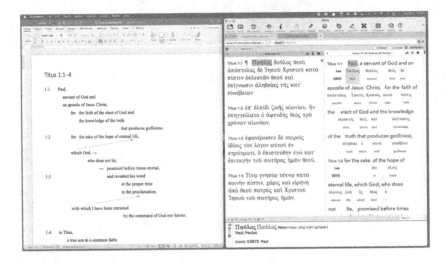

The lexical form also shows in Instant Details, but it is good to see it in the interlinear as you are doing mouse-overs. But like I said, experiment until you find what works best for you.

24.4 **Titus 1:1–2a**. As you mouse over the words, you should recognize a lot of them: Παῦλος, θεός, δέ Ἰησοῦς, Χριστός, κατά, πίστις, and καί. This will make phrasing much easier. Let's begin by placing the Greek over the English.

1:1   Παῦλος
       Paul,

          δοῦλος θεοῦ ... δὲ
          servant of God and

          ἀπόστολος ... Ἰησοῦ Χριστοῦ
          an apostle of Jesus Christ,

              κατὰ πίστιν ἐκλεκτῶν θεοῦ καὶ
              for   the faith of the elect of God and

                     ἐπίγνωσιν ἀληθείας
                     the knowledge of the truth

                            τῆς κατ᾽ εὐσέβειαν
                            that produces godliness,

1:2   ἐπ᾽   ἐλπίδι ζωῆς αἰωνίου
              for   the sake of the hope of eternal life,

Most of this is straightforward. The words δοῦλος and ἀπόστολος are both in apposition to Παῦλος. The words πίστιν and ἐπίγνωσιν are both accusative objects of the preposition κατά, as we suspected from the English, so that structure is confirmed. I try to indent a phrase under the Greek word it modifies and not the English; the modifier τῆς κατ᾽ εὐσέβειαν is under ἀληθείας.

24.5   What is interesting is the phrase τῆς κατ᾽ εὐσέβειαν. κατ᾽ is the elided form of the preposition κατά, but you knew that. εὐσέβειαν is in the accusative as the object of κατ᾽. But what is τῆς doing?

First of all, it is an inflected form of the article ὁ, genitive singular feminine. Why is it there? Do you remember that an articular prepositional phrase is modifying a word? How do you tell which word? Same case, number, and gender as the article. So what word is τῆς modifying? The closest possibility is ἀληθείας, and this makes sense in context. It also confirms our suspicions from the English that "that produces godliness" modifies "truth"; it is the truth that in fact produces godliness.

24.6   We also struggled a bit with how to phrase verse 2a. Options for what the prepositional phrase modifies are ἀπόστολος, πίστιν, and ἐπίγνωσιν. I discuss this a bit in my commentary and tentatively conclude that ἐπ᾽ indicates purpose, parallels κατά, and modifies ἀπόστολος.

Also, now that we know "for" is a translation of ἐπί, we understand how flexible the meaning of the preposition is and why the translations tend to use "in," which is pretty noncommittal in terms of meaning. The NLT starts a new sentence and writes, "This truth gives them confidence that they have eternal life," "confidence" being a theologically accurate translation of "hope" (ἐλπίς).

24.7   The words ζωῆς and αἰωνίου are both anarthrous, but it is clear from context that αἰωνίου is an attributive of ζωῆς. So the Greek has confirmed most of our decisions, and gave us clarity on a few phrases.

24.8   **Titus 1:2b–3a**. The words you recognize are the relative pronoun (inflected as ἥν), ὁ, and θεός. You may have guessed that πρό is a preposition meaning "before" and takes its object in the genitive.

And αἰωνίων is a genitive plural form of the same word αἰωνίου we saw in verse 2a, "eternal."

24.9 So here is the next section with the Greek added.

ἣν ἐπηγγείλατο ὁ ... θεὸς
which God, →

         ἀψευδὴς
         who does not lie,

    → ἐπηγγείλατο ... πρὸ χρόνων αἰωνίων
       promised before times eternal,

1:3 φανέρωσεν δὲ ... τὸν λόγον αὐτοῦ
and revealed his word

    καιροῖς ἰδίοις
    at the proper time

    ἐν κηρύγματι
    in the proclamation,

24.10 **English order**. But the words almost seem jumbled, don't they? Actually, this is pretty normal Greek. Let me start by listing the Greek in its original order and then reordering the Greek in English order. I do this at times when the Greek structure is challenging.

ἣν ἐπηγγείλατο ὁ ἀψευδὴς θεὸς πρὸ χρόνων αἰωνίων,
ἐφανέρωσεν δὲ καιροῖς ἰδίοις τὸν λόγον αὐτοῦ ἐν κηρύγματι

ἣν	ἐπηγγείλατο	ὁ θεὸς	ἀψευδὴς	πρὸ	χρόνων	αἰωνίων,
which	he promised	God	not lying	before	times	eternal

ἐφανέρωσεν	δὲ	τὸν λόγον	αὐτοῦ	ἰδίοις	καιροῖς	ἐν κηρύγματι
revealed	but	the word	his	in own	times	in proclamation

24.11 ὁ ἀψευδὴς θεός is the subject of ἐπηγγείλατο, and the adjective ἀψευδὴς is in the first attributive position between the article and the noun. There's no way in English to keep αψευδής as an adjective, so all major translations change it to a relative clause, "who does not lie."

24.12 The accusative noun clause τὸν λόγον αὐτοῦ is the direct object of ἐφανέρωσεν. What is confusing is that the dative noun clause καιροῖς ἰδίοις is before the direct object, even though it's parallel with the latter ἐν κηρύγματι.

This is a good example of why marketers are misleading when they say their translation reflects the underlying Greek structure. Sometimes they do; sometimes they don't. And if you don't know Greek, you don't know when they do or don't. Better to learn Greek than work with the misperception that you can see the Greek behind the English when you don't know Greek.

24.13 **Relative pronoun.** It's always critical to connect a relative pronoun (ἥν) back to its antecedent. What is the Greek linkage? Same gender and number. So what did God promise? He promised "life."

1:2

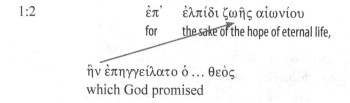

ἐπ' ἐλπίδι ζωῆς αἰωνίου
for the sake of the hope of eternal life,

ἣν ἐπηγγείλατο ὁ ... θεὸς
which God promised

What determines the case of the relative pronoun? Its function inside the relative clause. As I've said before, if this is confusing, replace the relative pronoun with its antecedent and treat the relative clause as its own sentence.

which God promised

life God promised

God promised life

ἣν is accusative because it is the direct object of the verb ἐπηγγείλατο.

24.14 **Dative of time when.** Do you remember that the dative is used to explain when an action occurs? καιροῖς ἰδίοις is when God revealed his word.

24.15 **Missing a word?** The other oddity in this section is the phrase ἐν κηρύγματι. In the proclamation of what? It is also typical of Greek to leave some of the meaning up to the context. Actually, this is done in all languages. What is being proclaimed? We know from verse 3a that it is God's word.

The NIV stretches a bit when they say, "he has brought to light through the preaching," citing 2 Timothy 1:10 ("It has now been revealed through the appearing of our Savior, Christ Jesus, who has destroyed death and has brought life and immortality to light through the gospel"). But I guess "brought to light" is an accurate explanation of "revealed."

24.16 **Titus 1:3b**. This phrase is pretty straightforward. You know the relative pronoun ὅ, πιστεύω (which has a slightly unusual meaning here of being "entrusted"), ἐγώ, σωτήρ, and the genitive plural form (ἡμῶν) of the person pronoun ἐγώ.

24.17
   ἐν κηρύγματι
   in the proclamation,

 ὃ ἐπιστεύθην ἐγὼ
 with which I have been entrusted

   κατ᾽ ἐπιταγὴν τοῦ σωτῆρος ἡμῶν θεοῦ
   by the command of God our Savior,

The antecedent of ὅ is κηρύγματι. I grayed out the text since we had already discussed it (i.e., it is not in verse 3b), but I needed it to be able to connect the relative pronoun to its antecedent. The prepositional phrase κατ᾽ ἐπιταγήν obviously modifies ἐπιστεύθην.

24.18 What might feel a little awkward is the phrase τοῦ σωτῆρος ἡμῶν θεοῦ. The basic modifier of ἐπιταγὴν is τοῦ … θεοῦ, σωτῆρος is in the first attributive position, and ἡμῶν modifies σωτῆρος. So the phrase is really straightforward.

24.19 Titus 1:4a. This verse begins the second part of the salutation and likewise is pretty straightforward.

1:4   Τίτῳ
     to Titus,

       γνησίῳ τέκνῳ κατὰ κοινὴν πίστιν
       a true son in a common faith:

τέκνῳ is in apposition to Τίτῳ (both are dative singular), which is modified by γνησίῳ and κατὰ κοινὴν πίστιν.

24.20 This brings up a common issue in phrasing. How many ways can you divide the text? The answer is, into as many as you need in order to be able to understand. If "a true son in a common faith" is sufficiently clear to you, then leave it on one line. If you are helped by more specificity, then divide that phrase further.

       γνησίῳ
       a true
     τέκνῳ
     son
       κατὰ κοινὴν πίστιν
       in a common faith:

Titus is Paul's son. He is his γνησίῳ son in that he carries his "father's" authority (in contrast to the false teachers in Crete), but his sonship is not biological but is κατὰ κοινὴν πίστιν.

24.21 **Titus 1:4b**. We now arrive at the third part of the salutation, the blessing.

     χάρις καὶ εἰρήνη ἀπὸ   θεοῦ πατρὸς καὶ
     Grace and peace from   God the Father and

                        Χριστοῦ Ἰησοῦ τοῦ σωτῆρος ἡμῶν
                        Christ Jesus our Savior.

If you wanted to highlight the parallelism between πατρὸς and σωτῆρος, you could add in two tabs. You could also put καί on its own line if you find that helpful.

χάρις καὶ εἰρήνη ἀπὸ θεοῦ πατρὸς

Grace and peace from God the Father

καὶ

and

Χριστοῦ Ἰησοῦ τοῦ σωτῆρος ἡμῶν

Christ Jesus our Savior.

24.22 The theologically important point to make here is one that you learned at 21.18. Did you notice that θεοῦ and Χριστοῦ are both objects of ἀπό? This is important. The construction does not mean that "God" and "Christ" are identical, but it does mean that Paul thinks of them as acting so closely together that both blessings of "grace" and "peace" come together from both members of the Godhead. If θεοῦ and Χριστοῦ where two totally separate beings, the preposition would have been repeated before Χριστοῦ.

If you wanted to stress this, then you could add some typographical element and do something like the line.

χάρις καὶ εἰρήνη ἀπὸ | θεοῦ πατρὸς

Grace and peace from | God the Father

| καὶ
| and

| Χριστοῦ Ἰησοῦ τοῦ σωτῆρος ἡμῶν
| Christ Jesus our Savior.

Or if you don't mind switching the word order a little, you could drop the greeting down a line.

| θεοῦ πατρὸς
| God the Father

χάρις καὶ εἰρήνη ἀπὸ | καὶ

Grace and peace from | and

| Χριστοῦ Ἰησοῦ τοῦ σωτῆρος ἡμῶν
| Christ Jesus our Savior.

24.23 So that's it. Congratulations. If you are able to do Method 2 phrasing, you have learned enough Greek to accomplish all our goals.

The next two chapters are a hodgepodge of Greek grammar that I thought you might want to know, but as of now you have covered the vast majority of what you need to know.

The video lesson for the chapter covers Titus 2:11–14, and your homework is Titus 3:1–7. Both start with your work in Phrasing 103.

DIAGRAMMING TOOLS IN SOFTWARE

24.24 There are some helpful tools in the software, and no doubt the software companies will continue to improve these. As is true of all tools, be sure not to let them ruin your fun; don't let them do your work of phrasing. But they are helpful as cross-references, or if you just don't have enough time to get ready for Sunday's sermon.

24.25 Accordance has a tool called the GNT Syntax module. You should read the instructions carefully in order to understand the diagramming, but this is pretty cool.

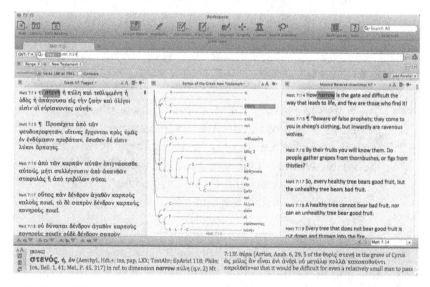

24.26 Logos also has a nice tool called the Lexham Syntactic Greek New Testament, which lays the phrases out and includes grammatical labels (see next page).

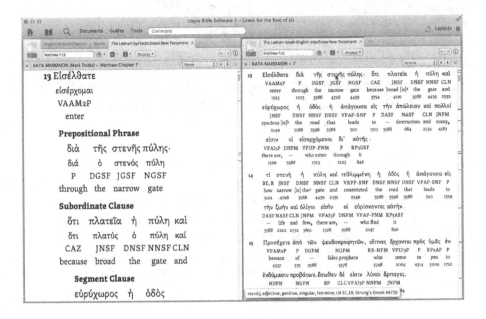

24.27 Recognize that these tools, and others like them, are helpful, but they represent exegetical decisions by the editors. Their editors are highly qualified scholars, but they still represent opinion; they are not infallible. So use them as you would any other tool, respecting the scholarship but making your own decisions.

SEMANTIC TAGS

24.28 The following is only for students who want to go further into phrasing. Much of the discussion in commentaries is concerned with the precise nature of the relationships between phrases, and the writer will use a label to describe the relationship such as "manner" or "temporal." These terms overlap some with the terms you have seen previously.

24.29 If you come up with your own labels for the connections between the major phrases, you are doing well. But sometimes it's difficult to come up with the right terminology, so here are some suggestions. They have been taken (with permission) from a textbook written by some good friends of mine, George Guthrie and Scott Duvall. If you want to know more, see their book *Biblical Greek Exegesis* (Zondervan, 1998). The terminology is also being employed in the *Zondervan Exegetical Commentary on the New Testament* series. I also included these terms on the laminated sheet for this textbook. Many of these terms listed below are the technical terms used in the better commentaries

24.30 You should add phrasing tags to Titus 1:1–4.

FOUNDATIONAL EXPRESSIONS

Many of the main phrases you come across can be categorized in one of these "foundational" categories.

1. **Assertion**. Making a statement.

   I am the true vine *(John 15:1)*.

2. **Event/Action**. Something that happened.

   The life was made manifest *(1 John 1:2)*.

3. **Rhetorical question**. A question used to make a declaration.

   For to which of the angels did God ever say, "You are my Son?" *(Heb 1:5)*.

4. **Desire** (wish/hope). Expression of a wish or hope.

   I hope to see you soon *(3 John 1:14)*.

5. **Exclamation**

   I am a miserable man *(Rom 7:24)*.

6. **Exhortation** (command/encouragement).

   "Get behind me, Satan!" *(Mark 8:33)*

7. **Warning**

   For if we go on sinning deliberately after receiving the knowledge of the truth, there no longer remains a sacrifice for sins *(Heb 10:26)*.

8. **Promise**

   I will never leave you nor forsake you *(Heb 13:5)*.

9. **Problem/Resolution**. The stating of a problem followed by its resolution.

   And you were dead in your trespasses and sins.... But God ... made us alive together with Christ *(Eph 2:1–5)*.

10. **Entreaty**. A polite request made to a superior.

Give us this day our daily bread *(Matt 6:11)*.

11. **Prayer** *(Col 1:9–10)*.

MODIFICATIONS

These are different ways to modify the main assertion.

TEMPORAL

12. **Time**. A simple statement of the time an event, action, or state occurred. It answers the question, "When did this occur?"

Then *after fasting and praying* they laid their hands on them and sent them off *(Acts 13:3)*.

13. **Simultaneous**. Two or more events or states expressed as happening at the same time.

Then, when they had *fasted and prayed* and laid hands on them, they sent them off *(Acts 13:3)*.

14. **Sequence**. Two or more events expressed as happening one after the other.

He appeared to Cephas, *then* to the twelve *(1 Cor 15:5)*.

15. **Progression**. Same as "sequence," but the emphasis is placed on the developmental nature of the actions.

I planted, Apollos watered *(1 Cor 3:6a)*.

LOCATION

16. **Place**. Where the event, action, or state occurred. Answers the question, "Where?"

They came *to Thessalonica (Acts 17:1)*.

17. **Sphere**. The domain or realm of existence.

But you are not in the flesh, you are *in the Spirit (Rom 8:9a)*.

18. **Source**. The point of origin. Answers the question, "From where?"

But we have this treasure in earthen vessels, to show that the transcendent power *belongs to God* and not to us *(2 Cor 4:7)*.

19. **Separation**. Creating distance between two parties.

And lead us not into temptation, but deliver us *from evil (Matt 6:13)*.

20. **Posture**. A frame of mind, an attitude, or an approach toward something or someone.

Unlike so many, we do not peddle the word of God *for profit* *(2 Cor 2:17)*.

ADVERBIAL

21. **Measure**. Answers the question, "How long?" "How many?" or, "How far?"

Why do you stand here idle *all day*? *(Matt 20:6)*.

22. **Circumstance**. Situations surrounding events or actions.

… leaving all they followed him *(Luke 5:11)*.

23. **Object**

… whom God presented as a propitiation through faith in his blood for a demonstration *of his righteousness (Rom 3:25)*.

24. **Cause**. An event or state that produces some result. Answers the question, "What brought this about?"

Therefore, *having been justified by faith,* we have peace with God through our Lord Jesus Christ *(Rom 5:1a)*.

25. **Result**. An outcome of some action or attitude.

Having shut your door, pray to your Father who is in secret, and *your Father who sees in secret will repay you (Matt 6:6)*.

26. **Purpose**. An outcome that one intends to take place. Answers the question, "What did he wish to occur?"

For God so loved the world, that he gave his only Son, *that whoever believes in him should not perish but have eternal life (John 3:16)*.

27. **Means**. The tool or instrument used in carrying out an action. Answers the question, "How did he do that?"

But *by the grace of God* I am what I am *(1 Cor 15:10a)*.

28. **Manner**. How the instrument is used. Answers the question, "In what way did he do this?"

Only that *in every way,* whether *in pretense* or *in truth,* Christ is proclaimed *(Phil 1:18)*.

29. **Agency**. The personal agent who performs the action. Answers the question, "By whom?" or, "Through whom?"

We have peace with God *through our Lord Jesus Christ (Rom 5:1)*.

30. **Substance**. The material or reality of which something is made.

Asking that you may be filled with the knowledge *of his will* (Col 1:9). ("His will" makes up the "knowledge.")

31. **Reference**. An expression of relation. Answers the question, "With reference to whom or what?"

You were taught, *with regard to your former way of life,* to put off your old self *(Eph 4:22)*.

32. **Advantage or Disadvantage**. For whom or against whom an action takes place.

For one will scarcely die *for a righteous person (Rom 5:7)*.

Thus you witness *against yourselves* that you are sons of those who murdered the prophets *(Matt 23:31)*.

33. **Association**. Expresses the idea of accompaniment.

And if anyone forces you to go one mile, go *with him* two miles *(Matt 5:41)*.

34. **Relationship**. Expresses some form of personal relationship.

We always thank God, the Father *of our Lord* Jesus Christ *(Col 1:3)*.

35. **Possession**. Expresses ownership.

And if anyone would sue you and take *your* tunic, let him have *your* cloak as well *(Matt 5:40)*.

36. **Basis**. The grounds upon which a statement or command is made.

    For the one who enters God's rest has also rested from his works, as God did from his. Let us, therefore, make every effort to enter that rest *(Heb 4:10–11)*.

37. **Inference**. The logical conclusion drawn from an idea.

    If anyone does not stumble in what he says, *he is a perfect man (Jas 3:2)*.

38. **Condition**. A requirement that must be fulfilled.

    If anyone does not stumble in what he says, he is a perfect man *(Jas 3:2)*.

39. **Concession/Contra-expectation**. A reservation or qualification.

    Although he was a son, he learned obedience through what he suffered *(Heb 5:8)*.

40. **Contrast/Comparison**. Two conditions, ideas, or actions put together in order to point out differences.

    Therefore *do not be foolish, but understand* what the will of the Lord is *(Eph 5:17)*.

41. **General/Specific**. When a general and a specific statement are put side by side to show the relationship between a broader and a particular concept, truth, or action.

    No one takes this honor for himself, but only when called by God, just as Aaron was. So also *Christ did not exalt himself to be made a high priest,* but was appointed *(Heb 5:4–5)*.

CLARIFICATION

42. **Restatement**. The same idea is expressed in a different way.

    For I will be merciful toward their iniquities, and *I will remember their sins no more (Heb 8:12)*.

43. **Description**. Functions to provide vivid detail of a person, event, state, or object.

    A *great red dragon,* with *seven heads and ten horns,* and on his heads *seven diadems (Rev 12:3)*.

44. **Identification**. Information used to specify a person or thing. Answers the question, "Which one?"

Now there was a man of the Pharisees *named Nicodemus,* a ruler of the Jews *(John 3:1).*

45. **Illustration/Example**. To elucidate by use of examples.

God, having promised to Abraham … swore by himself … And so having waited patiently [Abraham] obtained the promise *(Heb 6:13–15).* The whole of verses 13–15 functions as the illustration.

46. **Apposition**. A noun or participle that follows immediately another noun or participle with which it shares a common referent.

For this reason I, Paul, *a prisoner* for Christ Jesus *(Eph 3:1).*

47. **Explanation**. The addition of clarifying statements to a main proposition.

And when you pray, do not heap up empty phrases as the Gentiles do, *for they think that they will be heard for their many words (Matt 6:7).*

48. **Expansion**. Adding to a previous statement.

Therefore, it's necessary for an overseer to be above reproach: *a man of one woman, clear-minded, self-controlled (1 Tim 3:2).*

49. **Alternative** (either . . . or). When one condition, action, or place is expressed as a possible substitute for another.

Either he will hate the one and love the other, *or he will be devoted to the one and despise the other (Matt 6:24).*

50. **Question/Answer**. I'll let you figure this one out.

And he asked them, *"But who do you say that I am?"* Peter answered him, *"You are the Christ" (Mark 8:29).*

51. **Content**. The material or reality that something contains.

Therefore let us leave standing the elementary teaching about Christ and let us move on to maturity, not laying again a foundation of *repentance from dead works and of faith in God, instruction about cleansing rites and laying on of hands (Heb 6:1–2).*

52. **Verification**. Something by which a truth is established.

For David did not ascend into the heavens, but he himself says, *"The Lord said to my Lord, Sit at my right hand, until I make your enemies a footstool for your feet"* (Acts 2:34–35).

53. **Introduction**. A passage that presents the opening of a discussion or narrative, such as Hebrews 1:1–4 or Mark 1:1.

54. **Conclusion/Summary**. To bring to an end by way of summary or final decisive statement, such as Mark 7:28–29.

55. **List**. A number of things, normally of the same kind, mentioned one after the other.

To God's elect, strangers in the world, scattered throughout *Pontus, Galatia, Cappadocia, Asia and Bithynia (1 Pet 1:1)*.

56. **Series**. The joining of equally prominent assertions or commands in a loose association.

Rejoice always, pray without ceasing, give thanks in all circumstances (1 Thess 5:16–18).

57. **Parallel**. Two or more elements correspond verbally or conceptually.

You are the salt of the earth.... *You are the light of the world (Matt 5:13–14)*.

9a		And so,
b	duration	from the day we heard,
c	**assertion**	**we have not ceased to pray for you,**
d	content	asking that you may be filled
e	content	with the knowledge of his will
f	manner	in all spiritual wisdom and understanding,
10a	purpose	so as to walk
b	manner	in a manner worthy of the Lord,
c	manner	fully pleasing to him,
d	result	bearing fruit in every good work and
e	result	increasing in the knowledge of God.
11a	result	May you be strengthened
b	instrument	with all power,
c	accordance	according to his glorious might,
d	purpose	for all endurance and patience with joy,
12a	result	giving thanks to the Father,
b	description	who has qualified you to share in the inheritance of the saints in light.
13a	description	He has delivered us from the domain of darkness and
b	description	transferred us to the kingdom of his beloved Son,
14	description	in whom we have redemption, the forgiveness of sins.

This is the semantic tagging on Colossians 1:9–14 (ESV).

CHAPTER 25

VERBAL ODDS 'N ENDS

CONTRACT VERBS

25.1 You may have noticed that many of the verbs you have learned have a consonant before the personal ending (λέγω, γινώσκω, ἔχω, λαμβάνω, γράφω, εὑρίσκω, θέλω) or an ι (ἐσθίω) or υ (ἀκούω, πιστεύω). Others have a vowel like α (ὁράω) or ε (λαλέω, ποιέω).

What I am going to discuss does not apply to middle-only verbs (ἀποκρίνομαι, ἔρχομαι, γίνομαι, δύναμαι) or verbs whose lexical forms end in μι (δίδωμι, ἵστημι).

25.2 When the stem of a verb ends in α, ε, or o (you have not seen an example of the latter), the lexical form has a special rule. When learning Greek the traditional way, the student needs to know what that vowel is, so it is shown in the lexical form: ὁράω, λαλέω.

However, when that verb actually occurs in the text as a first person singular, the personal ending ω contracts with that final vowel, and the contract vowel is "swallowed up" by the ω.

So if the writer wants to say "I see," the lexical form of the verb is ὁράω, but in the text it will have contracted to ὁρῶ.

A well-known Greek word is ἀγαπάω, meaning "I love." But on the inside of my wedding band, Robin had inscribed ἀγαπῶ σε.

TRANSITIVE AND INTRANSITIVE

25.3 The issue of transitive and intransitive verbs is a mattter of the relationship between the verb and its object.

25.4 **Transitive** verbs require a direct object. The action of the verb carries over to an object (think of the Latin preposition *trans*, "across"), whether that object is expressed or implied.

ἔσωσεν ἡμᾶς
He saved us
He saved us *(Titus 3:5).*

The action of "he saved" has to carry over to a direct object, "us."

25.5 **Intransitive** verbs cannot have a direct object and cannot be passive.

στερεὸς θεμέλιος τοῦ θεοῦ ἔστηκεν, ἔχων τὴν σφραγῖδα ταύτην
firm   foundation of God *stands*   having seal   this
The firm foundation of God *stands*, having this seal *(2 Tim 2:19).*

STATIVE VERBS

25.6 Stative verbs describes a state of existence. The main stative verb in Greek is εἰμί, and includes predicate adjectives where εἰμί is supplied.

τὸ ... τέλος τῆς παραγγελίας ἐστὶν ἀγάπη ἐκ καθαρᾶς καρδίας
the ... goal of this charge   *is*   love from clean   heart
But the goal of this command *is* love from a clean heart *(1 Tim 1:5).*

οἴδαμεν δὲ ὅτι καλὸς ὁ νόμος, ἐάν τις   αὐτῷ νομίμως χρῆται
we know and that good the law if   someone it   lawfully uses
Now we know that the law *is* good if someone uses it lawfully
(1 Tim 1:8).

TIME FRAME OF THE SPEAKER

25.7 This point bears repeating one last time. While it may seem obvious, it's amazing how many times it's forgotten: *the time frame of the verb is from the perspective of the writer, not the reader.* Of course, what was presently true for Paul may still be presently true for you, but this is a function of theology and not grammar. This is especially important for the perfect tense.

τὸν καλὸν   ἀγῶνα   ἠγώνισμαι,   τὸν δρόμον   τετέλεκα,
the good   fight   *I have fought*   the race   *I have finished*

τὴν πίστιν   τετήρηκα
the faith   *I have kept*

I have fought the good fight, *I have finished* the race, *I have kept* the faith (*2 Tim 4:7*).

These statements were true for Paul, and the effects of the actions are felt by Paul, but not necessarily by others (unless, by implication, they too have fought, finished, and kept).

VOICE (ACTIVE)

25.8   **Simple**. We saw that the subject does the action of the active verb (8.26). This is the normal use of the active voice.

Χριστὸς   Ἰησοῦς   ἦλθεν   εἰς   τὸν κόσμον   ἁμαρτωλοὺς   σῶσαι
Christ   Jesus   came   into the world   sinners   to save

Christ Jesus *came* into the world to save sinners (*1 Tim 1:15*).

25.9   **Causative**. The subject is performing the action of the verb, not directly but through someone or something. You can often put "causes" before the verb and it will make sense, or you can make it passive.

τότε οὖν   ἔλαβεν ὁ Πιλᾶτος   τὸν Ἰησοῦν καὶ   ἐμαστίγωσεν
Then therefore he took Pilate   Jesus   and   *flogged*

ESV: Then Pilate took Jesus and *flogged* him (*John 19:1*).
CSB: Then Pilate took Jesus and *had him flogged*.

Pilate did not actually flog Jesus; he had someone else do it, but he was the ultimate cause of the flogging.

VOICE (PASSIVE)

25.10 **Simple**. We saw that the subject receives the action of the passive verb (8.27). Sometimes the agent of the action is expressed, sometimes not.

Ἀδὰμ γὰρ πρῶτος ἐπλάσθη, εἶτα Εὔα
Adam for first *was created* then Eve
For Adam *was created* first, then Eve *(1 Tim 2:13).*

Adam did not do the creating, but rather was the object of creation. The agent of the creating is left up to context, but it's generally not hard to determine.

ἐβαπτίζοντο ἐν τῷ Ἰορδάνῃ ποταμῷ ὑπ᾽ αὐτοῦ
they were being baptized in the Jordan River *by him*
They were being baptized in the Jordan River *by him (Matt 3:6).*

Here the agent of the baptism is stated—"him"—which the context makes clear is John.

25.11 **Divine passive**. Sometimes context shows that when a verb is passive, God is doing the action of the verb.

μακάριοι οἱ πενθοῦντες, ὅτι αὐτοὶ παρακληθήσονται
Blessed the mourning for they *will be comforted*
Blessed are those who mourn, for they *will be comforted (Matt 5:4).*

Comforted by whom? God. Hence, "divine" passive.

25.12 **English style**, however, prefers active verbs, and so many Greek passives are changed to actives in translation.

μετὰ τρεῖς ἡμέρας ἐγείρομαι
after three days *I will be raised*
After three days *I will be raised (Matt 27:63).*
ESV: After three days *I will arise.*

When it comes to the resurrection, it is unfortunate that the theologically rich passive is set aside for the sake of English style (see the ESV above). Jesus was raised by his Father through the work of the Spirit.

NEUTER PLURAL

25.13 A subject that is neuter plural can have a singular verb when the subject is being viewed as a collective whole.

τὰ   ἀρχαῖα   παρῆλθεν,   ἰδοὺ   γέγονεν   καινά
the   old   passed away   behold   has become   *new*

NASB: *The old things* passed away; behold, *new things* have come (2 Cor 5:17).

ESV: *The old* has passed away; behold, *the new* has come.

The ἀρχαῖα are the "old things" (plural) that all have passed away (παρῆλθεν, singular).

INFINITIVE

25.14 **Articular infinitive and preposition.** When the infinitive is preceded by a preposition and the article, there are specific rules of translation. This is the most difficult use of the infinitive to recognize and the most idiomatic. Any attempt to translate word for word must be abandoned because we have no construction like it in English. The translator sees what the phrase means in Greek and then says the same thing in English.

All of the pronouns below that act as the subject of the infinitive are accusative. I made up these examples; they are not in the Bible.

μετά indicating *antecedent time* (i.e., the infinitive happened *before* the main verb)

μετὰ τὸ βλέψαι τὸν Ἰησοῦν τοὺς ἁμαρτωλούς, ἔκλαυσεν

After Jesus saw the sinners, he wept.

ἐν indicating *contemporaneous time*

ὁ κύριος κρινεῖ ἡμᾶς ἐν τῷ ἔρχεσθαι αὐτὸν πάλιν

The Lord will judge us *when he comes* again.

πρό indicating *prior time* (i.e., the infinitive happened *after* the main verb)

> ὁ Ἰησοῦς ἠγάπησεν ἡμᾶς πρὸ τοῦ γνῶναι ἡμᾶς αὐτόν
>
> Jesus loved us *before we knew* him.

διά indicating *reason* or *cause*

> ὁ Ἰησοῦς χαρήσεται διὰ τὸ βλέπειν αὐτὸν ὅτι ἀγαπῶμεν αὐτόν
>
> Jesus will rejoice *because he sees* that we love him.

εἰς indicating *purpose*

> καθίζω ἐν τῷ ναῷ εἰς τὸ ἀκούειν με τὸν λόγον τοῦ θεοῦ
>
> I sit in the temple *in order that I might hear* the word of God.

πρός indicating *purpose*

> κηρύσσομεν τὸν εὐαγγέλιον πρὸς τὸ βλέψαι ὑμᾶς τὴν ἀλή-θειαν
>
> We proclaim the gospel *so that you may see* the truth.

25.15 **Purpose**. There are multiple ways to express purpose using the infinitive.

■ The simple infinitive (22.27).

> Μὴ νομίσητε ὅτι ἦλθον καταλῦσαι τὸν νόμον ἢ τοὺς προφήτας
> not think   that I came *to abolish*   the law   or the prophets
> Do not think that I have come *to abolish* the Law or the Prophets
> *(Matt 5:17).*

The purpose of Jesus' coming was not to abolish the Hebrew Scriptures.

- The articular infinitive with the article in the genitive case (τοῦ).

ἐτίθουν   καθ᾽ ἡμέραν πρὸς τὴν θύραν ... τοῦ αἰτεῖν ἐλεημοσύνην
he was placed every day   at   the door ...   *to ask for*   alms
NRSV: People would lay him daily at the gate ... *so that he could
ask* for alms (Acts 3:2).

The lame man was placed by the gate for the purpose of asking for alms.

- εἰς τό and the infinitive

παραδώσουσιν αὐτὸν τοῖς ἔθνεσιν εἰς τὸ ἐμπαῖξαι καὶ μαστιγῶσαι
hand over   him   to the Gentiles *into the mocked*   and *flogged*
NRSV: They will hand him over to the Gentiles *to be mocked* and
flogged (Matt 20:19).

Jesus was handed over for the purpose of being mocked and flogged.

- πρὸς τό and the infinitive

ὁ βλέπων   γυναῖκα πρὸς τὸ ἐπιθυμῆσαι αὐτὴν
the one looking at woman   *to*   *the lust*   her
ἤδη   ἐμοίχευσεν
already   committed adultery
ESV: Everyone who looks at a woman *with lustful intent* has
already committed adultery with her (Matt 5:28).

It is looking with purposeful intent that constitutes sin.

25.16 **Periphrastic.** There is a construction in which Greek uses εἰμί and
a participle together to state a single idea, and this is called a *periphrastic construction*. Originally, a periphrastic construction
emphasized the continuous force of the participle (which is why
the aorist participle never occurs in this construction). However,
by the time of Koine Greek, this emphasis is often lost. In fact,
Koine Greek normally uses a periphrastic construction for the
third person plural, perfect middle/passive.

ἦν   γὰρ διδάσκων αὐτοὺς ὡς ἐξουσίαν ἔχων
he was for *teaching* them as authority having
For *he was teaching* them as one who had authority *(Matt 7:29).*

τῇ γὰρ χάριτί ἐστε σεσῳσμένοι διὰ πίστεως
by for grace *you are having been saved* through faith
For by grace *you have been saved* through faith *(Eph 2:8).*

25.17 Here are all the different forms a periphrastic construction can take. The form of εἰμί and the participle can be separated by several words.

periphrastic tense	construction		
Present	present of εἰμί	+	present participle
Imperfect	imperfect of εἰμί	+	present participle
Future	future of εἰμί	+	present participle
Perfect	present of εἰμί	+	perfect participle
Pluperfect	imperfect of εἰμί	+	perfect participle
Future perfect	future of εἰμί	+	perfect participle

25.18 A **genitive absolute** is a noun or pronoun and a participle in the genitive that are not grammatically connected to the rest of the sentence. In other words, there will be no word in the remaining part of the sentence that the noun, pronoun, or participle modifies.

These are common constructions especially in narrative passages. They usually occur at the beginning of the sentence and are usually temporal. Translation is often idiomatic.

αὐτοῦ λαλοῦντος παραγίνεται Ἰούδας
he speaking comes Judas
NASB: *While He was still speaking*, Judas … came up *(Mark 14:43).*
NIV: *Just as he was speaking*, Judas … appeared.

ὁ ... Ἰησοῦς   ἐξένευσεν   ὄχλου ὄντος   ἐν τῷ   τόπῳ
Jesus   departed   *crowd being*   in the   place

NASB: Jesus had slipped away *while there was a crowd* in that place
(*John 5:13*).

ESV: Jesus had withdrawn, as there was a crowd in the place.

NET: Jesus had slipped out since there was a crowd in that place.

NRSV: Jesus had disappeared in the crowd that was there.

Notice how the genitive αὐτοῦ ("he") in the first example functions as the "subject" of the participle, even though technically a
participle cannot have a subject. The genitive absolute is often
used when the noun or pronoun doing the action of the participle
is different from the subject of the sentence.

QUESTIONS

25.19   Greek can ask a question and give no indication of the expected
        response.

        ποῦ ἐστιν ὁ τεχθεὶς βασιλεὺς τῶν Ἰουδαίων;
        where is   *the one born King*   *of the Jews*
        Where is the one born King of the Jews? (*Matt 2:2*)

25.20   Greek can ask a question such that the expected answer is, "Yes."
        They do this by introducing the question with οὐ (or the strength-
        ened form οὐχί).

        οὐχὶ ἡ ψυχὴ πλεῖόν ἐστιν τῆς τροφῆς;
        not   *life*   *more than is*   *food*
        Life is more than food, *isn't it*? (*Matt 6:25*)

25.21   Greek can also ask a question such that the expected answer is,
        "No." They do this by introducing the question with μή.

        μὴ πάντες χαρίσματα ἔχουσιν ἰαμάτων;
        not *all*   *gifts*   *they have* *of healing*
        Not all have the gifts of healing, *do they?* (*1 Cor 12:30*)

25.22 Translations rarely indicate the expected answer since to do so is considered clumsy English style.

25.23 We have seen that the subjunctive can also be used in a question in which the answer is in doubt, or the question is rhetorical ("Deliberative subjunctive," 22.12).

τί   φάγωμεν; ἤ, τί   πίωμεν, ἤ, τί   περιβαλώμεθα;
what *we eat*   or what *we drink*   or what *we wear*

"What *should we eat?*" or "What *should we drink?*" or "What *should we wear?*" (Matt 6:31)

ESV: "What *shall we eat?*" or "What *shall we drink?*" or "What *shall we wear?*"

OPTATIVE

25.24* There is another mood called the optative. If the subjunctive describes an action one step removed from reality (uncertain but possible), the optative describes an action two steps removed. It is sometimes called the mood of "wish."

25.25* Since the days of Classical Greek, the optative has been falling out of use. There are only sixty-eight uses of the optative in the New Testament, and fifteen are the expression μὴ γένοιτο, "may it not be," sometimes translated idiomatically as, "God forbid."

MORPHOLOGY FOR THE CURIOUS*

25.26* Although the Bible Study Greek approach does not require you to be able to identify the parts of the Greek verb, it can be helpful to understand the concepts. I discussed this briefly at 8.3.

25.27* The **stem** of a verb is the part of the verb that carries its basic meaning. The form λύομεν means "we destroy." The stem is *λυ (I put an asterisk in front of a stem). While it is possible for the stem of a verb to undergo some changes, most of the changes are made to the beginning and the ending of the verb.

25.28* Some of the more common verbs use totally different stems to form their different tense forms. ἔρχομαι (I go) → ἐλεύσομαι (I will go) → ἦλθον (I went) → ἐλήλυθα (I have gone). The software will parse these confusing forms properly, but you may notice they are significantly different.

25.29* Greek often adds a **connecting vowel** between the stem of a verb and its personal ending. This is to aid in pronunciation. For example, λέγετε means "You say." The stem is *λεγ, the connecting vowel is the second ε, and τε is the second person plural personal ending. λέγτε is an awkward sound for the Greek speaker, so they smoothed it out with the connecting vowel, λέγετε.

25.30* In order to mark a verb as indicating a past event, an **augment** is added to the beginning of the word.

If the verb begins with a consonant, the augment is an ε, such as in λέγω → ἔλεγεν, "I lose → I was loosing."

If the verb begins with a vowel, the vowel is lengthened, such as α → η. ἀγαπῶ → ἠγάπησα, "I love" → "I loved."

25.31* Some tenses use a **tense formative** like a σ or a κ that is placed between the word's stem and the connecting vowel/personal ending to form different tenses. ἀγαπάω (I love) → ἀγαπήσω (I will love) → ἠγάπησα (I loved) → ἠγάπηκα (I have loved).

25.32* Here is the present active indicative paradigm.

1 sg	λύω	I loose
2 sg	λύεις	You loose
3 sg	λύει	He/she/it looses
1 pl	λύομεν	We loose
2 pl	λύετε	You loose
3 pl	λύουσι(ν)	They loose

CHAPTER 26

ODDS 'N ENDS

IDIOMS

26.1 Idioms are collections of words, usually two, that have a special meaning when the words occur together, a meaning that the words don't have when they are isolated.

- εἰ μή means "except" or "unless," even though the two words separately mean "if" and "not."

- διὰ τοῦτο, "through this," means "on account of this" or "therefore."

PARTIALLY INFLECTED AND UNINFLECTED

26.2 Some words inflect in some cases but not in others. For example, the four forms of Ἰησοῦς are Ἰησοῦς, Ἰησοῦ, Ἰησοῦ, Ἰησοῦν. The genitive and dative are identical.

26.3 Other words never inflect, such as many personal names and words borrowed from other languages. For example, Ἀβραάμ ("Abraham") will always be Ἀβραάμ regardless of its function in the sentence.

26.4 Even though the form does not change, the computers will parse these with the relevant case. Ἰησοῦ will be parsed as either a genitive or a dative. If there is an article before the word, it will be fully declined, τοῦ Ἰησοῦ and τῷ Ἰησοῦ.

FOUR OR EIGHT CASES

26.5 In years past there has been a debate as to whether there are four or eight cases in Greek. You may see remnants of this discussion in the commentaries, so I thought I should summarize the issues.

26.6 There are four distinct *forms* of words in the Greek noun system, and the argument (among others) is that form should be the deciding factor: nominative, accusative, dative, and genitive.

26.7 Others have argued that there are eight distinct *ideas*, and form should take a back seat to meaning. In this arrangement, the genitive and ablative have the same form (e.g., θεοῦ), but the genitive is the basic idea of "of," and the basic idea of the ablative is "from."

Likewise, what we have been calling the dative can actually be broken down into three basic ideas: "to" (*dative*, indicating personal interest or reference/respect), "in" (*locative*), and "by" (*instrumental*). I introduced these terms in 16.1.

26.8 The four case system has won the day, partially because there are many more meanings of nouns than eight. Form wins over function, and I think in this case that is a good decision (pun intended).

CONDITIONAL SENTENCES

26.9 A "conditional sentence" is an "if… then… " type sentence. The "if" clause is called the **protasis**, and the "then" clause is the **apodosis**. There are four basic types of conditional sentences in Greek, and each one has its own nuance of meaning.

Type	Protasis	Apodosis
First class	εἰ + indicative any tense	any mood or tense
Second class	εἰ + indicative past tense	(ἄν) + indicative past tense
Third class	ἐάν + subjunctive any tense	any mood or tense
Fourth class	εἰ + optative present or aorist	ἄν + optative present or aorist

26.10 **First class conditional sentence**. Also called a "condition of fact." The protasis begins with εἰ ("if") and the verb is in the indicative. These sentences are saying that if something is true, and let's assume for the sake of the argument that it's true, then such and such will occur.

εἰ δὲ ὁ ὀφθαλμός σου ὁ δεξιὸς σκανδαλίζει σε, ἔξελε αὐτόν
if but the eye   your right   causes to sin   you tear out it
If your right eye causes you to sin, tear it out *(Matt 5:29)*.

Sometimes the apodosis is clearly true, and translators might use "since" instead of "if." But it seems to me that there is often something to be gained by saying "if ..." even when you know it's true. It causes you to affirm the truthfulness of the apodosis.

εἰ υἱὸς εἶ   τοῦ θεοῦ, εἰπὲ τῷ λίθῳ τούτῳ ἵνα γένηται ἄρτος
if son   you are of God   say   to the stone this   that it become   bread
NRSV: If you are the Son of God, command this stone to become a loaf of bread *(Luke 4:3)*.

Satan certainly knew who Jesus was.

However, there are times in which saying "if" makes something sound conditional when it's not.

εἰ δὲ ἐν πνεύματι θεοῦ ἐγὼ ἐκβάλλω τὰ δαιμόνια
if but by Spirit   of God I   cast out   the demons
But *if* I, by the Spirit of God, cast out demons *(Matt 12:28)*

Jesus knew he was casting out demons by God's Spirit, and some people would translate εἰ as "since." Galatians 5:25 is another example.

εἰ ζῶμεν πνεύματι, πνεύματι καὶ στοιχῶμεν
if we live by spirit   with spirit   also   let's keep in step
NIV: Since we live by the Spirit, let us keep in step with the Spirit.
CSB: If we live by the Spirit, let us also keep in step with the Spirit.

26.11 Second class conditional sentence. Also called "contrary to fact." The protasis begins with εἰ ("if") and the verb is a past tense in the indicative. These sentences are saying that if something is true, even though it's not, then such and such would occur. The falseness of the protasis is assumed in the argument.

εἰ   γὰρ ἐπιστεύετε Μωϋσεῖ, ἐπιστεύετε ἂν   ἐμοί
if   for   you believed   Moses   you believe   would me

If you believed Moses, you would believe me *(John 5:46)*.

Jesus is claiming that they did not really believe Moses.

26.12 Third class. The protasis begins with ἐάν ("if") and the verb is in the subjunctive mood. There are two subcategories of the third class condition, although they are identical in form. We learned this in 22.9.

1. Future More Probable. Sometimes a third class condition is used to say that if some specific event in the future happens, and it probably will, then something else will happen.

ἐὰν ἅψωμαι κἂν   τῶν ἱματίων αὐτοῦ σωθήσομαι
if   I touch   might clothes   his   I will be healed

If I can only touch his clothes, I will be healed *(Mark 5:28)*.

She thought that if she could only touch Jesus's clothing—and it was likely that she could—then she would be healed.

ταῦτά σοι   πάντα δώσω, ἐὰν πεσὼν   προσκυνήσῃς μοι
these   to you all   I will give if   falling down you worship   me

All these I will give you, if you will fall down and worship me *(Matt 4:9)*.

I mentioned this example earlier. Did Satan really believe it was likely Jesus would do this? Seems unlikely, although we do not know what Satan did know and did not know about Jesus. Perhaps the use of this particular grammatical form was meant to suggest to Jesus that he might do this. Satan was wrong! This points to the problem of this label, "more probable." There are many examples in the Greek Testament where the "if" clause is not likely to happen.

2. Present General. This same form is also used to state a general truth, an axiomatic truth. The subjunctive mood is appropriate because the truth of the statement is timeless.

ἐάν τις   περιπατῇ ἐν τῇ ἡμέρᾳ, οὐ προσκόπτει
if   anyone walks   in   the day not he stumbles

If anyone walks in the day, he does not stumble *(John 11:9)*.

Jesus is not thinking of any particular event in the future; he is stating a general truth.

26.13 **Fourth class**. Also called a "less probable future" condition. The writer is saying that if something happens, and it's *not* likely to happen, then something else would happen. There is no complete illustration of this form in the New Testament. Moreover, it uses a mood you are not learning here—the optative mood (25.24–25).

GREEK-ENGLISH INTERLINEARS

26.14 **Word order**. It's difficult to speak of "normal" Greek word order, since most Greek sentences do not follow it. But in general, the normal word order is conjunction, verb, subject, object.

26.15 Why would a Greek speaker alter the order? Mostly for emphasis. If they wanted to emphasize a word, they would tend to move it to an "unusual" location, normally forward in the sentence. Sometimes English can translate the nuance of the word order, but normally not. What is the point of the word order here?

πάντας ἀνθρώπους θέλει   σωθῆναι
all   people   he wishes to be saved

[God] desires *all* people to be saved *(1 Tim 2:4)*.

τῇ γὰρ χάριτί ἐστε σεσῳσμένοι
by for *grace* you are having been saved

NASB: For by *grace* you have been saved *(Eph 2:8)*.
NIV: For *it is* by *grace* you have been saved.

26.16 **Nuance**. The significance of word order is highly nuanced. Don't put too much weight on the perceived significance of a word's order in the sentence.

MORPHOLOGY FOR THE CURIOUS*

26.17* "Morphology" refers to how Greek actually forms a word (25.26-27). A **morpheme** is the smallest amount of information in a word. For a noun, the root (e.g., λογο) and the case ending (e.g., ν) are two morphemes that together form the inflected form λόγον.

29.18* A **declension** is a basic pattern for inflecting a noun or adjective. There are three of these basic patterns for nouns and adjectives, each with many subpatterns. Declensions have only to do with form; they have no effect on meaning. Here are some sample paradigms of nouns.

nom sg	ὥρα	λόγος	σάρξ	ὄνομα
gen sg	ὥρας	λόγου	σαρκός	ὀνόματος
dat sg	ὥρᾳ	λόγῳ	σαρκί	ὀνόματι
acc sg	ὥραν	λόγον	σάρκα	ὄνομα
n/v pl	ὧραι	λόγοι	σάρκες	ὀνόματα
gen pl	ὡρῶν	λόγων	σαρκῶν	ὀνομάτων
dat pl	ὥραις	λόγοις	σαρξίν	ὀνόμασι(ν)
acc pl	ὥρας	λόγους	σάρκας	ὀνόματα

If you were not learning Bible Study Greek but were following a more traditional path, you would be memorizing many paradigms such as this. In Bible Study Greek, we let the interlinear and the software do the parsing. But I thought you might enjoy actually seeing a paradigm, even if you don't have to memorize it, although you did memorize the paradigm of the article and hopefully that of the relative pronoun.

CONGRATULATIONS

You did it! You made it to the end. Good job. Now the trick is to keep using it. Read commentaries that require you to know a little Greek, like the volumes in Zondervan's *Exegetical Commentary on the New Testament*. Only do word studies in Greek. Keep comparing translations to see where they are the same and where they are different, and find out why. Using Greek and the tools is key to you remembering and fine-tuning all that you have learned. It will make a difference; I promise.

VOCABULARY

NOUNS

ἄγγελος, angel; messenger

ἀδελφός, brother

ἁμαρτία, sin

ἀνήρ, male, husband; man

ἄνθρωπος, man; person, human being; people, mankind

βασιλεία, kingdom

γῆ, earth, land; region; humanity

γυνή, woman; wife

δόξα, glory

ἔθνος, nation, plural: Gentiles

ἔργον, work, deed

ἡμέρα, day

θεός, God, god

Ἰουδαῖος, Jewish; noun: a Jew

Ἰησοῦς, Jesus, Joshua

καρδία, heart

κόσμος, world

κύριος, Lord; master, sir

λόγος, word, Word, statement, message

μαθητής, disciple

νόμος, law

ὄνομα, name

οὐρανός, heaven; sky

ὄχλος, crowd

πατήρ, father

Παῦλος, Paul

Πέτρος, Peter

πίστις, faith, belief; trust; teaching

πόλις, city; town

πνεῦμα, spirit, Spirit; wind, breath

σωτήρ, savior
υἱός, son; descendant
χάρις, grace
χείρ, hand
Χριστός, Christ, Messiah

ADJECTIVES

ἅγιος, adjective: holy; plural noun: saints
ἄλλος, other, another
εἷς, one
μέγας, large, great
ὁ, the
πᾶς, singular: each, every; plural: all
πολύς, much, many; great, large
πρῶτος, first

PRONOUNS

αὐτός, he, she, it (they, them)
ἑαυτοῦ, himself/herself/itself
ἐγώ (ἡμεῖς), I (we)
ἐκεῖνος, that (those)
ὅς, who (whom)
οὐδείς, no one (nothing)
οὗτος, this (these)
σύ (ὑμεῖς), you
τίς, who? what? which? why?
τις, someone/thing, anyone/thing

VERBS

ἀκούω, I hear; understand, obey
ἀποκρίνομαι, I answer
γίνομαι, I become; am
γινώσκω, I know; understand

γράφω, I write
δίδωμι, I give
δύναμαι, I am able
εἰμί, I am (is, are; was, were)
εἰσέρχομαι, I come in(to), enter
ἐξέρχομαι, I come out
ἔρχομαι, I come
ἐσθίω, I eat
εὑρίσκω, I find
ἔχω I have
θέλω, I want
ἵστημι, intransitive: I stand; transitive: I cause to stand
λαλέω, I speak
λαμβάνω, I take; receive
λέγω, I say, tell
οἶδα, I know; understand
ὁράω, I see
πιστεύω, I believe, trust
ποιέω, I do; make
πορεύομαι, I go; live

PREPOSITIONS

ἀπό (ἀπ', ἀφ'), gen: from ("away from")
διά (δι'), gen: through, by; acc: on account of
εἰς, acc: into; in
ἐκ (ἐξ) gen: from; out of
ἐν, dat: in; by; with
ἐπί (ἐπ', ἐφ'), gen: on, when; dat: with; acc: beside
κατά (κατ', καθ'), gen: against; acc: according to; throughout
μετά (μετ', μεθ') gen: with; acc: after
παρά, gen: from; dat: beside, in the presence of; acc: alongside of
περί, gen: concerning; acc: around
πρός, acc: to ("towards"); with
ὑπέρ, gen: for ("in behalf of"); acc: above
ὑπό (ὑπ', ὑφ') gen: by; acc: under

CONJUNCTIONS

COORDINATING

ἀλλά (ἀλλ᾽), but
γάρ, for
δέ (δ᾽), and; but
ἤ, or; than
καθώς, as, even as
καί, and; even, also
οὖν, therefore; so
τε, and

SUBORDINATING

ἐάν, if
εἰ, if
ἵνα, in order that; so that; that
ὅτι, that; because
ὡς, as ("like")

INTERJECTIONS, ADVERBS, PARTICLES

ἄν, Untranslatable. Makes a statement contingent.
ἰδού, Look! Behold!
μέν, on the one hand
μή, not, lest
οὐ (οὐκ, οὐχ), not
οὕτως, thus, so, in this manner
τότε, then

INDEX

B

Beetham, Chris 93
Bible Study App x, 83, 233
BillMounce.com x, xxv, xxvi, 6, 16, 82, 88
breathing marks 11–12
   rough breathing mark 11
   smooth breathing mark 12
Bromiley, Geoffrey W. 93

C

case endings 23
cases 23, 27, 34
Church Greek x, 111
clause 124
compound word 17
conditional sentences 288–292
   apodosis 289
   protasis 289
conjunction 181–193
   adversative 184, 185, 188
   ascensive 183
   "because" 190
   conditional 192
   continuation 184, 185, 186, 187, 190
   coordinate 183–188
   coordinating 181, 184
   copulative 183
   correlative 181, 192–193
   direct / indirect speech 191
   explanatory 187
   inferential 189
   purpose 191
   result 191
   subordinate 181, 190–191
consonant cluster 17
contract verbs 277
cursive 10

D

dative case 29, 171–174
   "by" 173
   direct object 174
   object of preposition 172
   reference 174
   simple apposition 173
   time 175
   "to" 172
   "with" 173
declension 293
definite article 113
demonstratives 139–140
dependent clause 123
deponent 62–63
diacriticals 229
diaeresis 15
diphthong 11, 12, 15, 17
   improper 9
direct object 18, 20, 29, 168, 278
double consonant 17

E

eight cases 288–289
elision 15, 33
enclitic 141
English cases 19
   objective 19
   possessive 19
   subjective 19

F

Foundational Greek x, 1
future tense 212, 222
   gnomic 223
   Imperatival 222
   predictive 57, 222
   prohibition 244

G

gamma nasal 9
gender 21, 25–26, 114, 137
   natural 25
   natural and grammatical
     137–138
genitive case 29
   apposition 177–178
   attributive 179
   descriptive 30, 175
   direct object 176
   epexegetical 177
   Hebraic genitive 179
   objective 177
   object of a preposition 176
   object of preposition 176
   possessive 30, 175
   simple apposition 176
   subjective 177
   time 179
gerund 72
GK Numbers 26
gloss 27
Greek
   Classical 3
   Koine 3
Greek alphabet 6–10
Greek Grammar Beyond the Basics x
Greek language 3–5

H

head noun 29, 175, 177
Hebrew 5

I

imperative mood 44, 66, 241–242
   command 66, 241
   entreaty 241
   person 66

imperfect tense 56, 58, 62, 213,
     217, 223–224, 226, 284
   conative 226
   customary 226
   ingressive 225
   iterative 226
   progressive 225
   tendential 226
   voluntative 226
independent clause 123
indicative mood 44, 51, 63,
     239–240
   declarative 63, 239
   interrogative 239
indirect object 20, 23, 29
infinitive 45, 67–68, 245–246,
     281–283
   appositional 247
   articular 281
   complementary 67, 246
   purpose 68, 246, 282
   result 246
   subject 169, 247
inflected form 26
inflection 18, 51–52
   partially inflected 288
   uninflected 288
Interlinear for the Rest of Us ix, x,
     81
intransitive 278
iota subscript 9

L

Latin 4
lexical form 26, 29, 54
Logos x, 27, 84, 136, 233, 267
Louw and Nida 86

M

minuscule 10
mood 44–46
morphology 52
  augment 287
  connecting vowel 286
  morpheme 293
  stem 23, 286
  tense formative 287
  verbs 286–287
Mounce Greek Dictionary 85
Mounce's Expository Dictionary 85,
    92, 102, 105–108
Mounce translation x, xv

N

negation 242–243
neuter plural subject 281
nominative case 27–28, 53,
    164–166
  predicate nominative 165
  simple apposition 166
  subject 164
noun phrases 125–126
  dative 125
  genitive 125
nouns 18
number 21, 25, 42

O

objective 99
online class 7, 9, 11, 12, 26, 81, 104
optative mood 286–287
  μὴ γένοιτο 243

P

paradigm 51
parsing 27, 52

participle 45–46, 68, 248–257
  absolute time 255
  adjectival 46, 255
  adverbial 45–46, 68–70, 124,
    151, 245, 248–252
  anarthrous 69
  attendant circumstances 253
  attributive 70–71
  cause 252
  concessive 253
  conditional 252
  genitive absolute 284
  gerunds 46
  means 252
  participial phrase 45
  periphrastic 283
  purpose 251
  relative time 70, 255–257
  result 251
  substantival 72
  temporal 69, 251
passive voice 62, 280
  divine passive 280
  simple 60, 280
perfect tense 58–59, 227
  consummative 227
  intensive 227
  periphrastic 283
person 41
personal endings 51
personal pronoun 140
phrase 123
phrasing 38–39, 46, 125, 126, 131,
    144–163, 195–213, 229–238,
    259–276
possessive 30, 134
postpositive 63–64
predicate nominative 53

middle 60–61, 73–74
middle reflexive 61
passive 43

W

Wallace, Daniel 219
word order 21, 45, 292
word studies 74–109

anachronism 101
cognates 101
etymological fallacy 102
Septuagint 100

Z

Zondervan 26, 93, 268